SKETCHBOOK
LUGANO SWITZERLAND
MILAN ITALY
And a bonus:
SIFF SONOMA CALIFORNIA

STORIES, JOURNAL/COLORING BOOK
(A book you can make your own)

DEAMER DUNN

LUGANO SWITZERLAND is surrounded in beauty, whether you are enjoying its lush green hills, its Alps drop back, its shimmering winding lake or its old-world cobblestone nooks and crannies. This book and its sister novel, Omar T in Lugano Switzerland, were inspired by Lugano's Franklin University celebrating turning 50! Fifty plus years of offering one of the world's most diverse student body and staff. One of the best decisions of my life was to attend Franklin. Switzerland's most southern Canton of Ticino, of which Lugano is the largest city, is an unofficial crossroad between Europe's north and south. For the author and its diverse alumni, Franklin ties us to others all over the globe. For these two books, connections to MILAN ITALY and SONOMA CALIFORNIA are also shared…

Available to resellers through:

<u>KDP</u> ISBN-13: 9798352560167

<u>INGRAM SPARK</u> ISBN-13:

Editor: Dani Cyrer

All Art by Deamer

**First Addition
Pajaro Street Publishing**

SKETCHBOOK – LUGANO SWITZERLAND

Book Notes & Disclosures

Most of my sketch victims were unaware that my camera, eye and pencil clad fingers had focused upon them. For the most part, the tales I write for this series of sketchbooks are on individuals I know nothing of, beyond what I observed from drawing them. Consider these as bonus material for inspiring you to make this book your own.

The drawings of this Sketchbook open with Lugano Switzerland and my alma mater, Franklin University. It finishes with a few of Milian Italy and some of Sonoma California and SIFF, the Sonoma International Film Festival.

Most of my Sketchbooks are matched with a novel. This book corresponds with OMAR T IN LUGANO: Omar T and Sissy head to Lugano Switzerland via Sonoma California and Milan Italy, to assist with the food service for Franklin University's 50-year Celebration. This Omar school reunion inspires love and introspection, as Omar returns to his school, more than a decade after its profound influence on his life.

ABOUT THE SERIES: Omar and his family travel to a different location for each of these culinary adventures. The travel fiction aspect is enhanced with descriptions of actual sites, restaurants, bookstores, galleries and shops—including sketches, favorite lists and recipes. Diversity in race, religion, culture, language and sexual orientation not only exists within Omar's family, it is celebrated in these tales. Each Omar T book is independent, you do not need to read them in the order of their publication, though, as the collection grows, there are more references between the novels. For a fun additional Ticino, Switzerland, Milan & Sonoma California adventure, get yourself a copy of Omar T in Lugano Switzerland.

ENJOY!

Artist/Author Deamer Dunn
Author Web Site: http://artbz.bz
Amazon Author Page: https://www.amazon.com/author/deamerdunn
(Please pass on your impressions; write a review on Amazon and/or other sites)
You can also support your local bookstore via: https://bookshop.org/shop/deamerdunn

YouTube Author/Artist Page (music videos of art & book sketches):
https://www.youtube.com/user/deamerdunn
https://www.instagram.com/deamerauthor/
Friend me on Facebook: Deamer Dunn Author
I would love to hear from you: deamer@artbz.bz

As a Journal/Coloring Book:
A BOOK YOU CAN MAKE YOUR OWN

In case you haven't heard, coloring books for all ages are becoming quite a passion. Perhaps, for many, a little coloring can still feed a passion for getting into a book, as well as allowing the satisfaction of finishing something. A few of these sketches are accompanied with a fictional story influenced by the scene. Deamer Sketchbooks are meant to inspire you. Each sketch is partnered with a blank page— you can add notes, comments, poems, words of a song, or your own artistic doodles—innovation inspired by creative human activity. The idea is that this is a book that you can make your own. It is a travel companion, whether you take it along, or it takes you…

Cheers! *Salud! A Votre Sante! Saluti!*

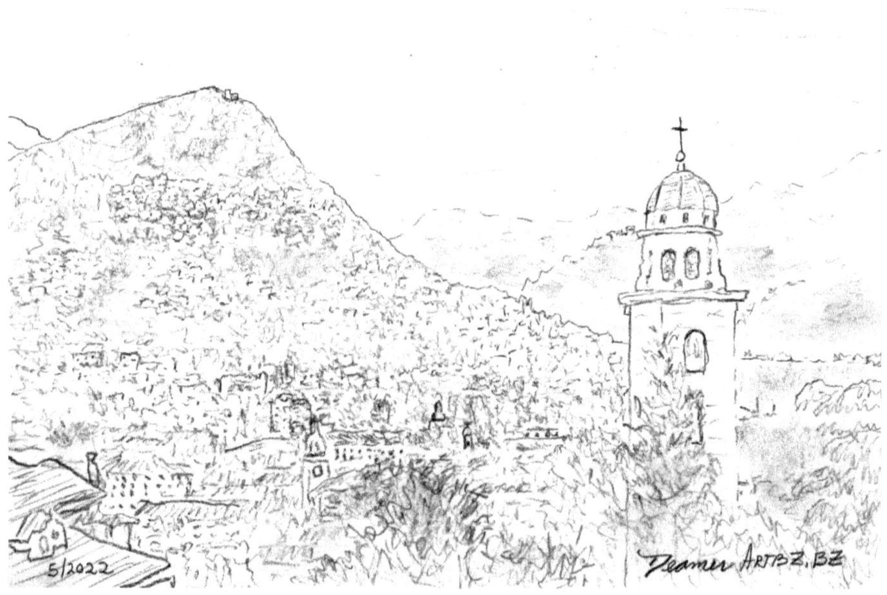

Index

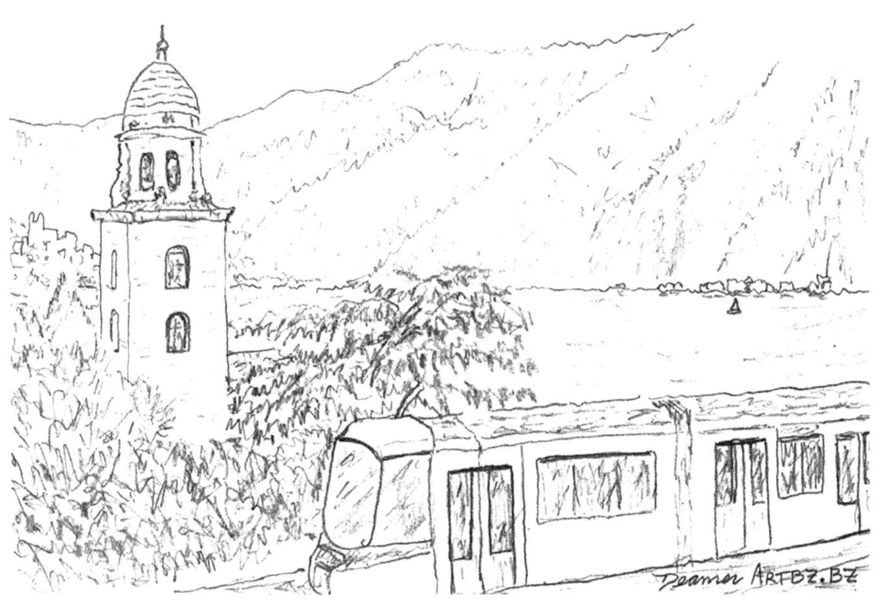

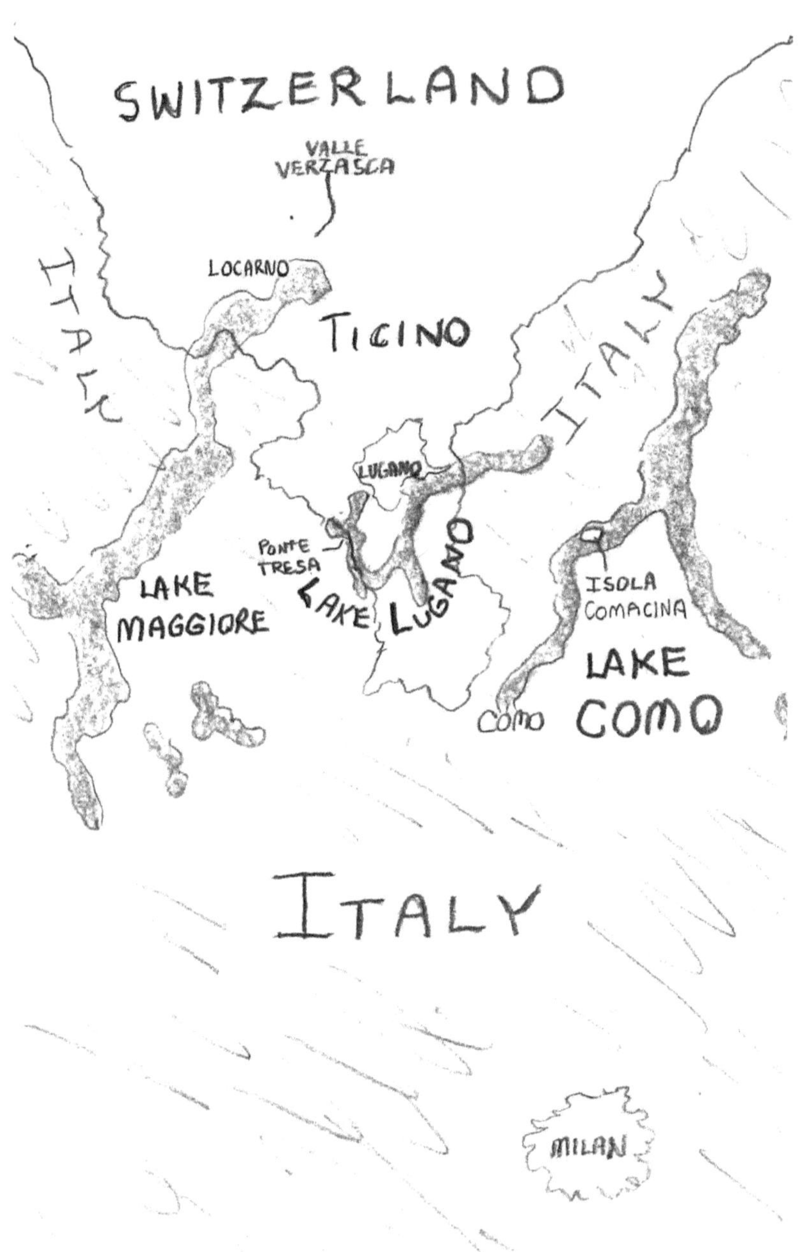
SWITZERLAND
VALLE VERZASCA
LOCARNO
TICINO
ITALY
LUGANO
PONTE TRESA
LAKE MAGGIORE
LAKE LUGANO
ITALY
ISOLA COMACINA
LAKE COMO
COMO
ITALY
MILAN

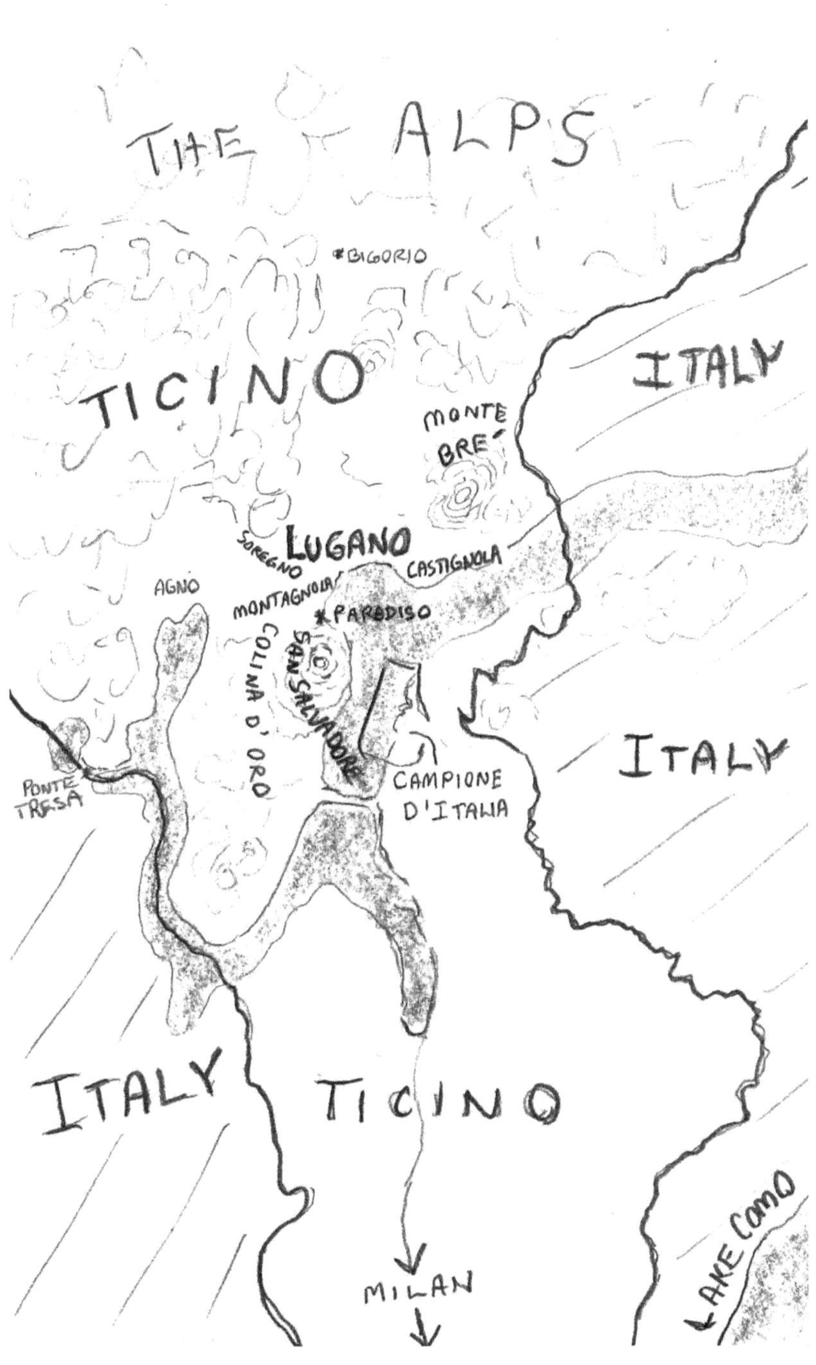
THE ALPS
#BIGORIO
TICINO
ITALY
MONTE BRE
SOREGNO
LUGANO
CASTIGNOLA
AGNO
MONTAGNOLA
*PARADISO
COLINA D'ORO
SAN SALVADORE
ITALY
CAMPIONE D'ITALIA
PONTE TRESA
ITALY
TICINO
MILAN
LAKE COMO

LUGANO AND FRANKLIN UNIVERSITY·

Wandering

I did not come into this world with a sense of how I fit into it. I mean, you could argue that is how all of us arrive, blank slate babies, randomly a part of some family, in some land. Though, I don't really believe that. We seem to come to this world with some kind of past. At least, that is how I felt growing up, going to school, making friends and getting to know my parents and siblings. Somehow, none of these things ever felt comfortable to me. Not that I could ever figure out what did make sense. I guess you could say I always felt removed whether at school or at home. Two things did inspire me, music and reading. Neither of these pleasures seemed to help me bridge the gaps between myself and those I interacted with. Being a reader did sometimes connect me to a teacher here and there, but my habits of following a trend with my often distracted me from the books a teacher assigned me. Maybe if I would have made it to college, I could have melded my reading habits into studies of my choice. But that wasn't meant to be my path. None of my family was into music. An older brother who was in lust for a guitar playing girl, bought himself a guitar in an attempt to impress her. When that didn't work out, the instrument found a home in our garage. I picked it up one day; I liked the feel of it. I still have it, his name is Bernard. We have been traveling the world together. I still haven't been able to define myself, well maybe, I can call myself a professional wanderer. People and places come and go, but Bernard and the thoughts expressed in my songs are the friends that travel with me. Music has brought some sheckels to my purse and assisted in me making connections while traveling. And, everywhere I go I can find books. Something I can hold, an object for learning, a source of new friends. While in Lugano, I discovered the stories of Hermann Hesse, a long-term resident of this beautiful crossroad between the north and south of Europe. His characters are so real and alive. Some of them will stay with me, in my brain and my soul, as I continue my journey…

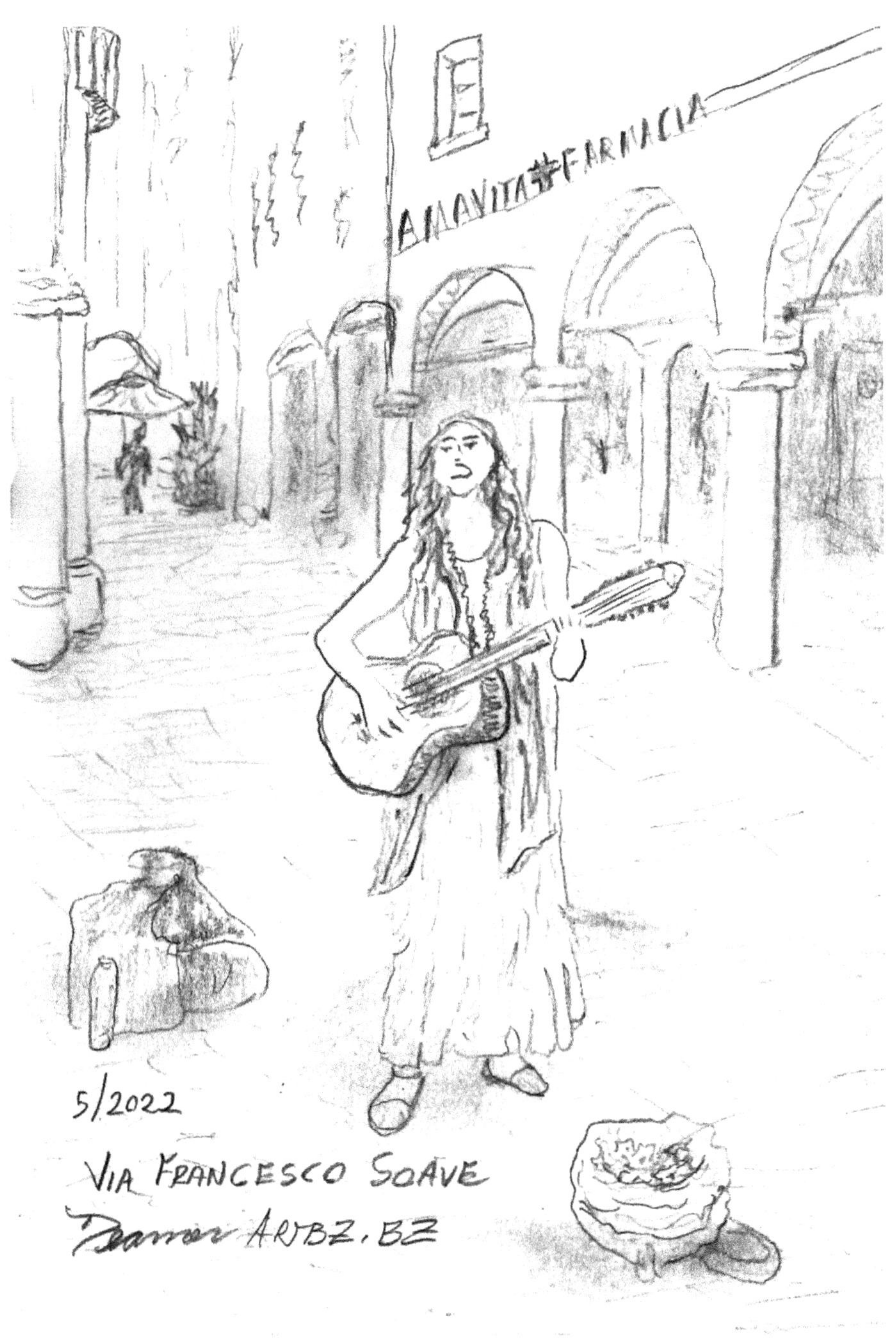
AMAVITA FARMACIA
5/2022
VIA FRANCESCO SOAVE

Teaching

For me, teaching has always been about connecting. Whether it is the thrill of coming up with a lesson plan to direct young minds, or the light in their eyes upon an enlightenment. This really hasn't changed whether I was instructing little ones, teenagers or cocky college students. Though, as I have matured, I think I appreciate the connection that much more. Being a part of Franklin University has enhanced this feeling. There is something special about teaching at an international school. Somehow, these connections feel that much richer. Guiding the kids assembled at Franklin, virtually from every part of the world, gives me an additional pride. There have been times when a classroom discussion between kids of different cultures, different backgrounds, has moved me to tears. We touch on all the controversies that the political science and sociology teachers deal with, but I think the kids approach topics within literature with more curiosity and more open-minded. Somehow, I think, the arts help us let go of our tribal affiliations and just try to understand. I have had some interesting exchanges with both students and staff on these types of thoughts. I guess I just want everyone to get along. Even when I was at a much bigger university, with lecture auditoriums, teaching still was mostly about my one-on-one interactions. Weather permitting, I love to take a student outside, surround us with the beauty of the hillside of Sorengo and its views of the city and lake Lugano. Being surrounded by beauty seems loosen the shackles of one's background and inspire the mind. History is so filled with so many writers of thought and emotion. I still find my own ideas changing as I share my interpretations. What a wonderful journey of discovery, contemplation and teaching…

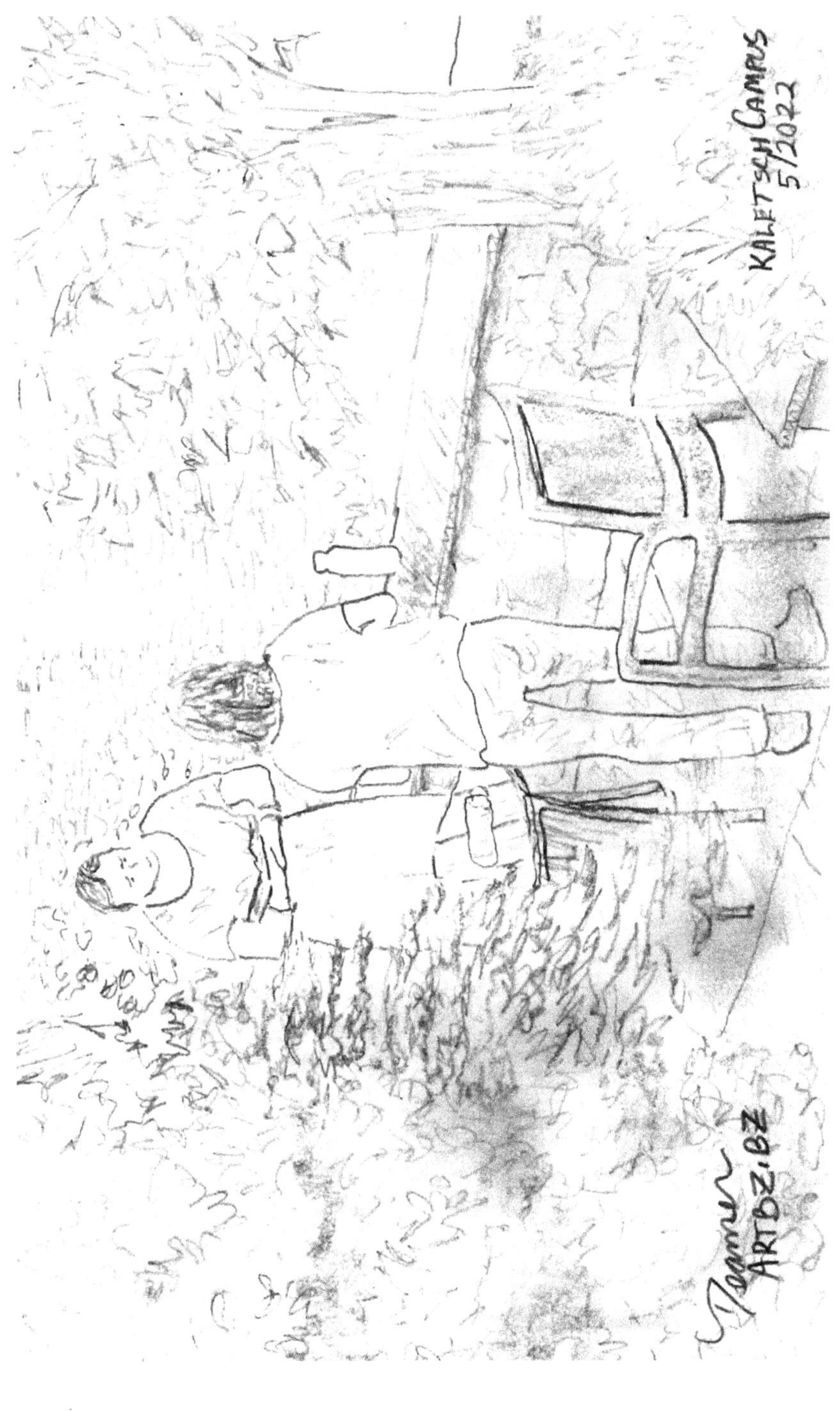
KALETSCH CAMPUS
5/2022
Joann
ARTDZ.BZ

12

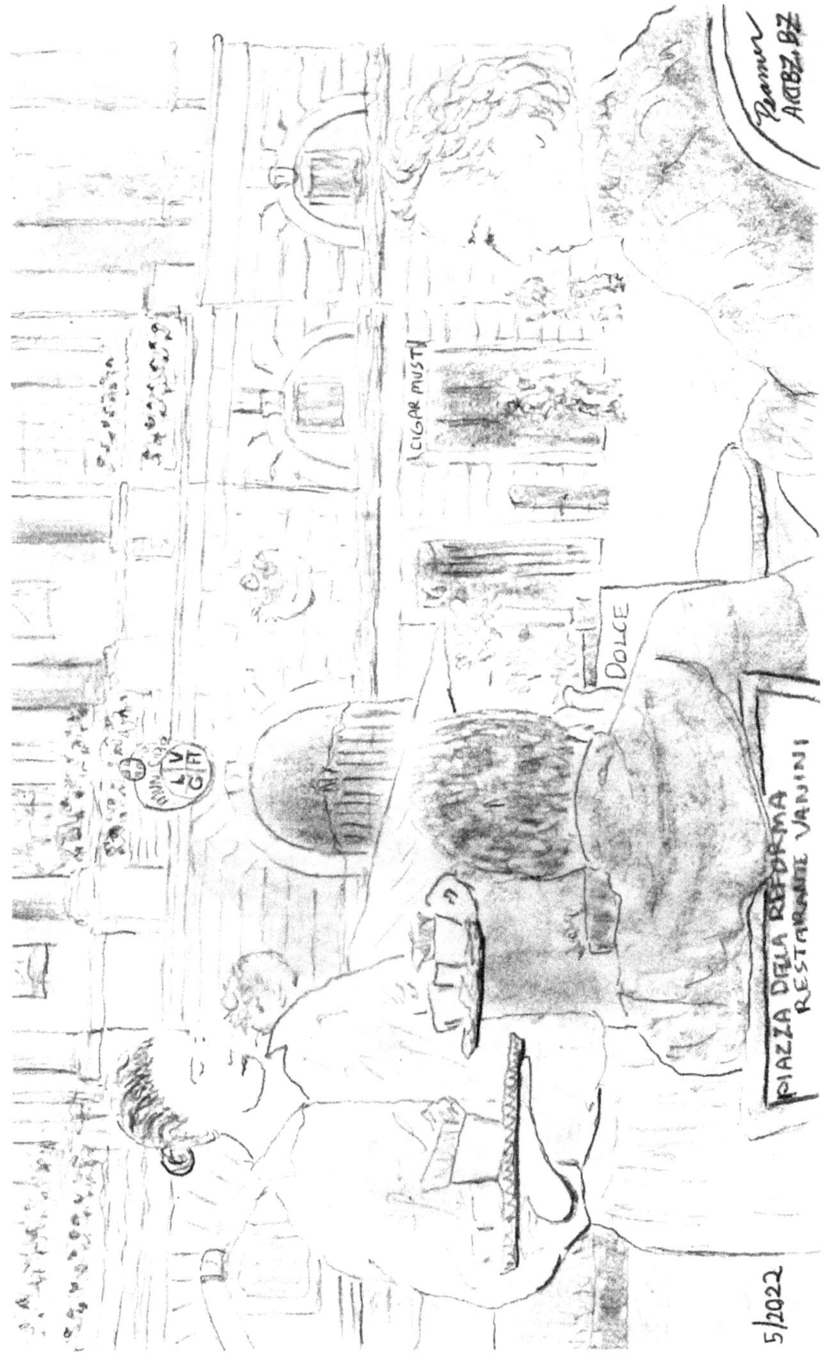

CIGAR MUSTI
DOLCE
PIAZZA DELA REFORMA
RESTAURANTE VANINI
5/2022

14

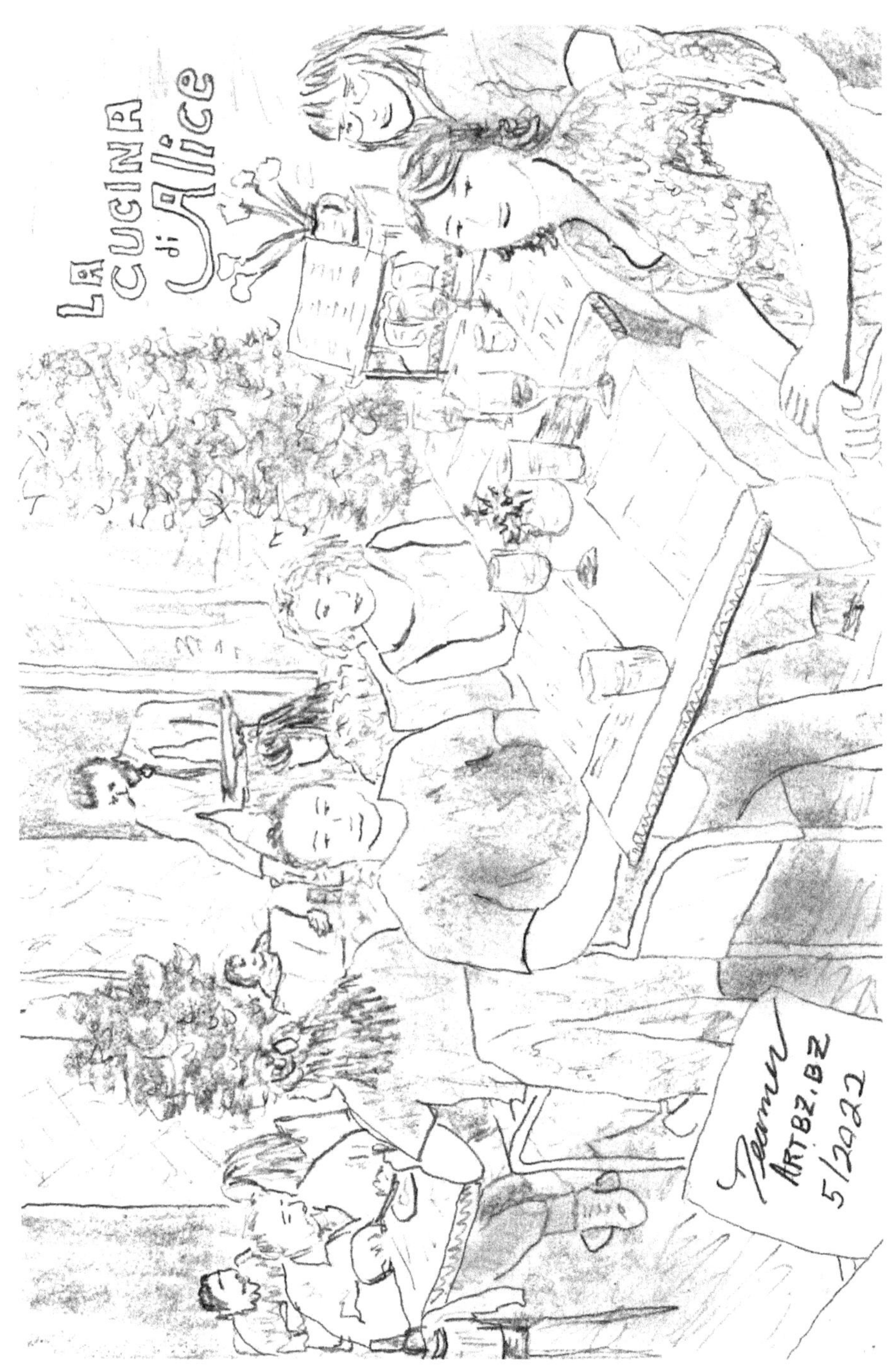
LA CUCINA di Alice

16

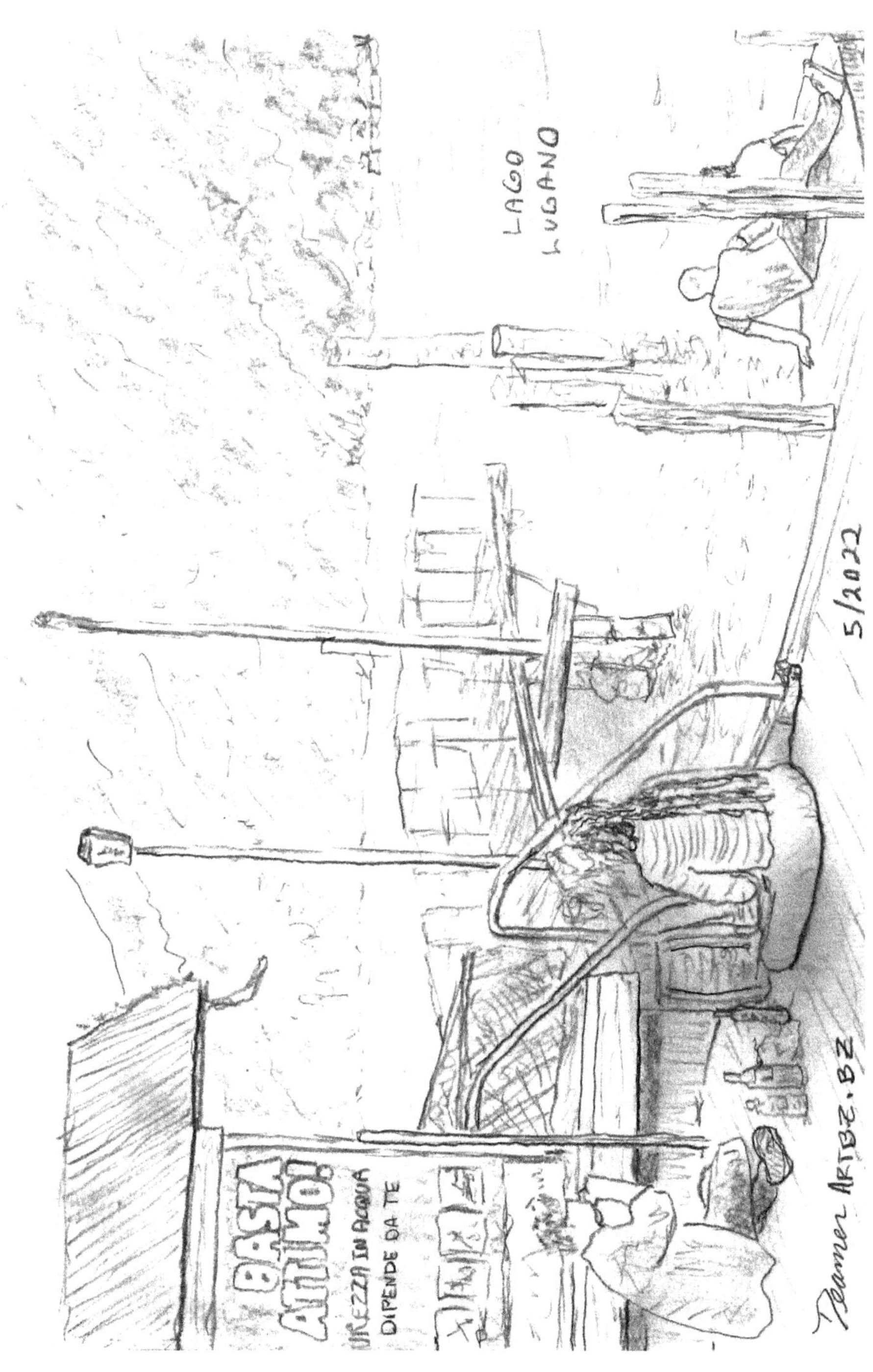
LAGO
LUGANO
BASTA
ANIMO!
UREZZA IN ACQUA
DIPENDE DA TE
5/2022
Dreamer ARTBZ.BZ

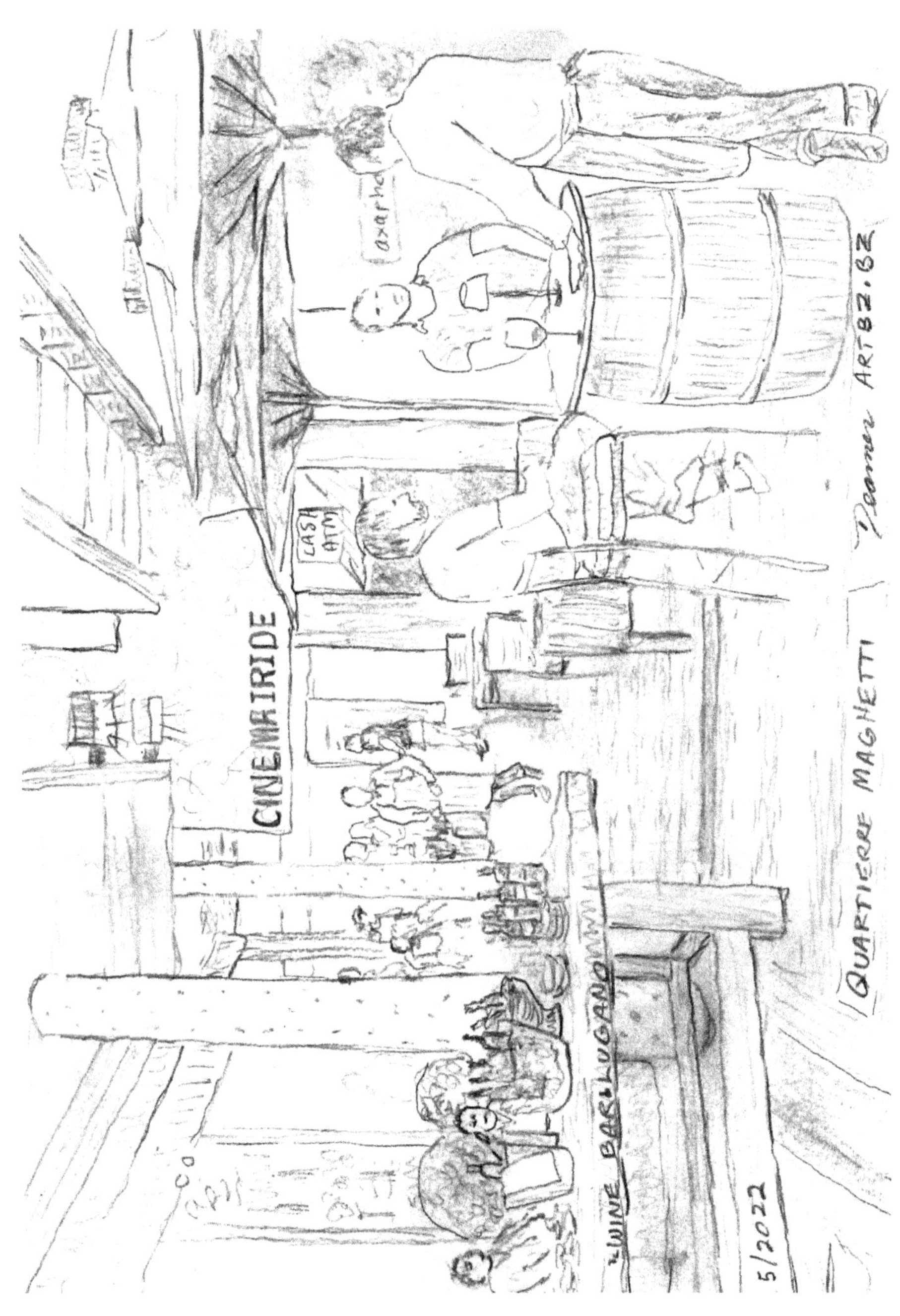
CINEMA IRIDE
CASH ATM
oxarka
WINE BAR LUGANO
QUARTIERRE MAGHETTI
Drawn ART82.BZ
5/2022

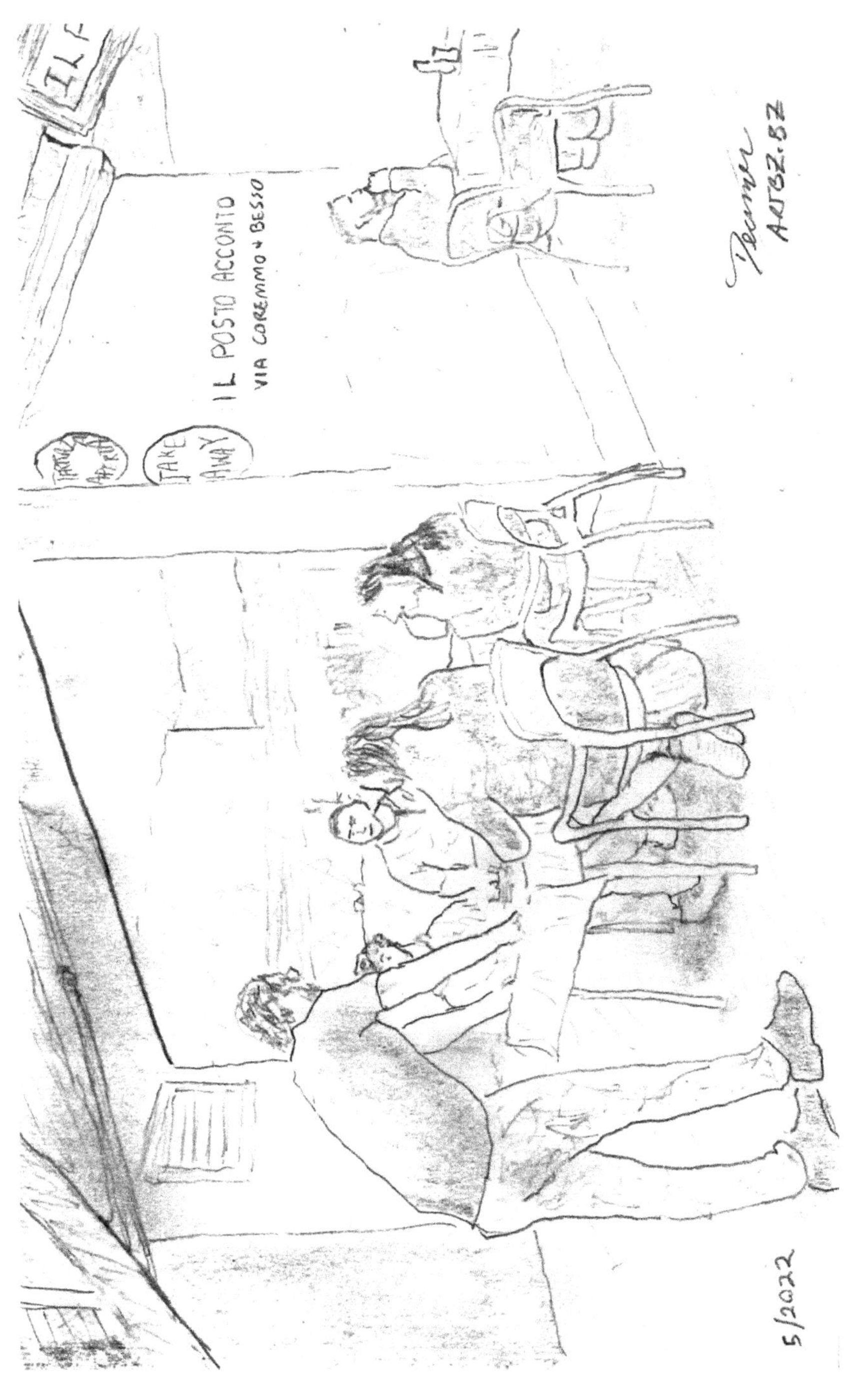
IL POSTO ACCONTO
VIA COREMMO ↓ BESSO
TAKE
AWAY
5/2022

22

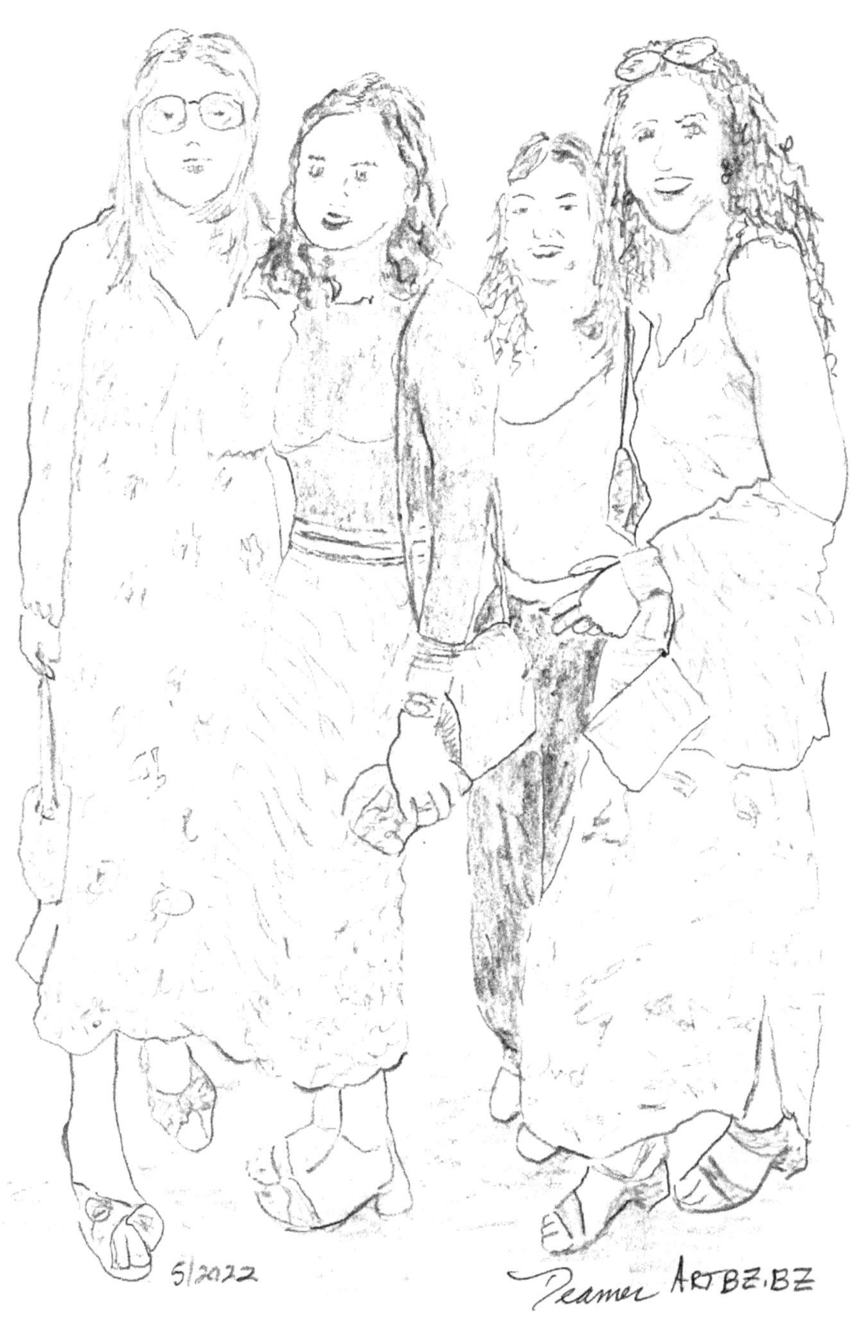

5/2022
Dreamer ARTBZ.BZ

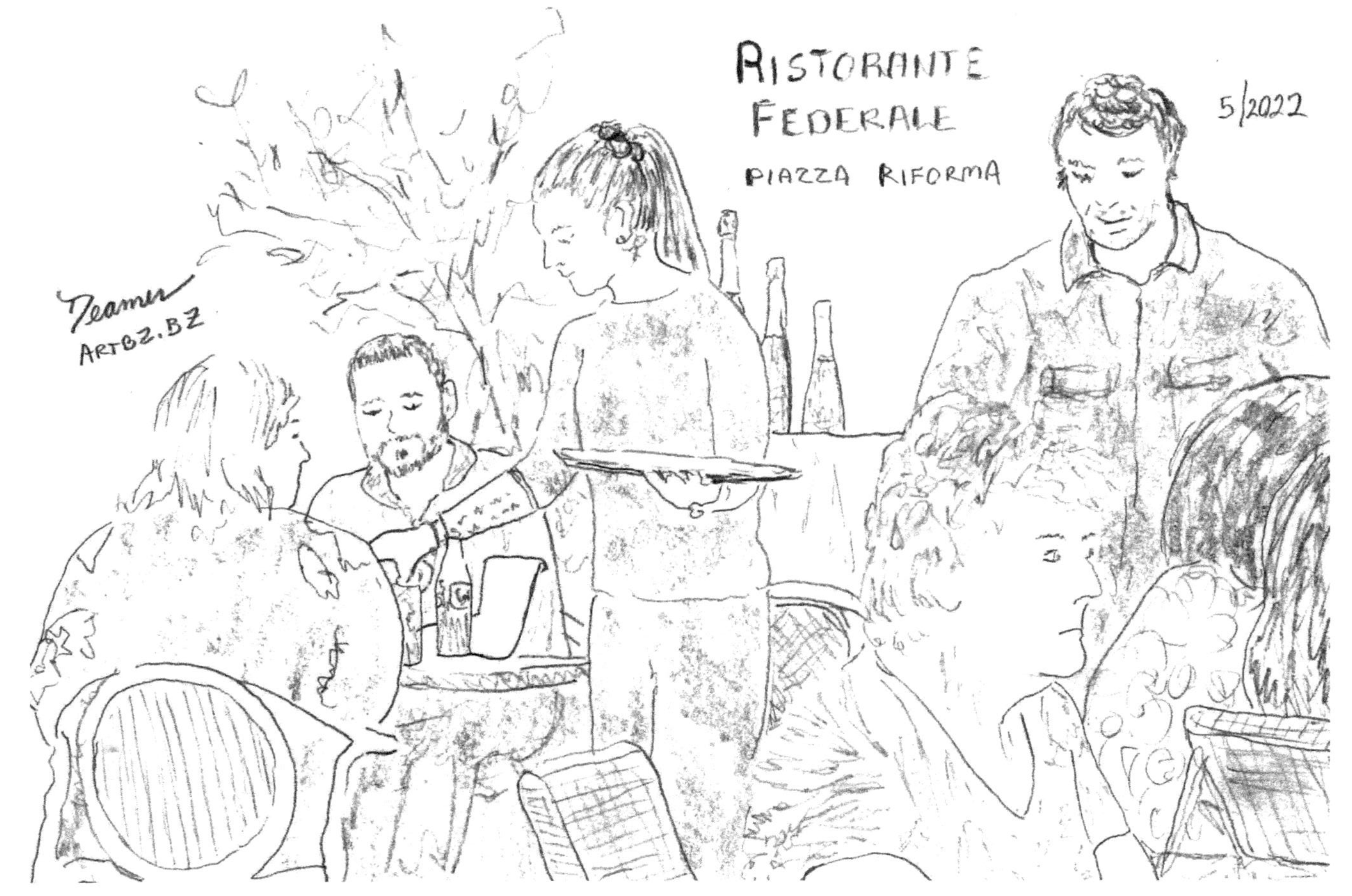
RISTORANTE
FEDERALE
PIAZZA RIFORMA
5/2022
ARTBZ.BZ

26

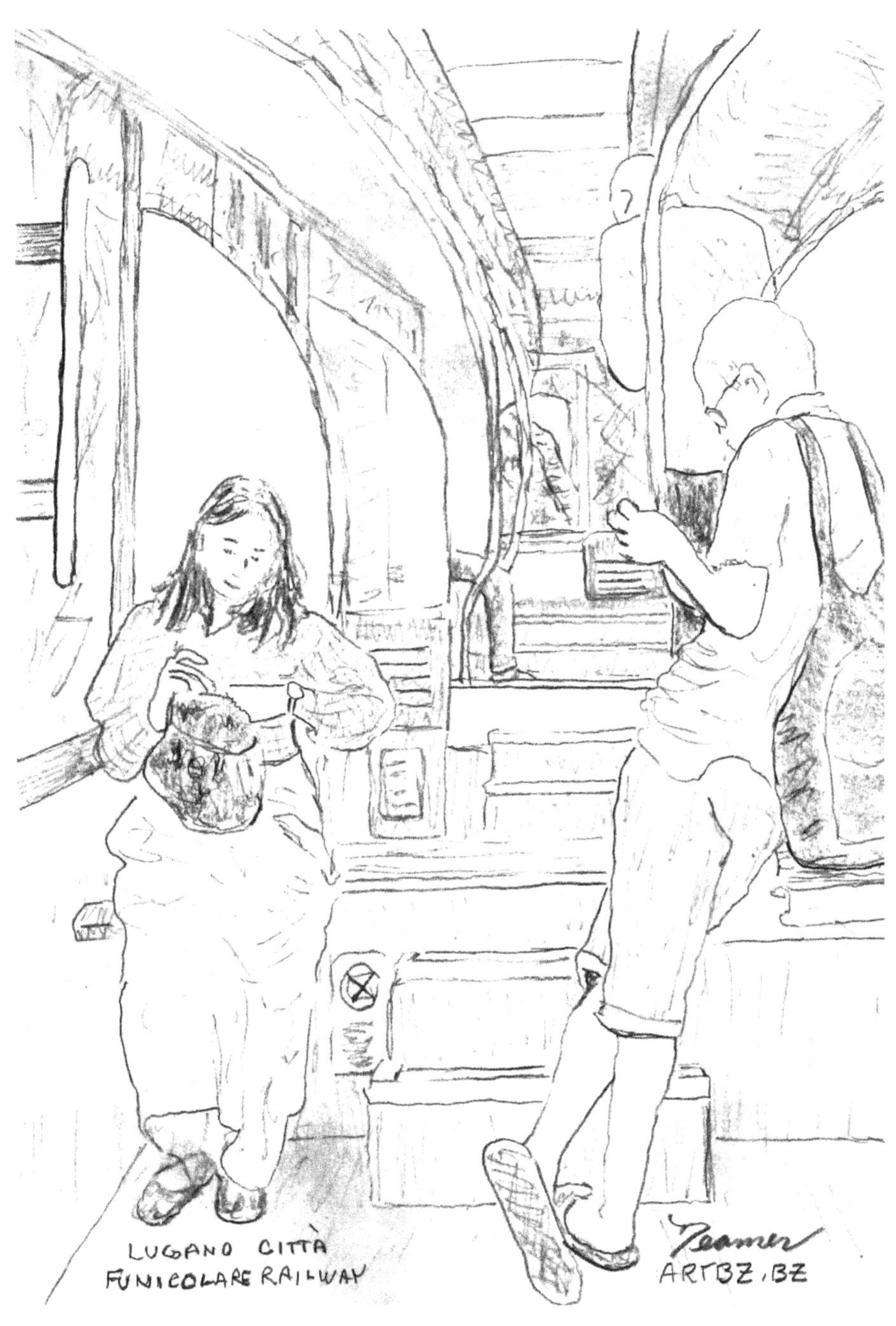

LUGANO CITTÀ
FUNICOLARE RAILWAY
ARTBZ.BZ

28

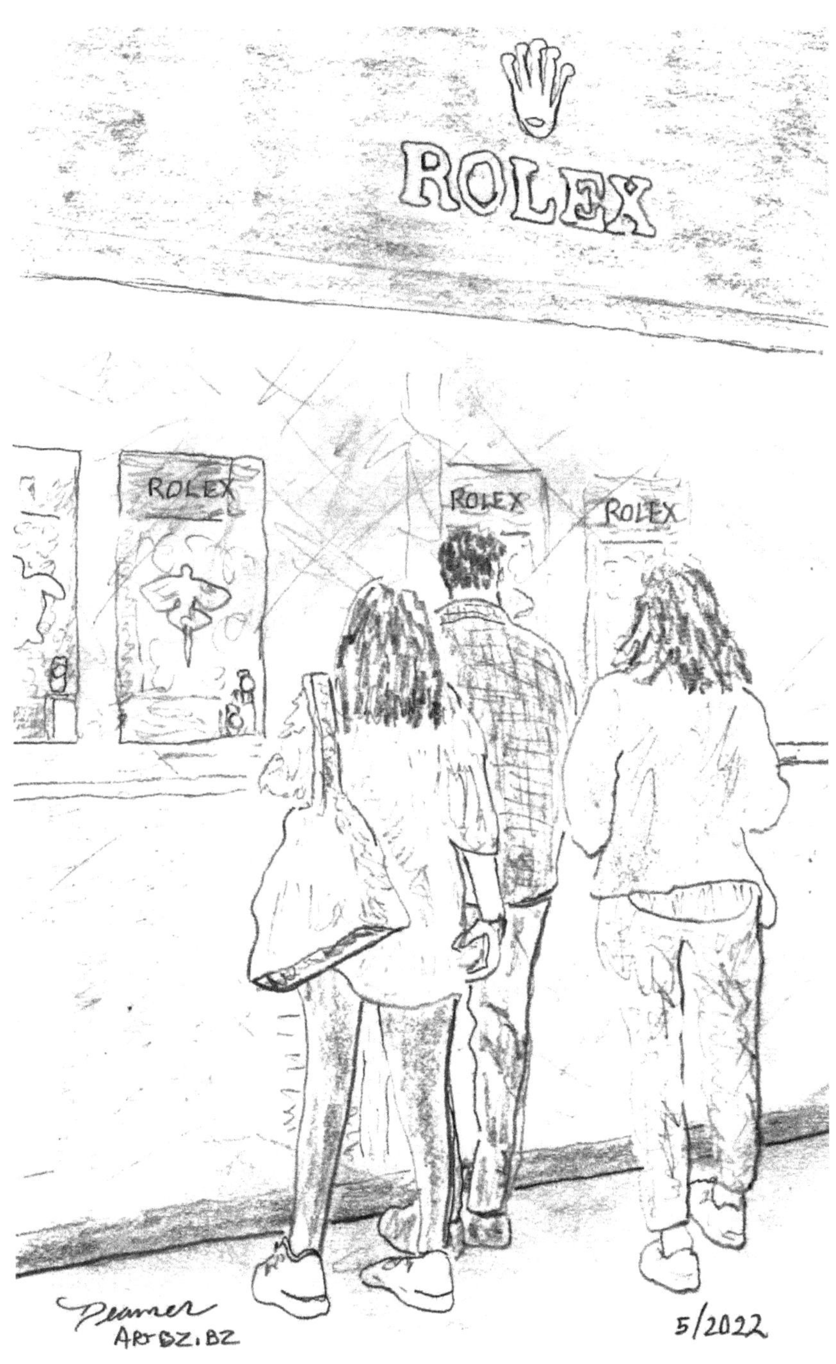
ROLEX
ROLEX
ROLEX
ROLEX

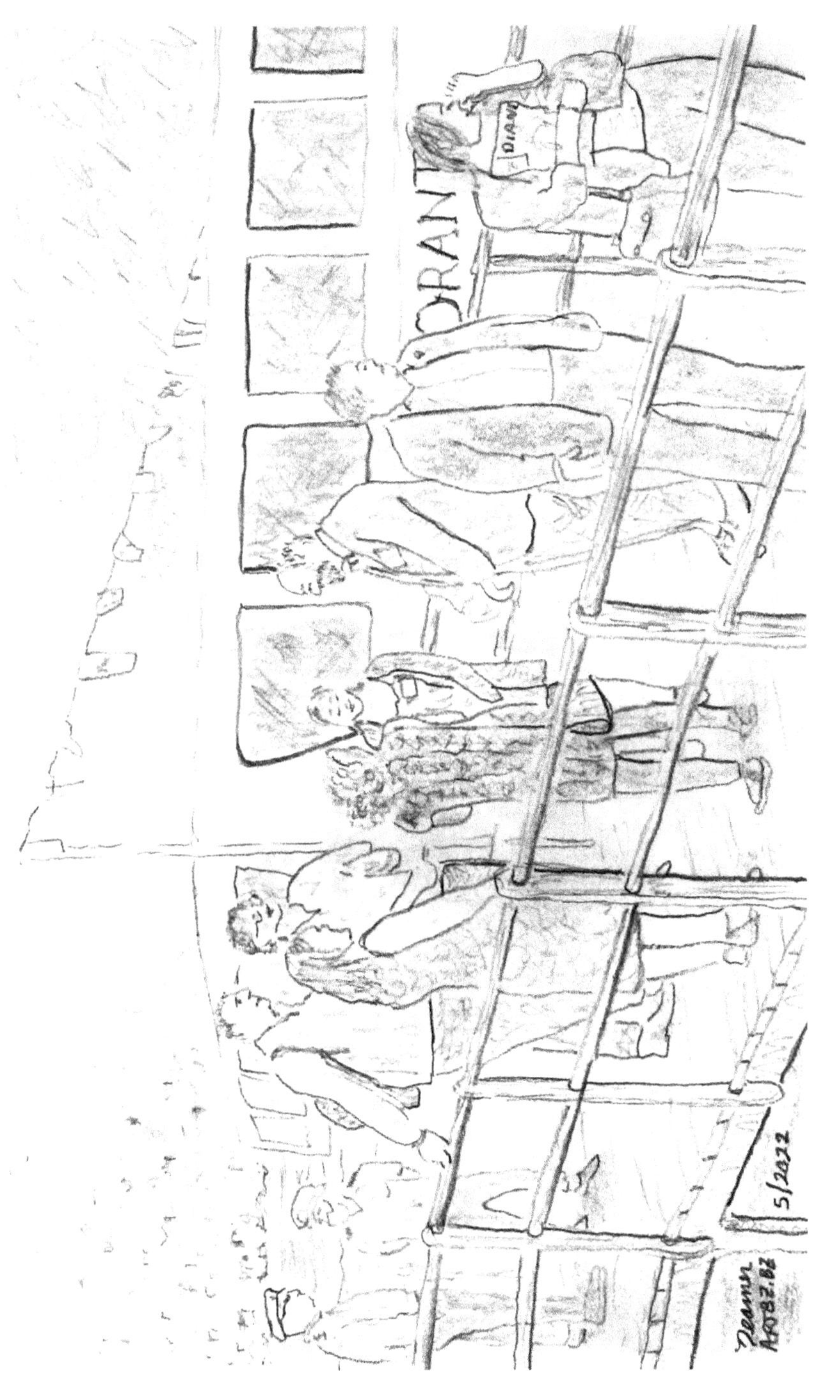

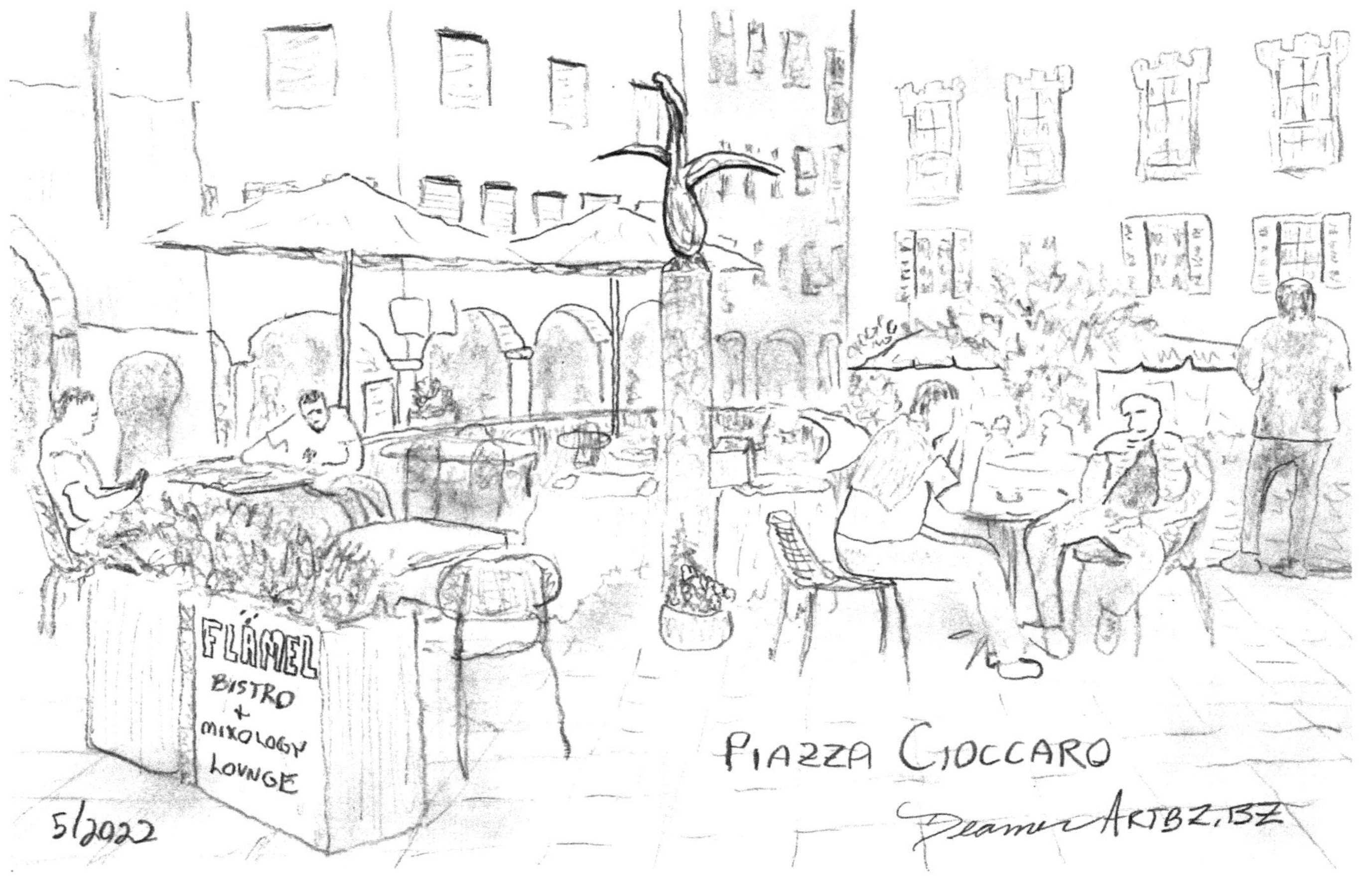
FLÄMEL
BISTRO
+
MIXOLOGY
LOUNGE
5/2022
PIAZZA CIOCCARO
Deamer ARTBZ.BZ

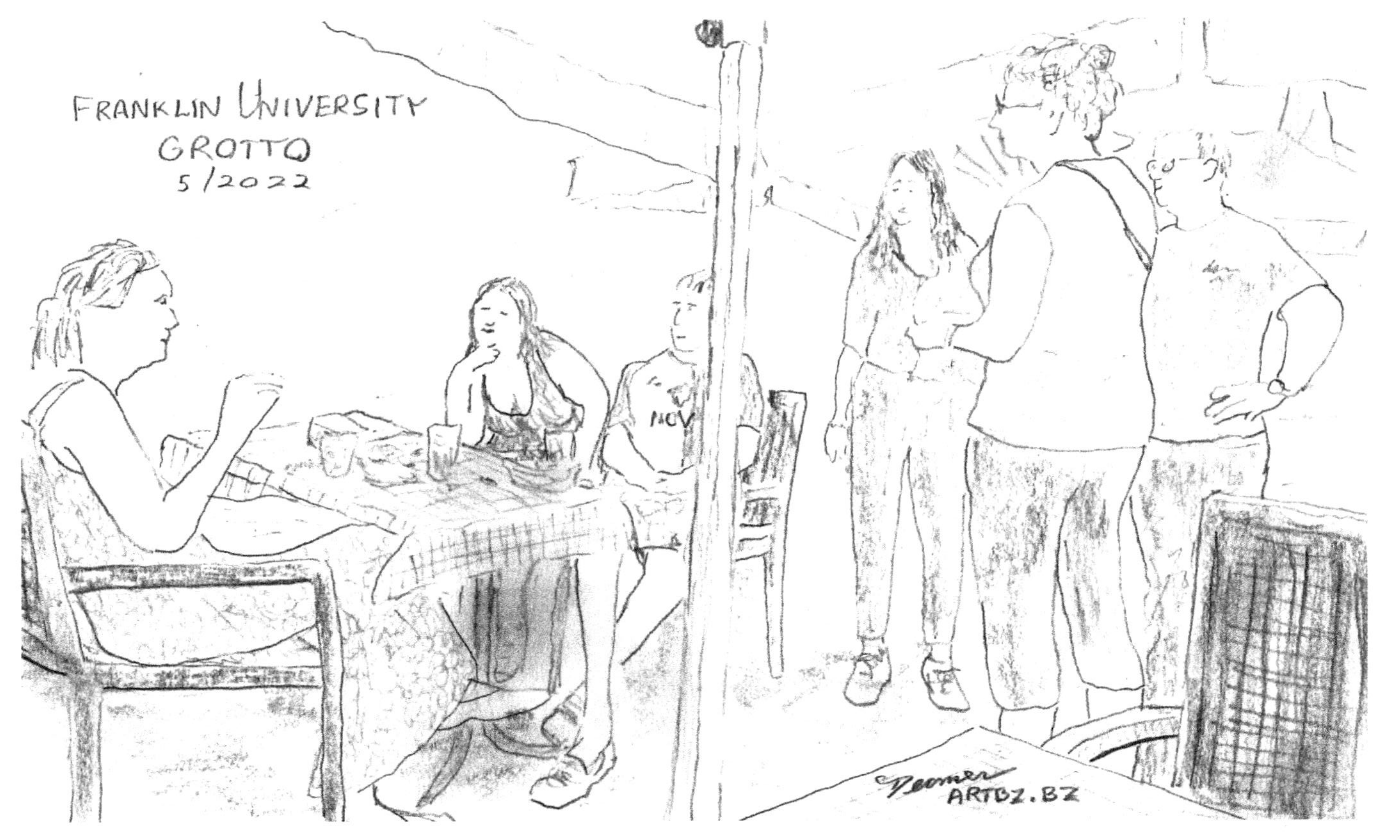
FRANKLIN UNIVERSITY
GROTTO
5/2022
ARTBZ.BZ

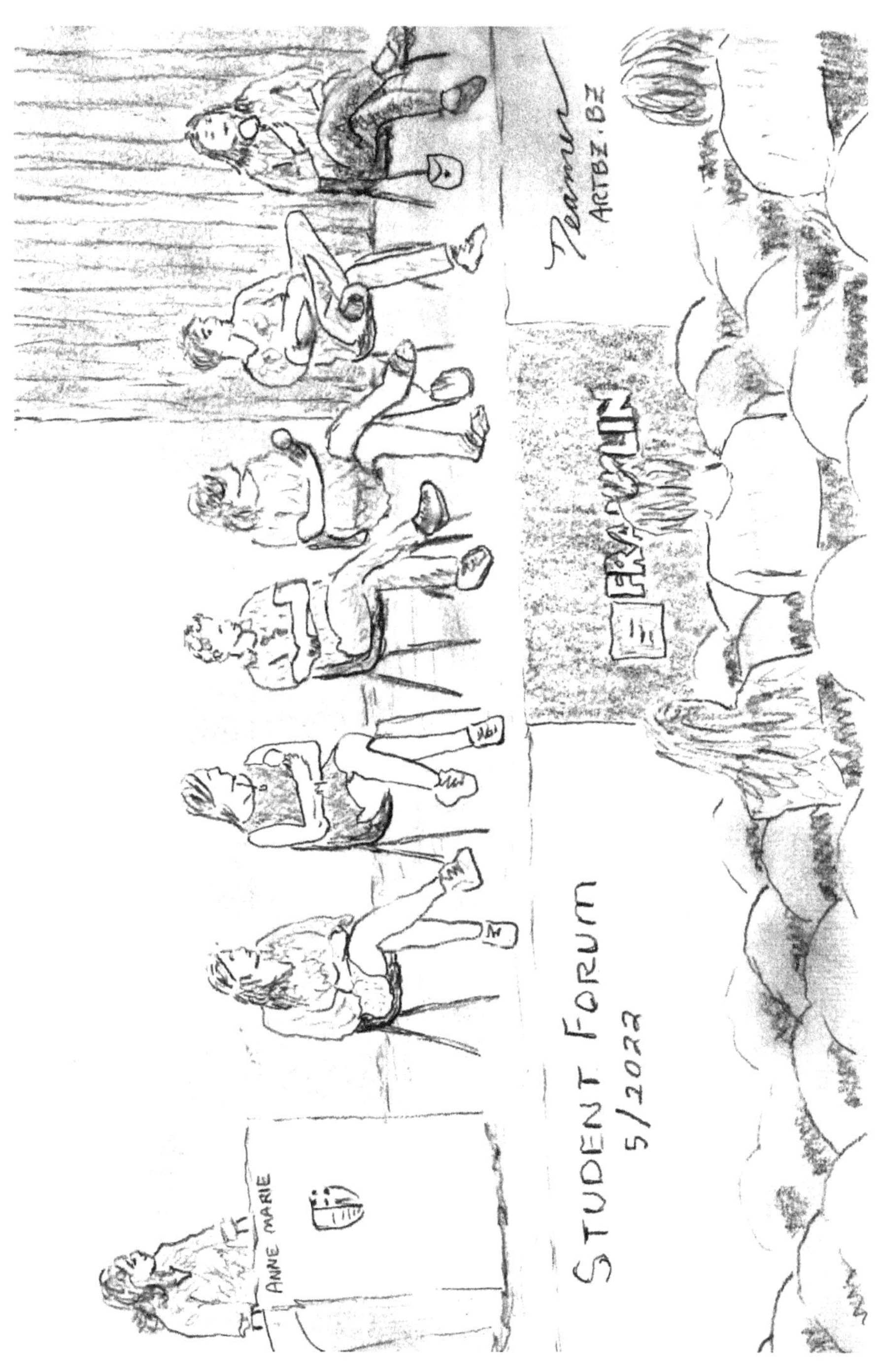
Team
ARTBZ.BZ
FRANKLIN
STUDENT FORUM
5/2022
ANNE MARIE

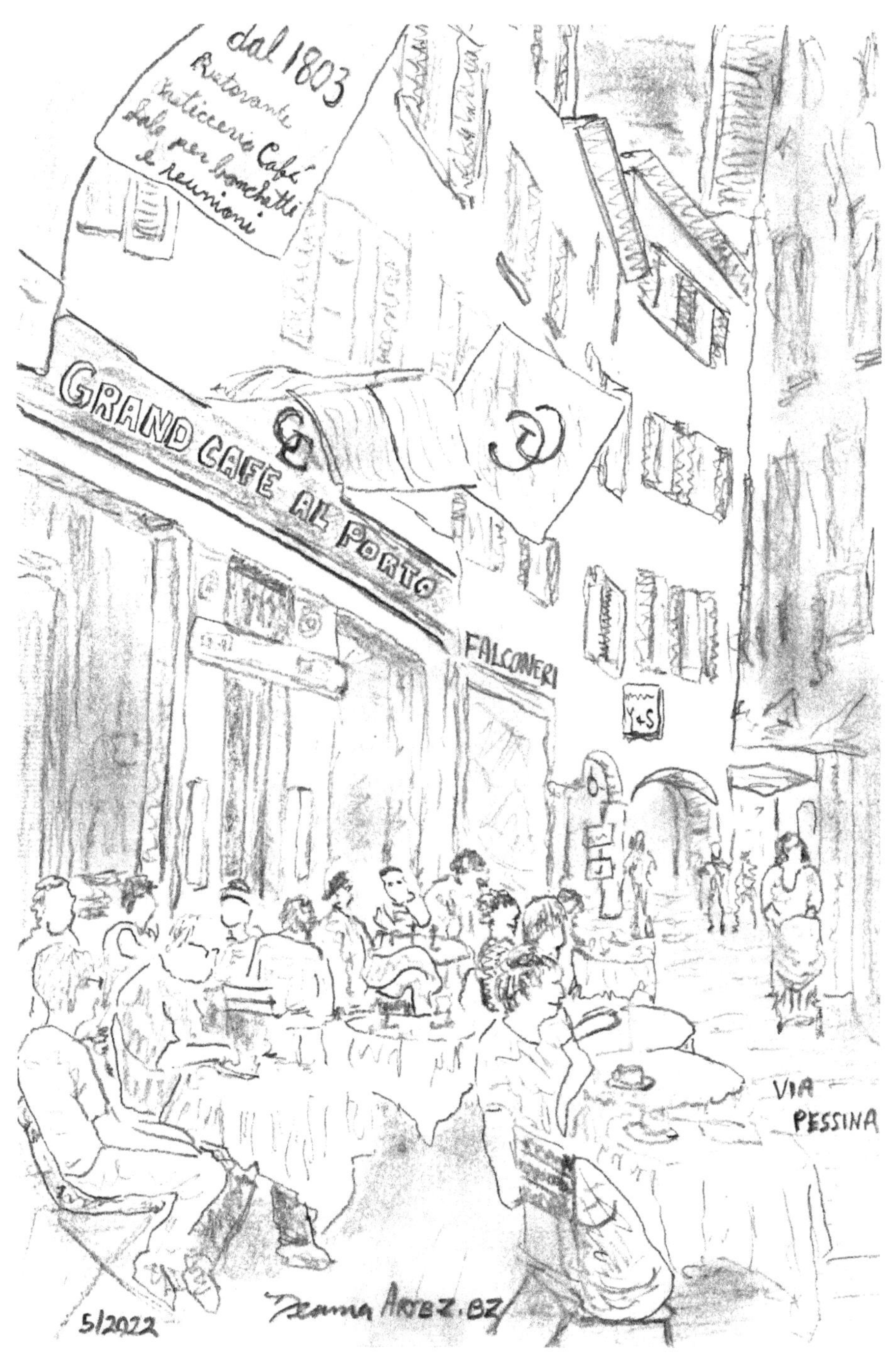

dal 1803
Ristorante
Pasticceria Café
Sale per banchetti
e reunioni
GRAND CAFE AL PORTO
FALCONERI
Y+S
VIA PESSINA
5/2022

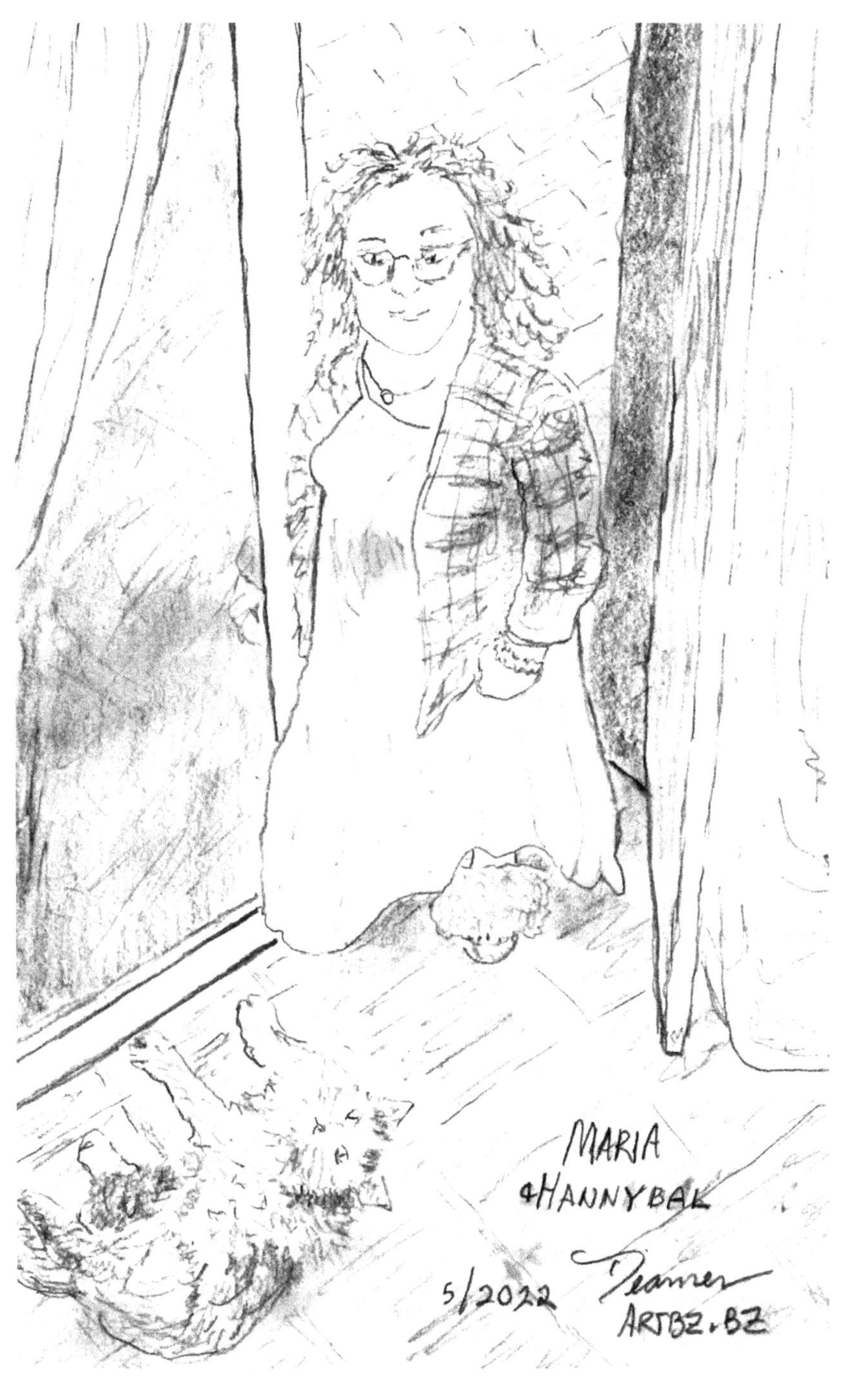
MARIA
&HANNYBAL
5/2022
ART82.BZ

42

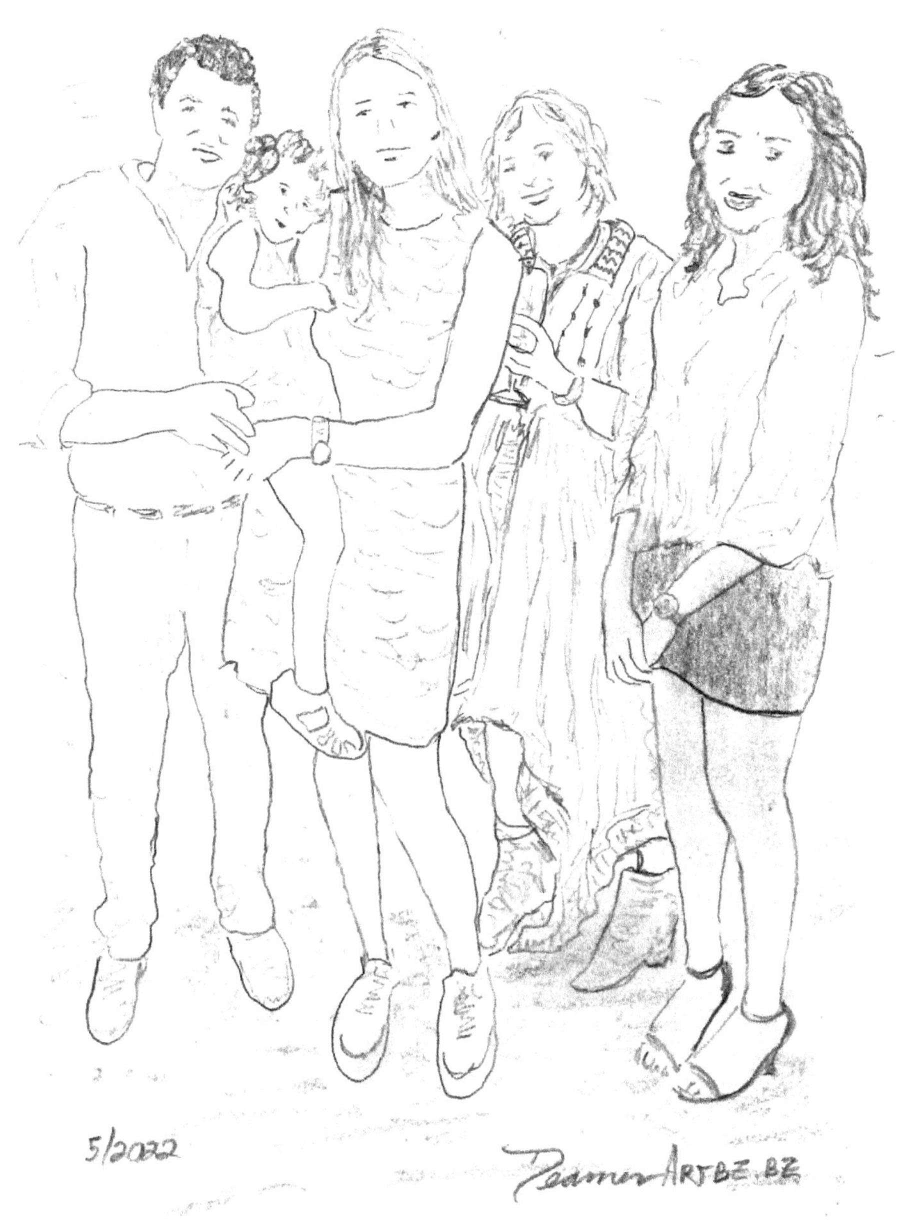
5/2022

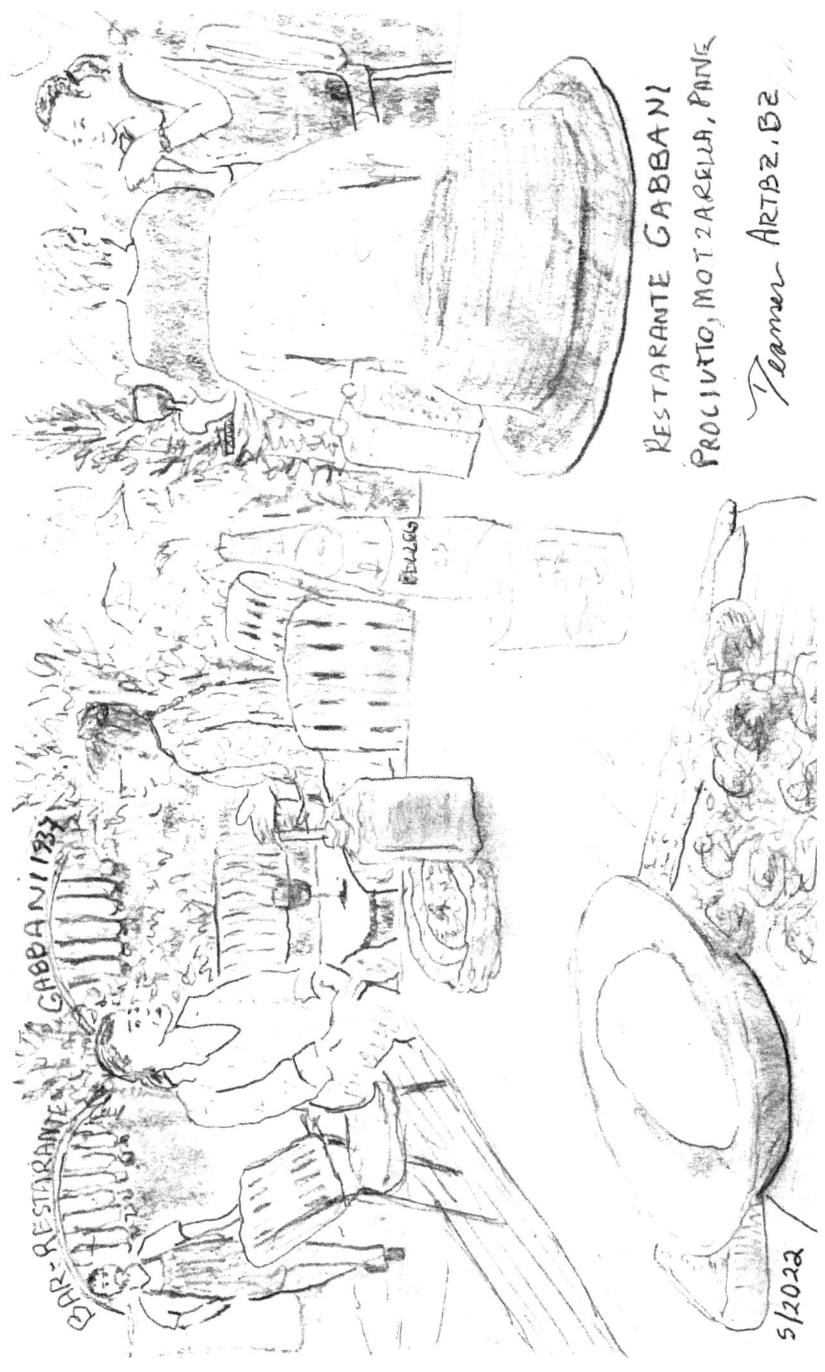
RESTARANTE GABBANI
PROCIUTTO, MOTZARELLA, PANE
ARTBZ.BZ
BAR-RESTARANTE GABBANI 1937
5/2022

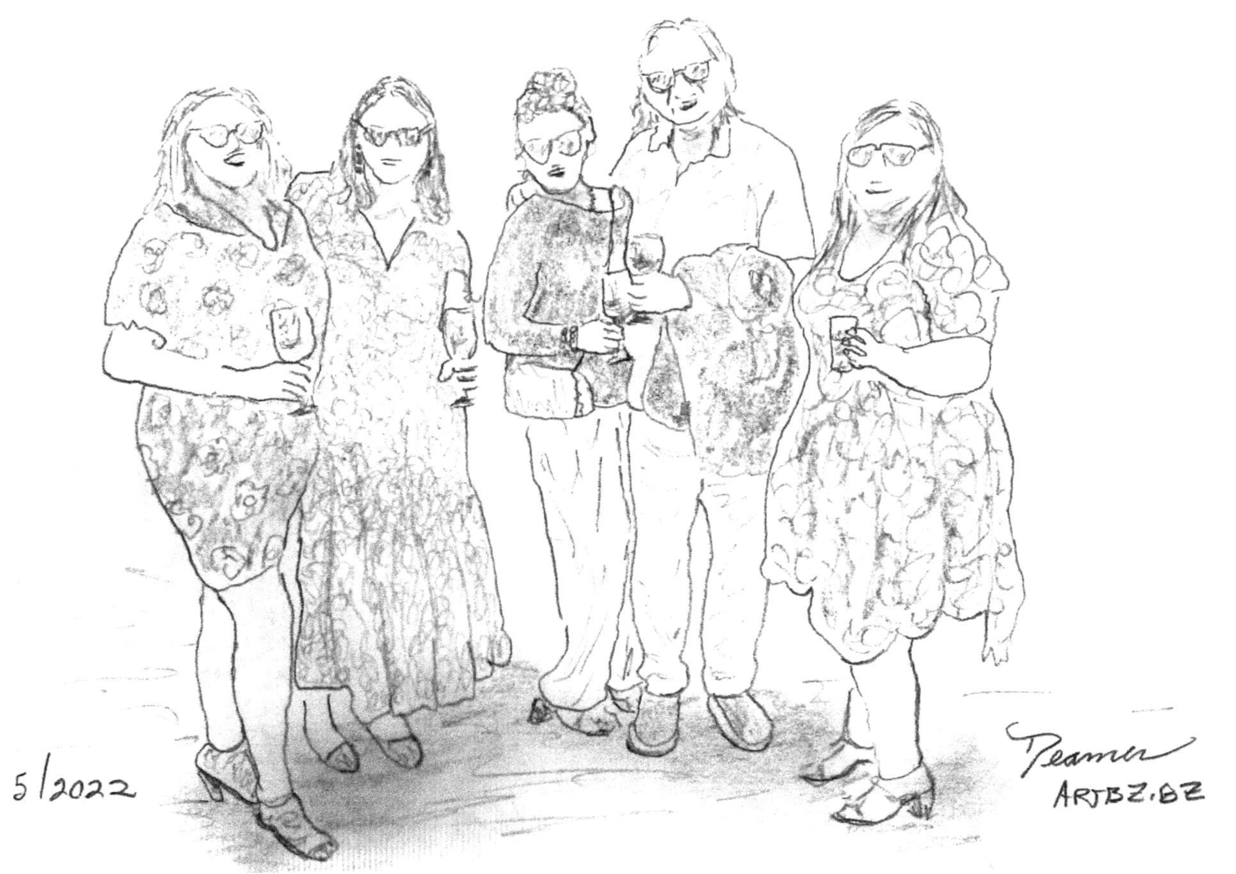

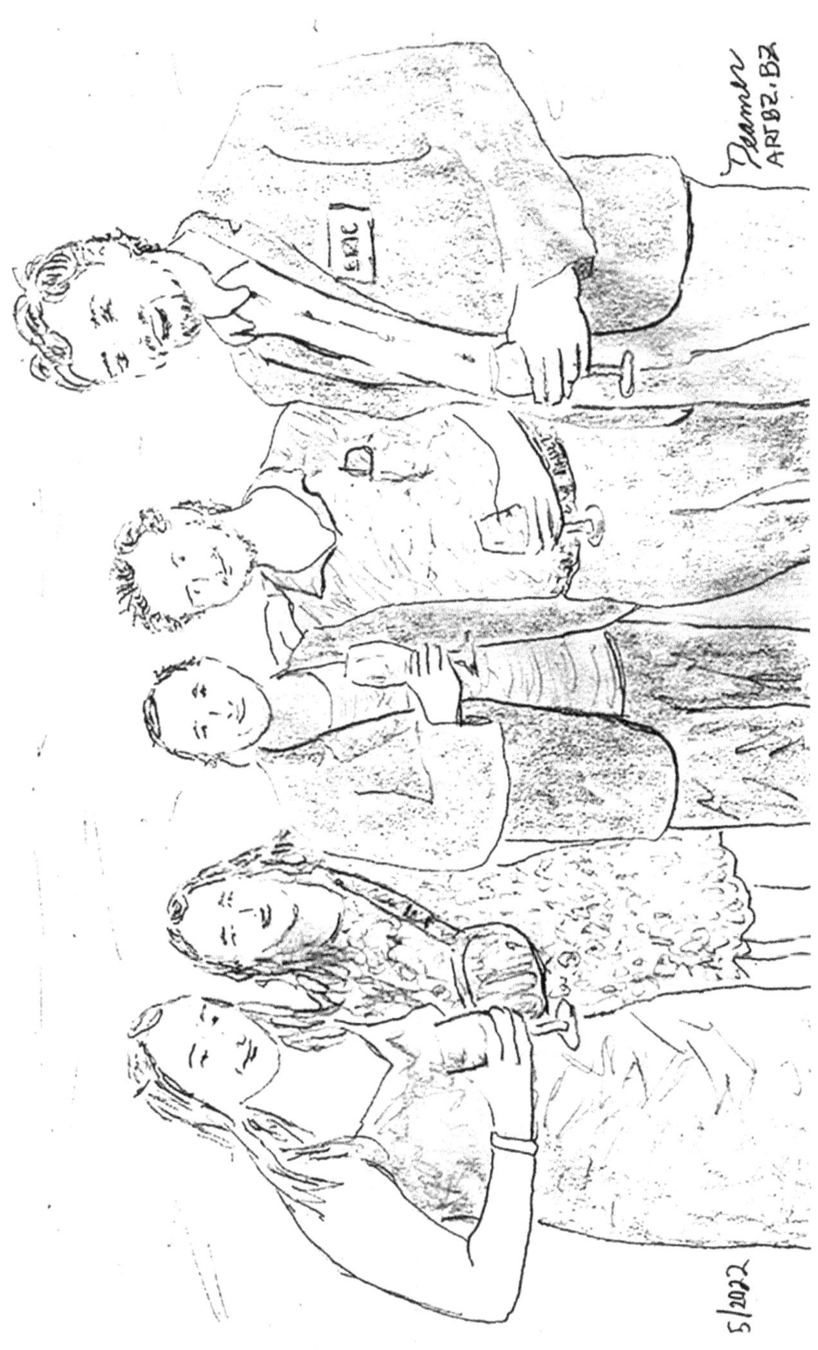

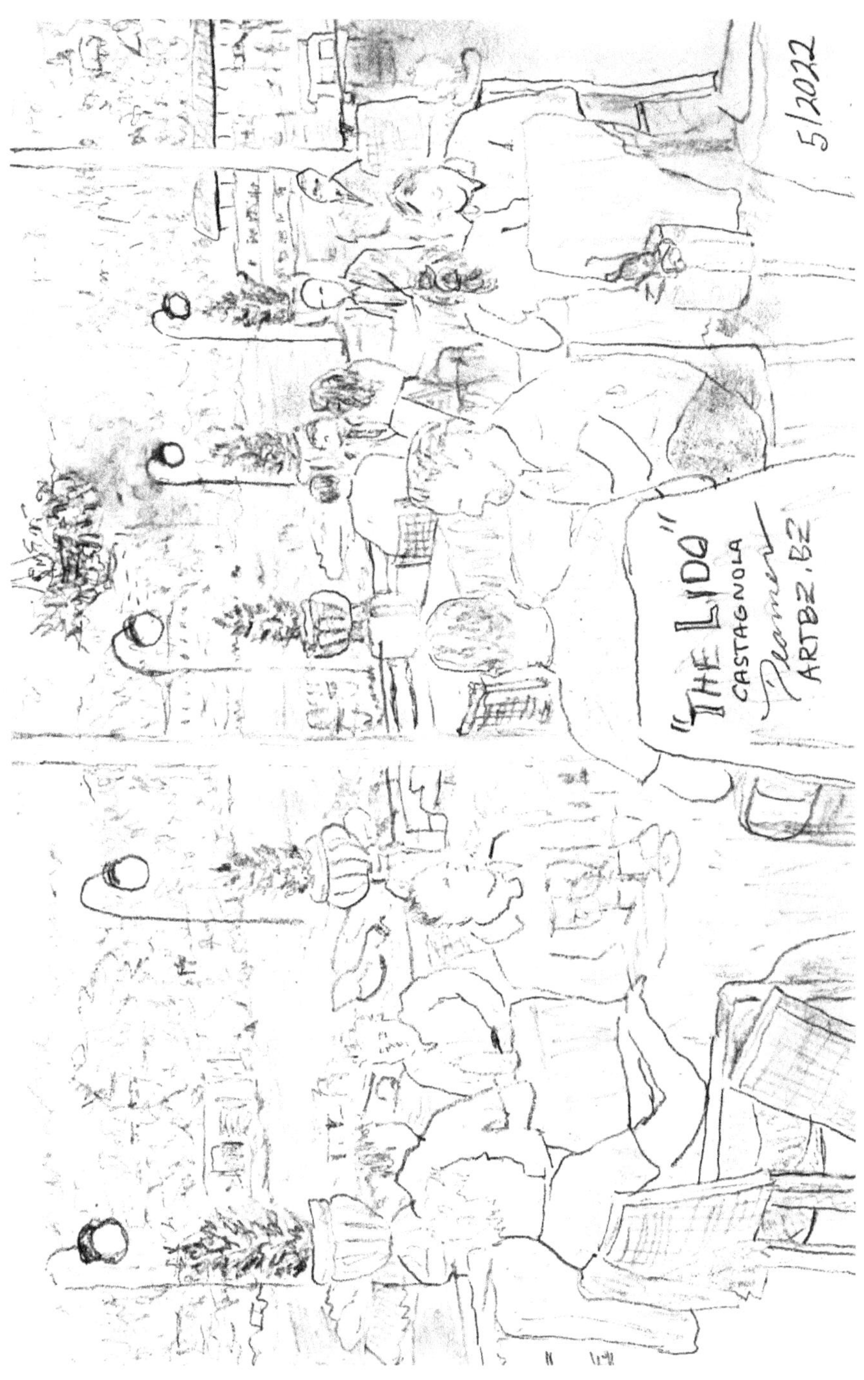
5/2022
"THE LIDO"
CASTAGNOLA
ARTB2.B2

52

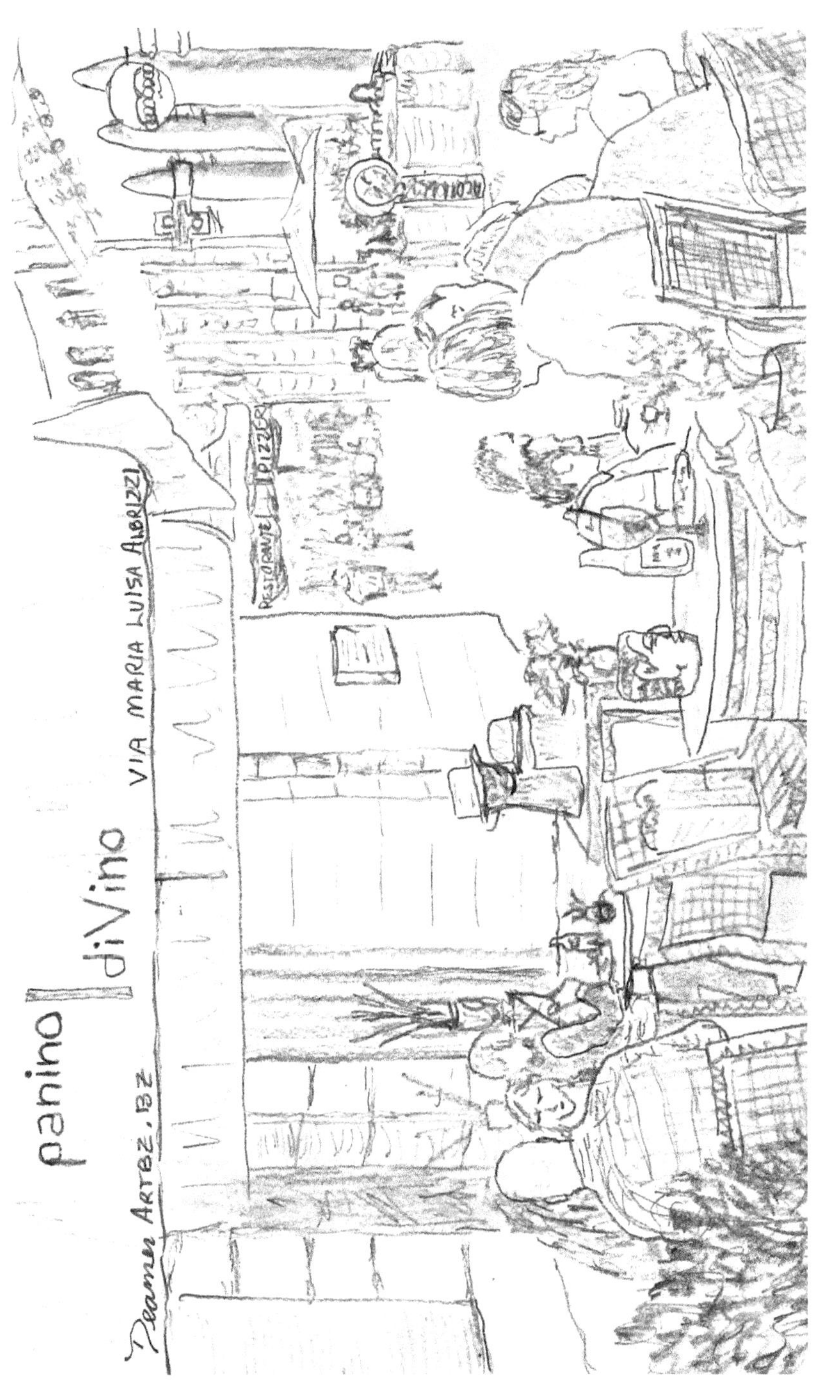
panino diVino
VIA MARIA LUISA ALBRIZZI
RISTORANTE PIZZERI
Dreamer Artez, BZ

54

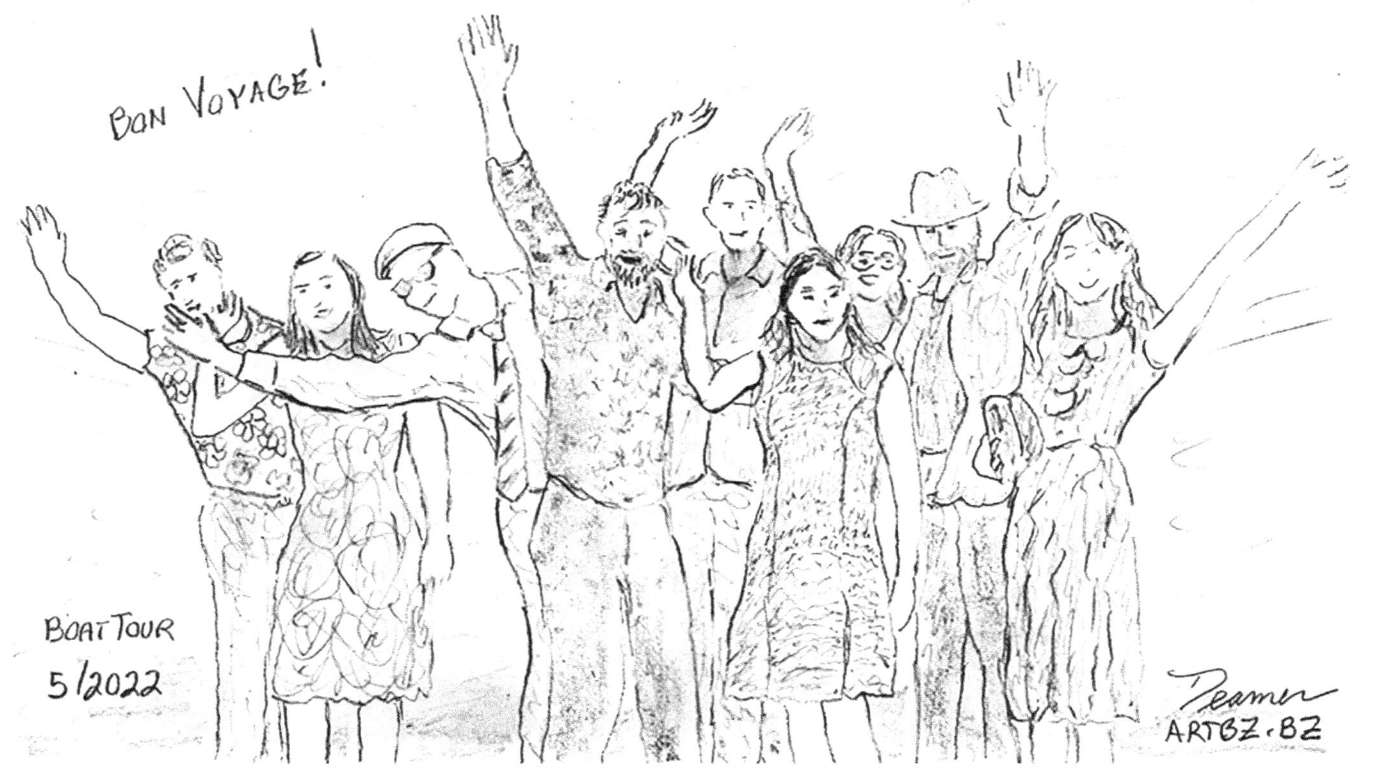
Bon Voyage!
Boat Tour
5/2022

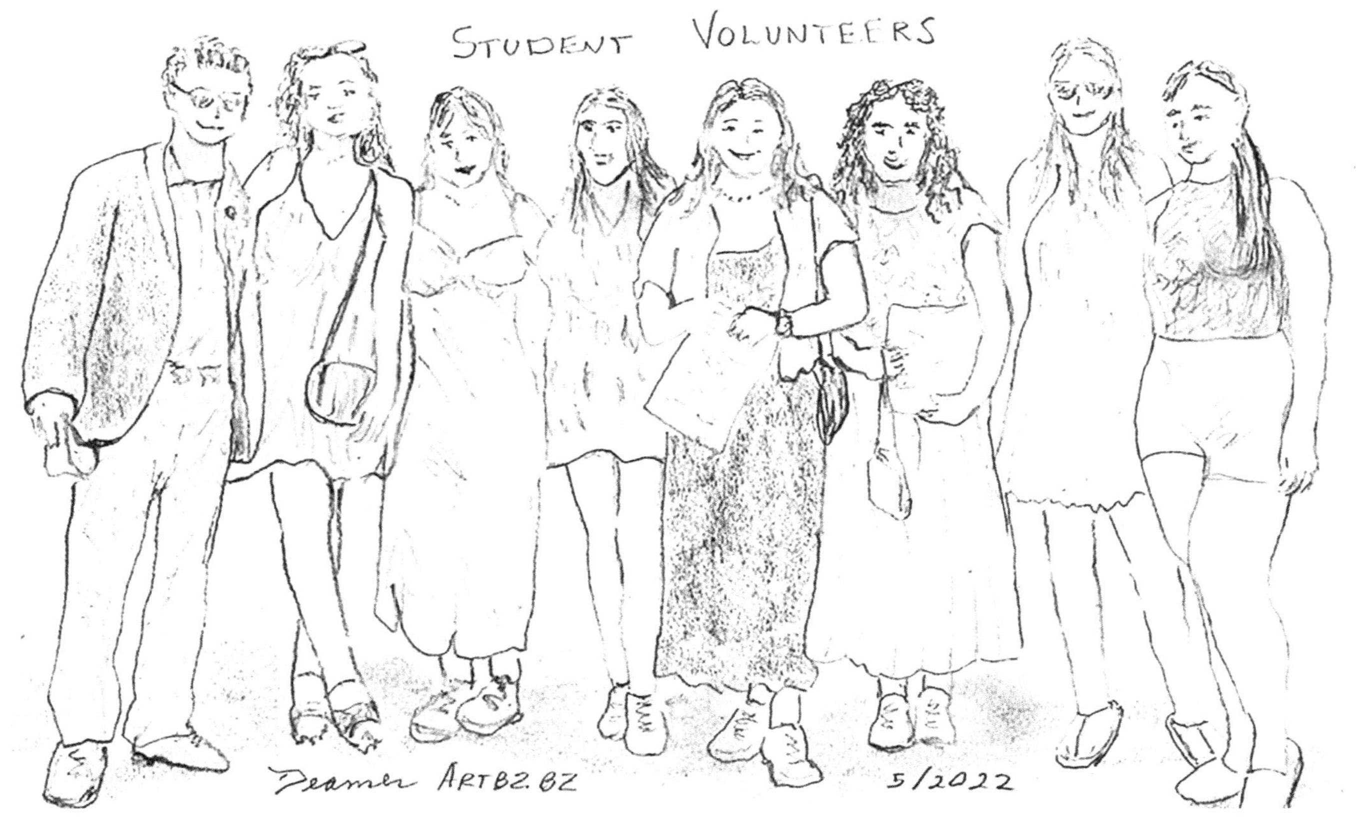
STUDENT VOLUNTEERS
Deamer ARTB2.BZ
5/2022

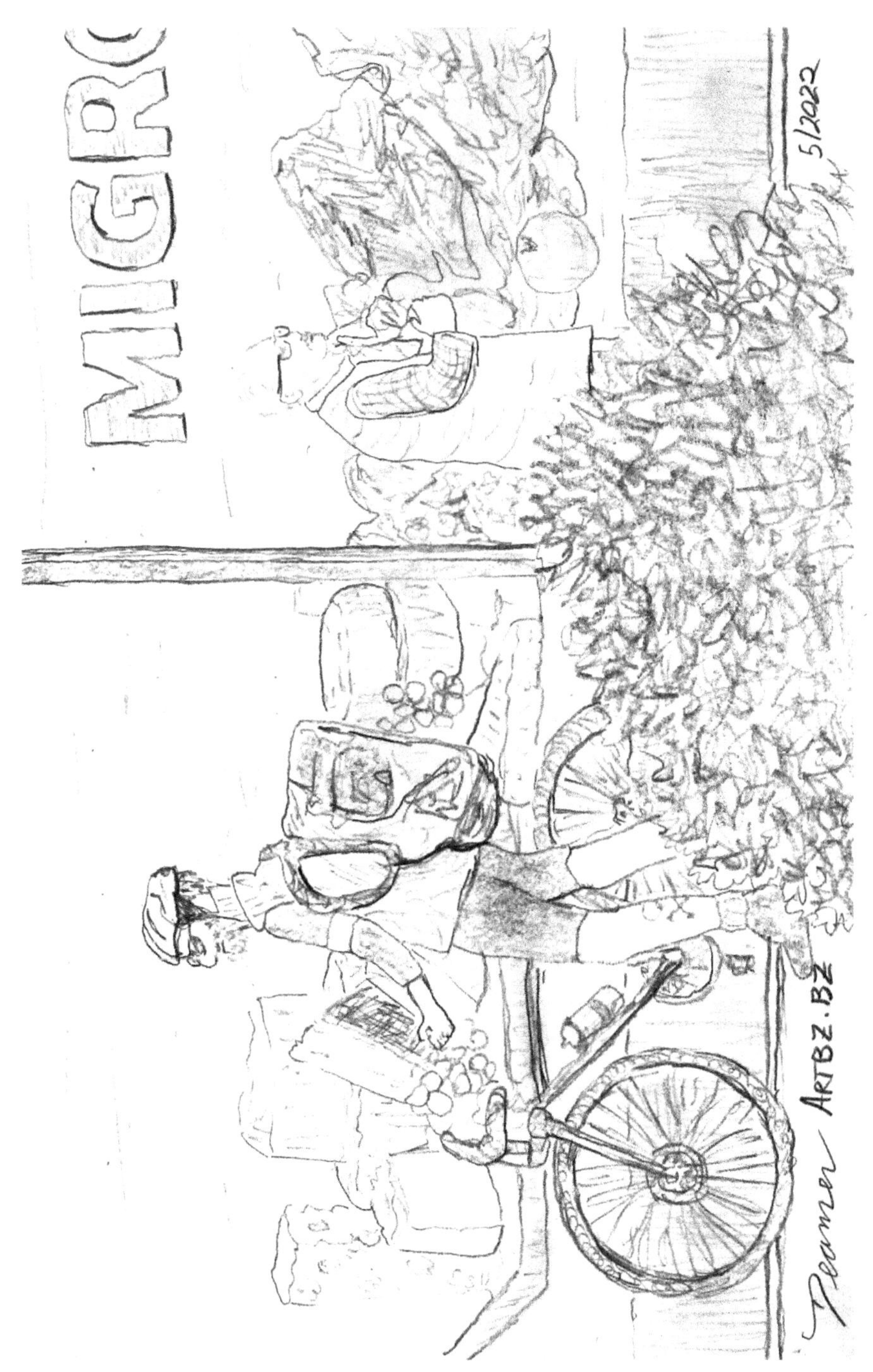
MIGRO
Reamer ArtBz.BZ
5/2022

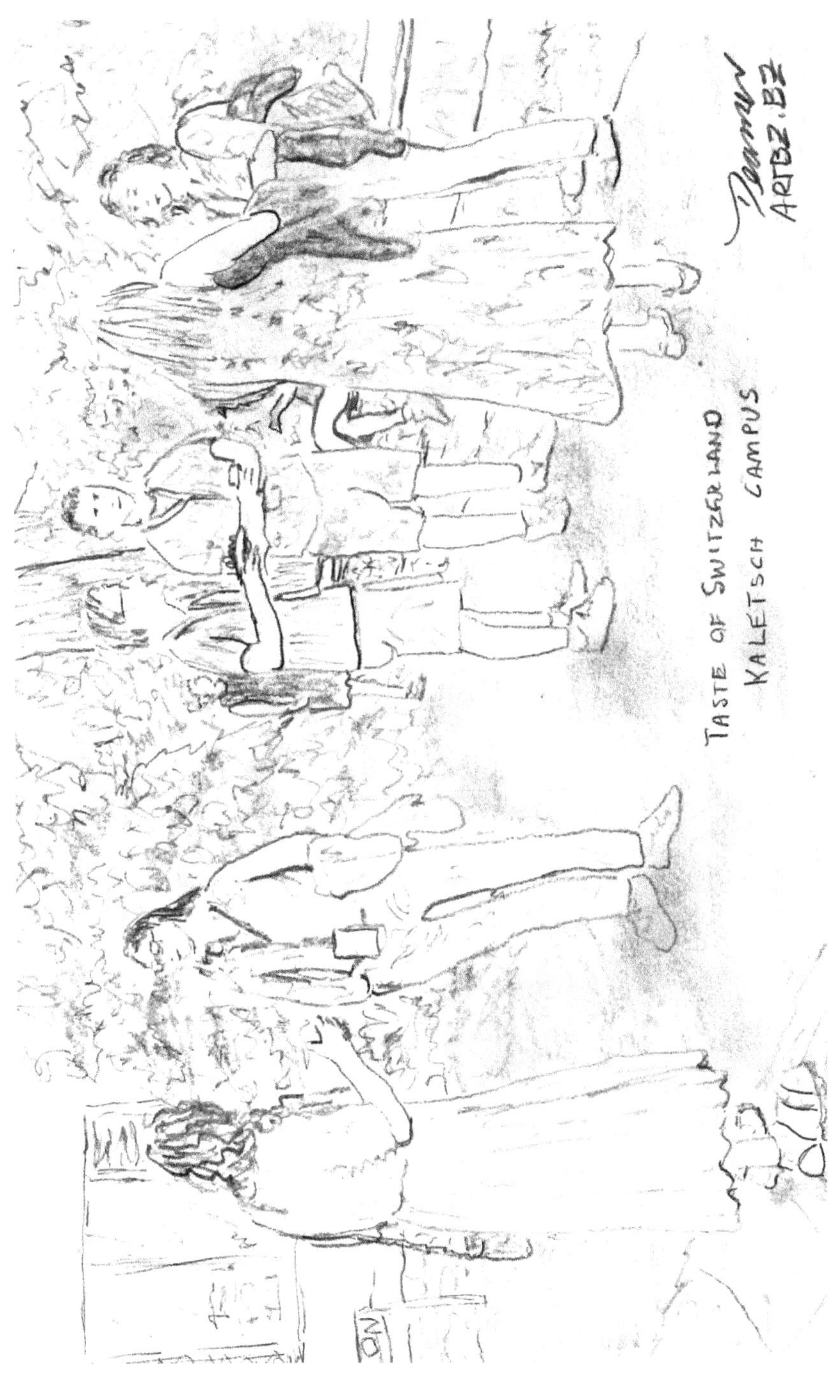
Taste of Switzerland
Kaletsch Campus

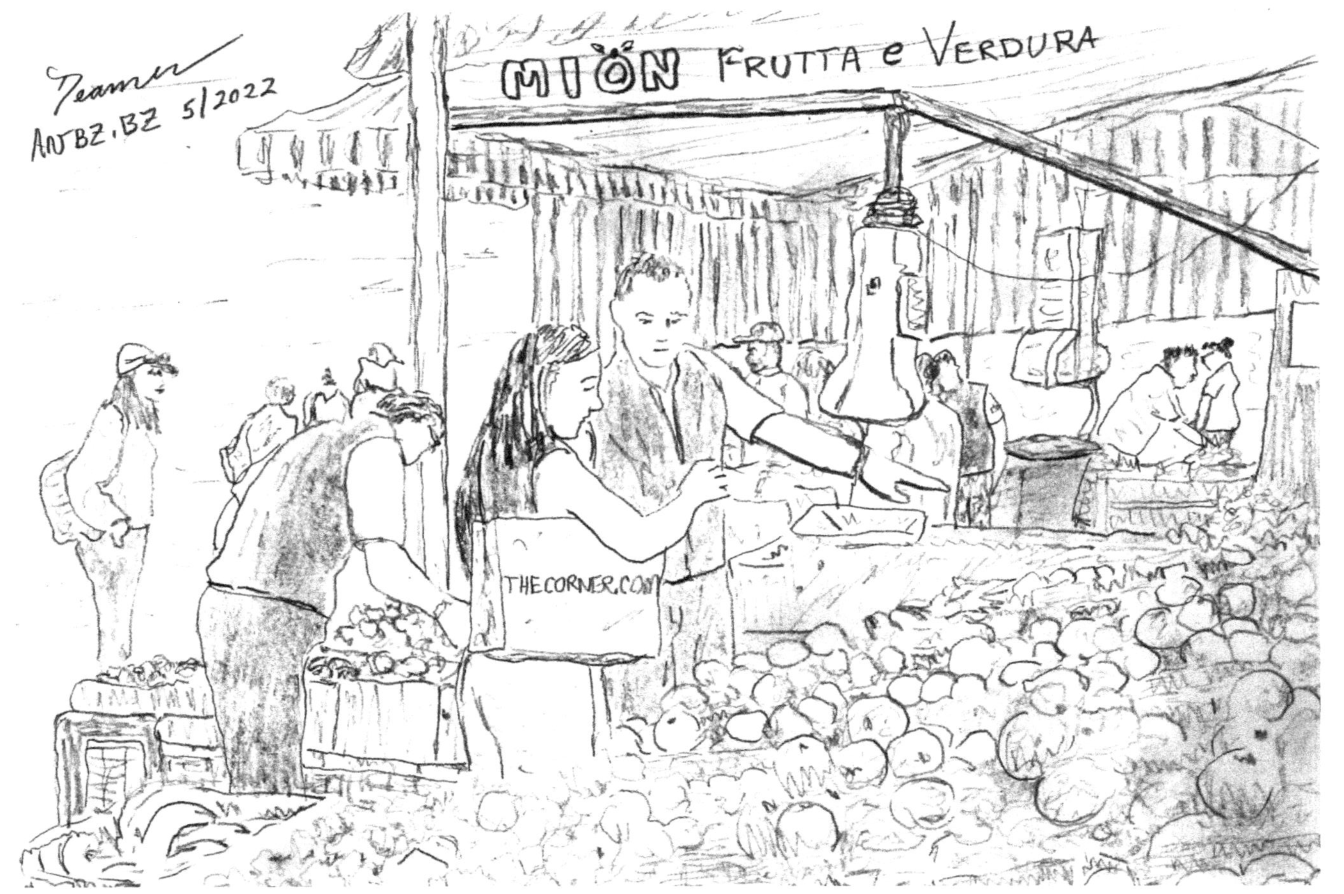
MIÖN FRUTTA e VERDURA
THECORNER.COM
Teamer
ANTBZ.BZ 5/2022

64

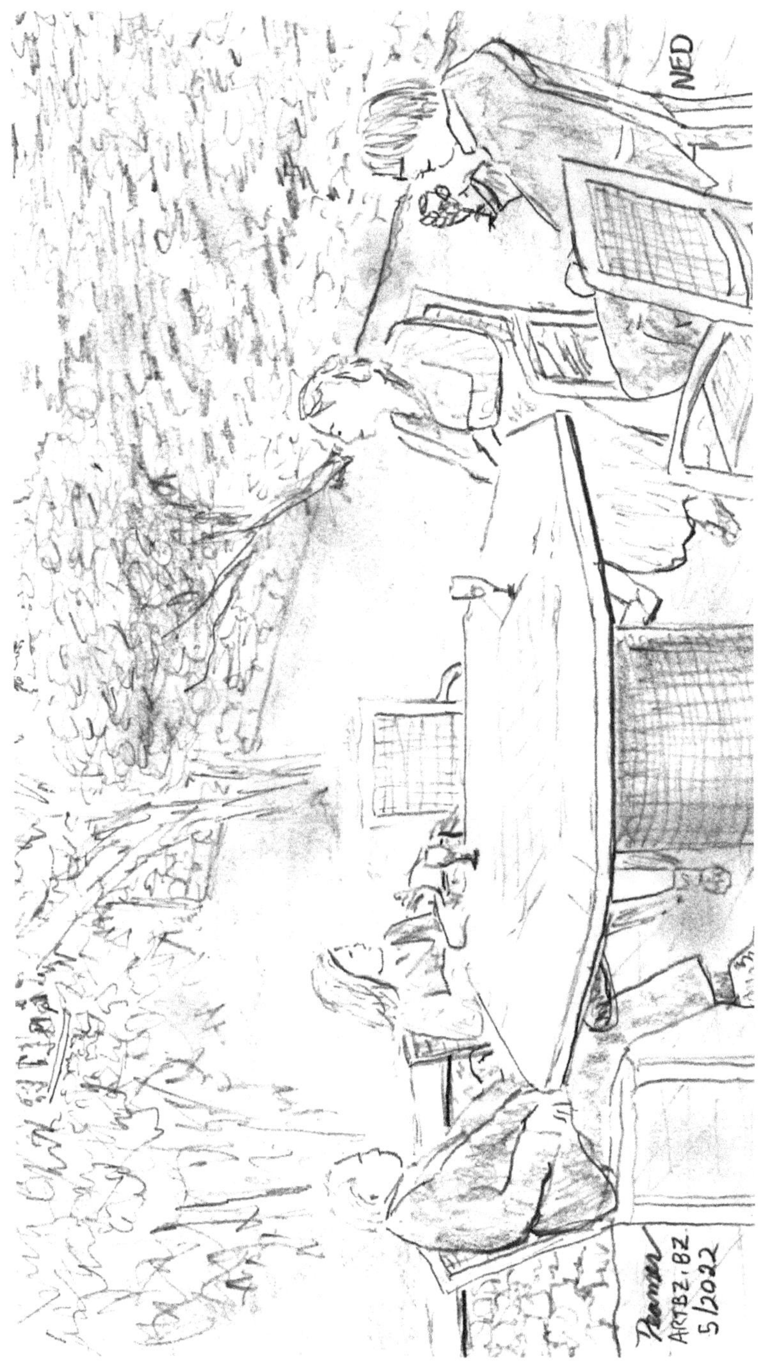

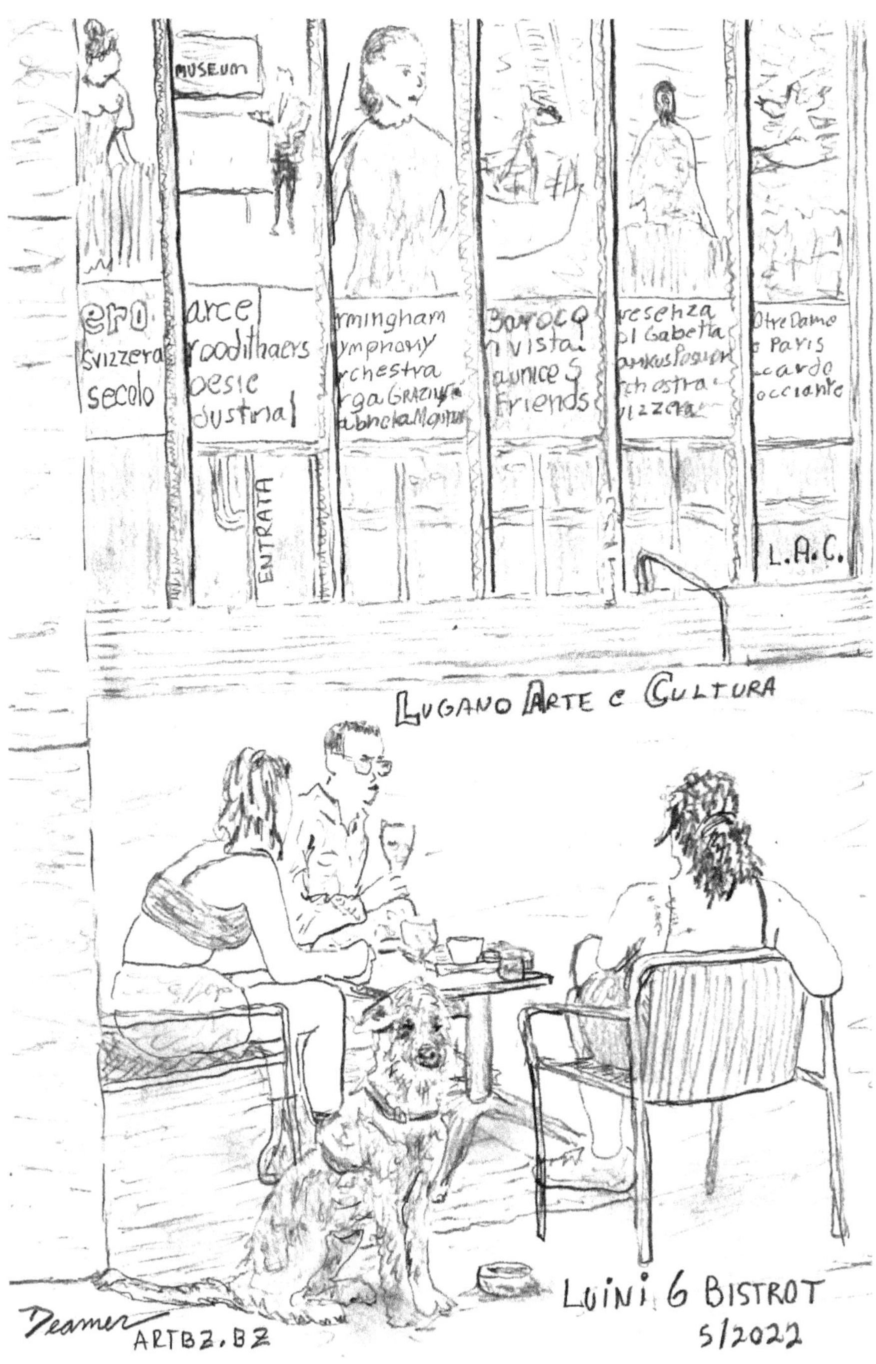

MUSEUM
ero
svizzera
secolo
arce
roodithaers
oesie
dustrial
ENTRATA
rmingham
ymphony
rchestra
rga GRAZIA
bhelaMonn
Baroco
n vista
unice S
Friends
resenza
l Gabetta
nkusPosuer
chestra
vizzera
Otre Dame
e PARIS
carde
occiante
L.A.C.
Lugano Arte e Cultura
Deamer
ARTBZ.BZ
Luini 6 Bistrot
5/2022

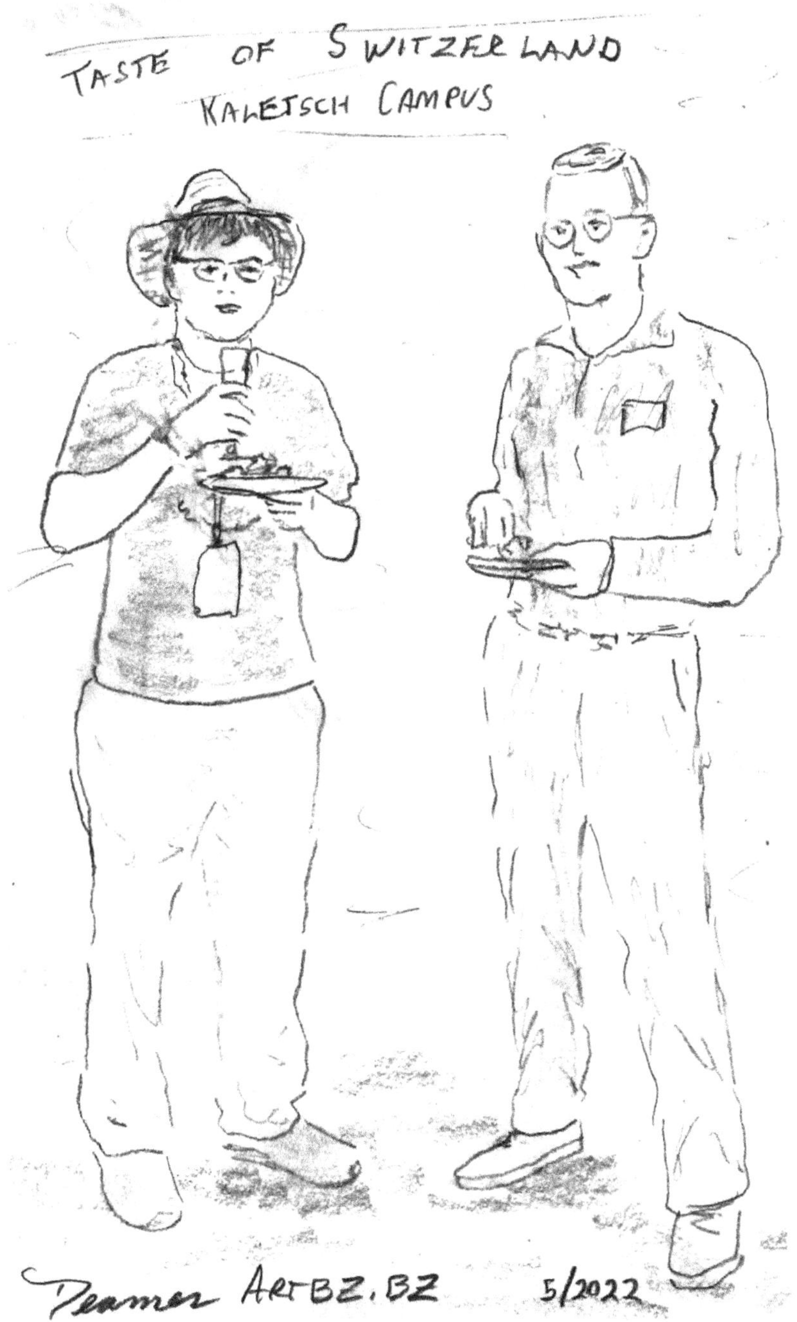
TASTE OF SWITZERLAND
KALETSCH CAMPUS
Deamer ArtBZ.BZ   5/2022

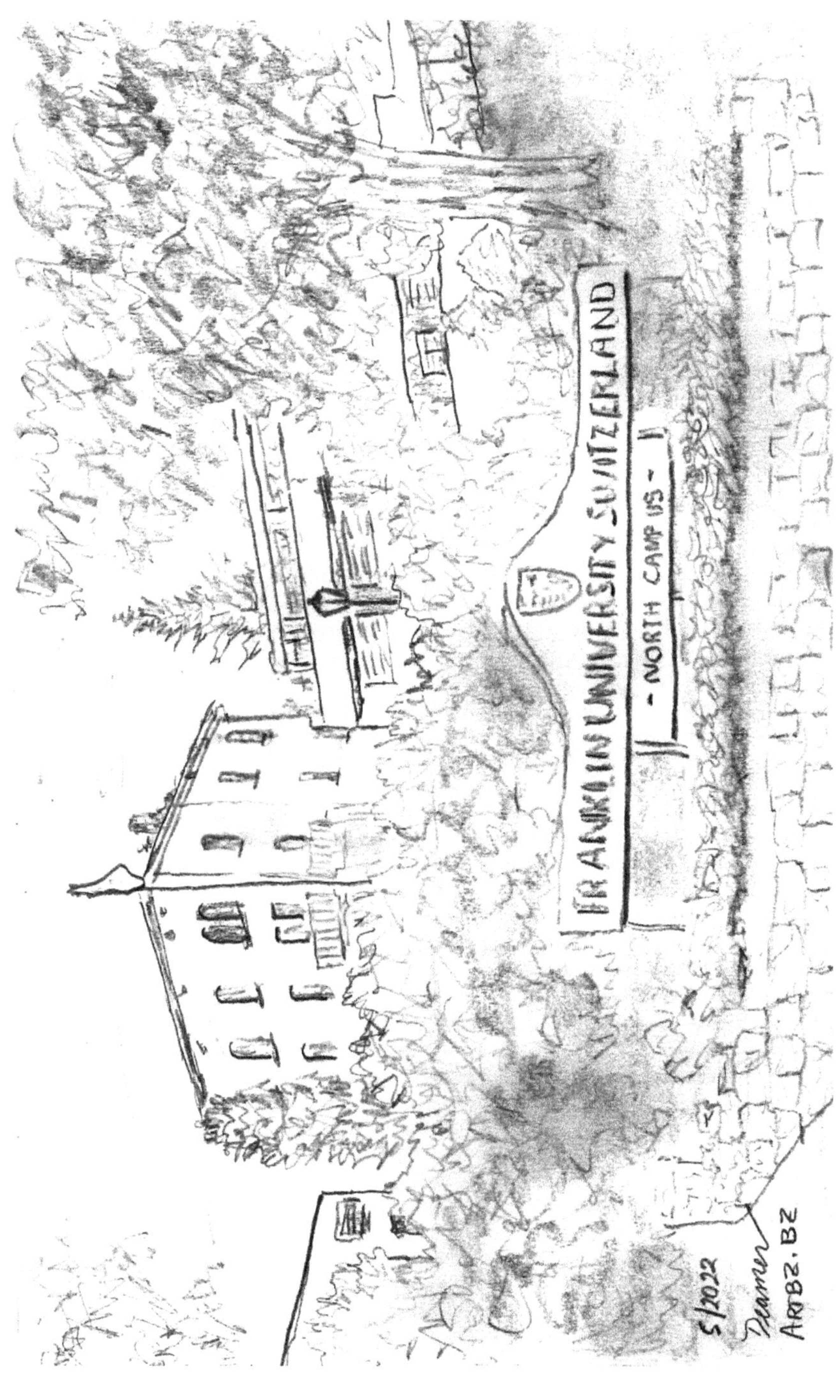
FRANKLIN UNIVERSITY SWITZERLAND
- NORTH CAMPUS -
5/2022
Deamer
ArtB2.B2

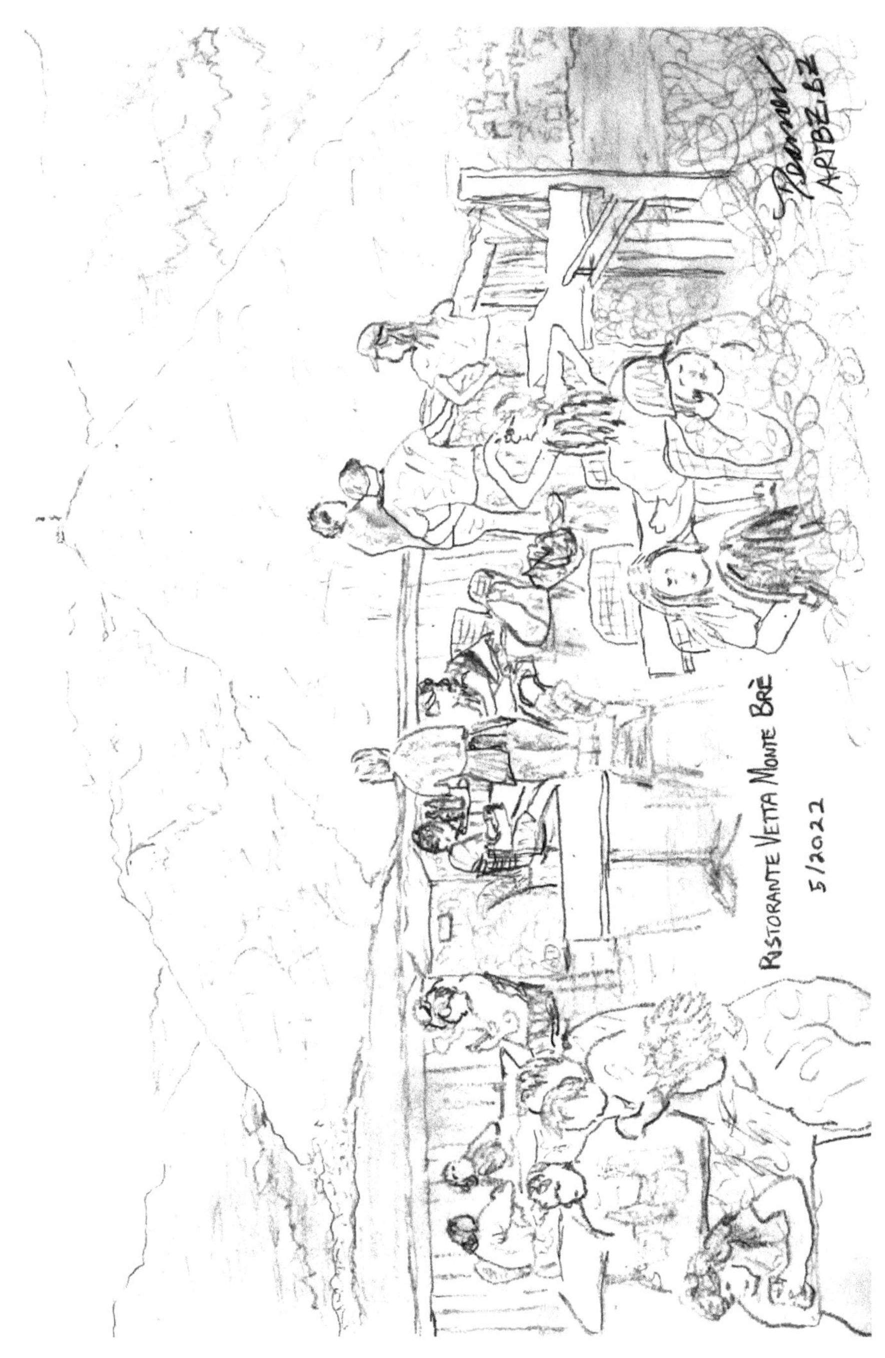

Ristorante Vetta Monte Brè
5/2022

74

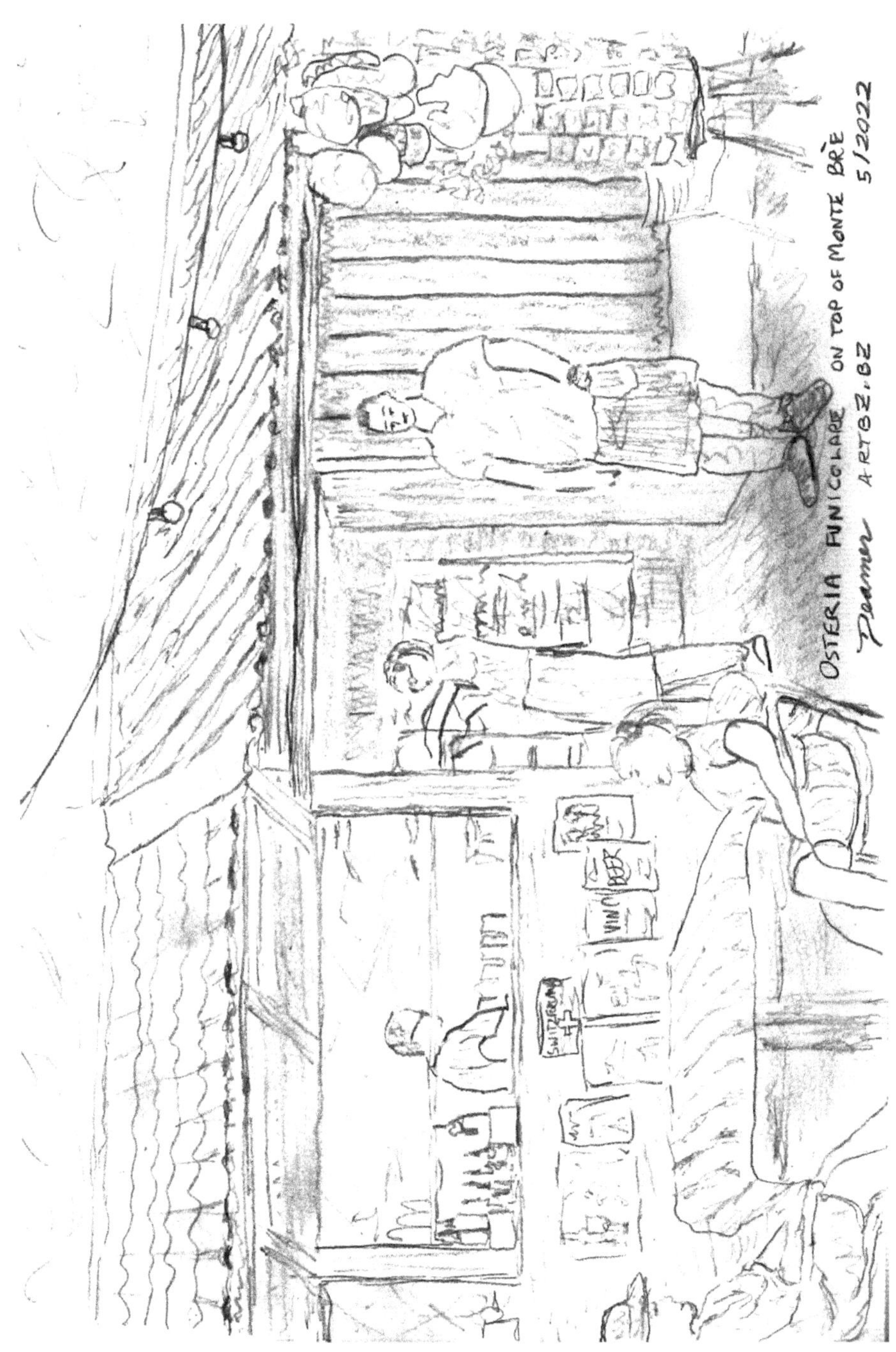

OSTERIA FUNICOLARE ON TOP OF MONTE BRÈ
Palmer ARTBZ.BZ
5/2022
SWITZERLAND
VIN DE PAYS

76

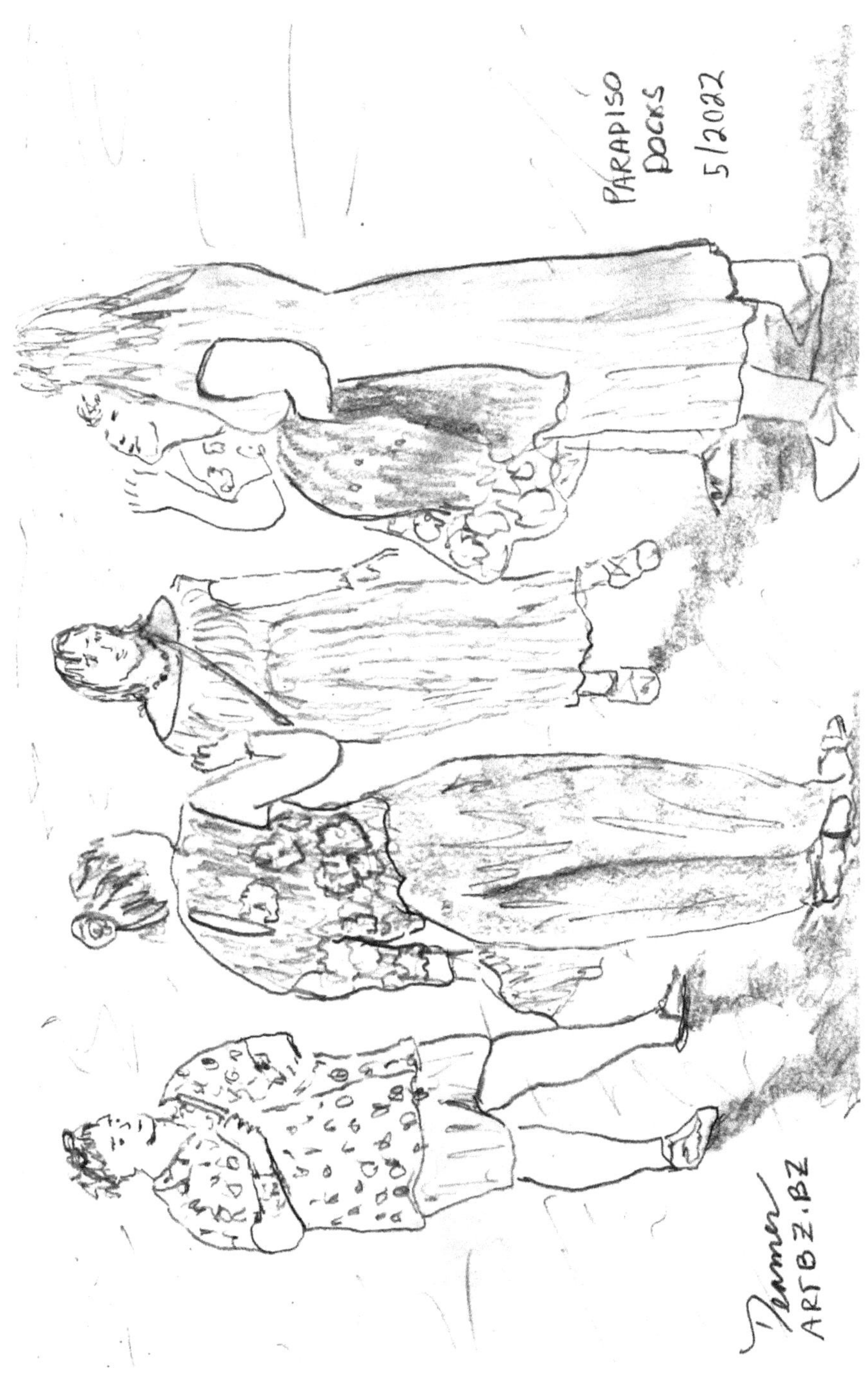
PARADISO
DOCKS
5/2022
ARTBZ.BZ

SUSTAINABLE GARDEN DEDICATION
FOR PROFESSOR ANN GARDINER
NORTH CAMPUS

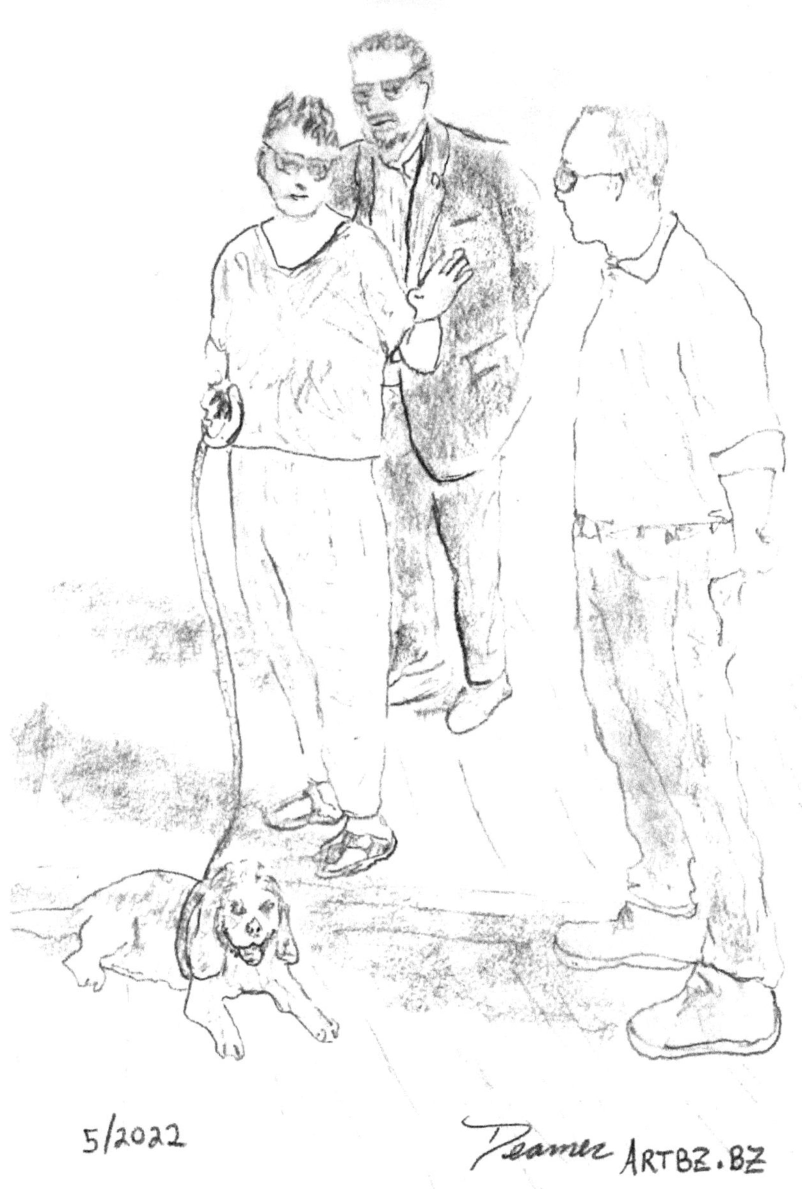

5/2022 Deamer ARTBZ.BZ

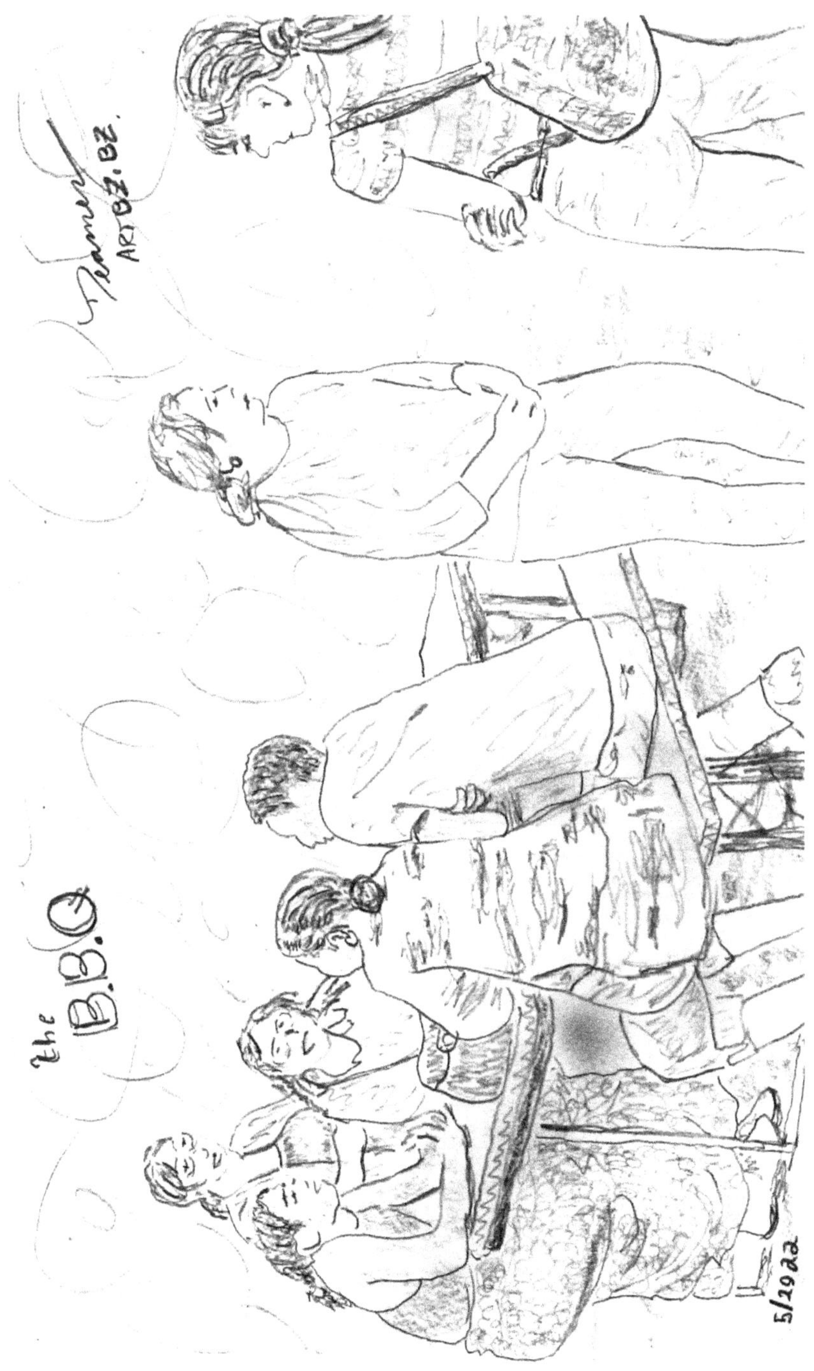

82

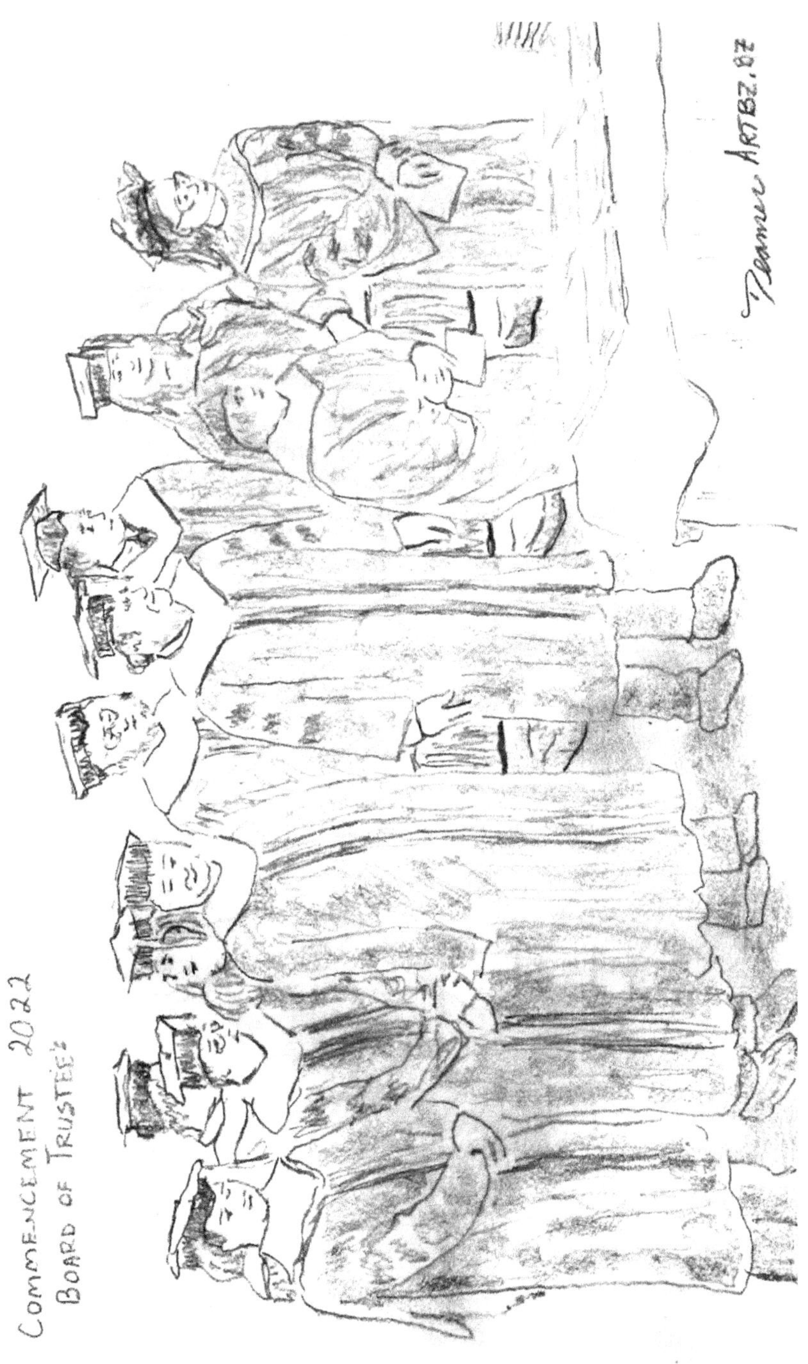
COMMENCEMENT 2022
BOARD OF TRUSTEES
Reamer ARTBZ.02

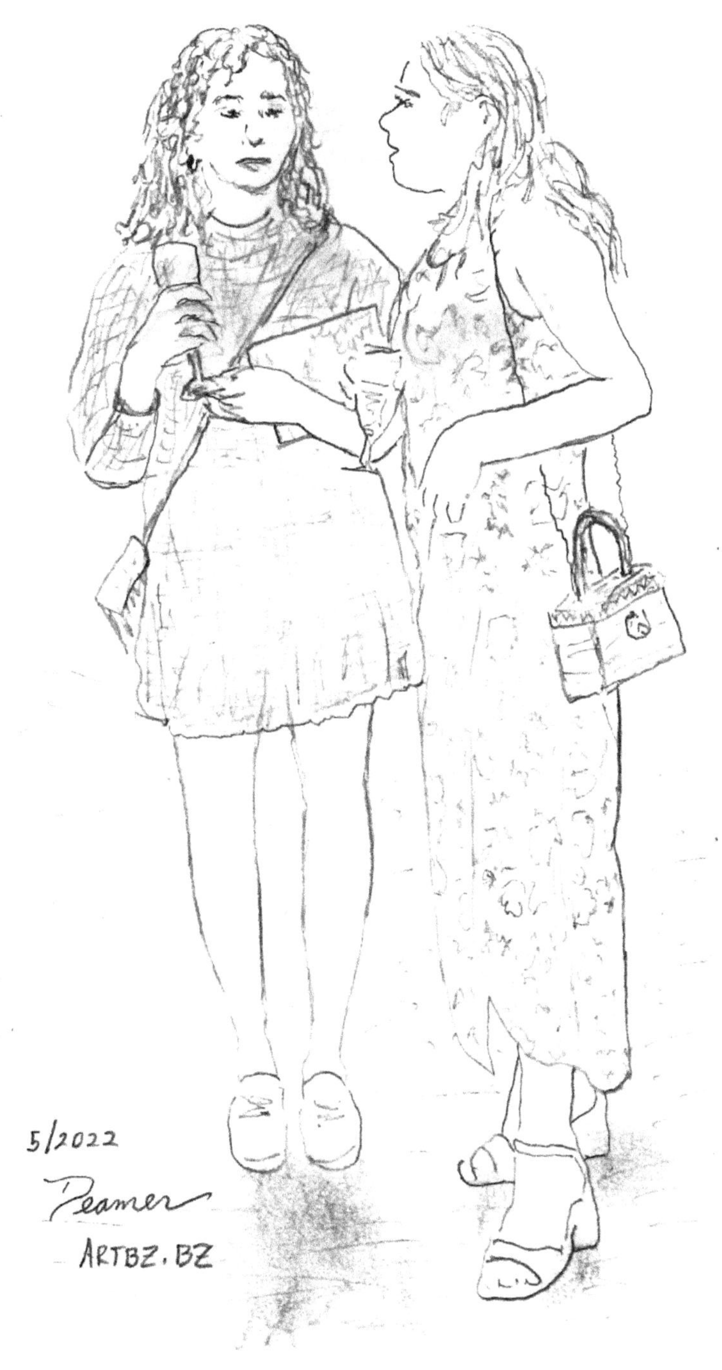

5/2022

Deamer

ARTBZ.BZ

86

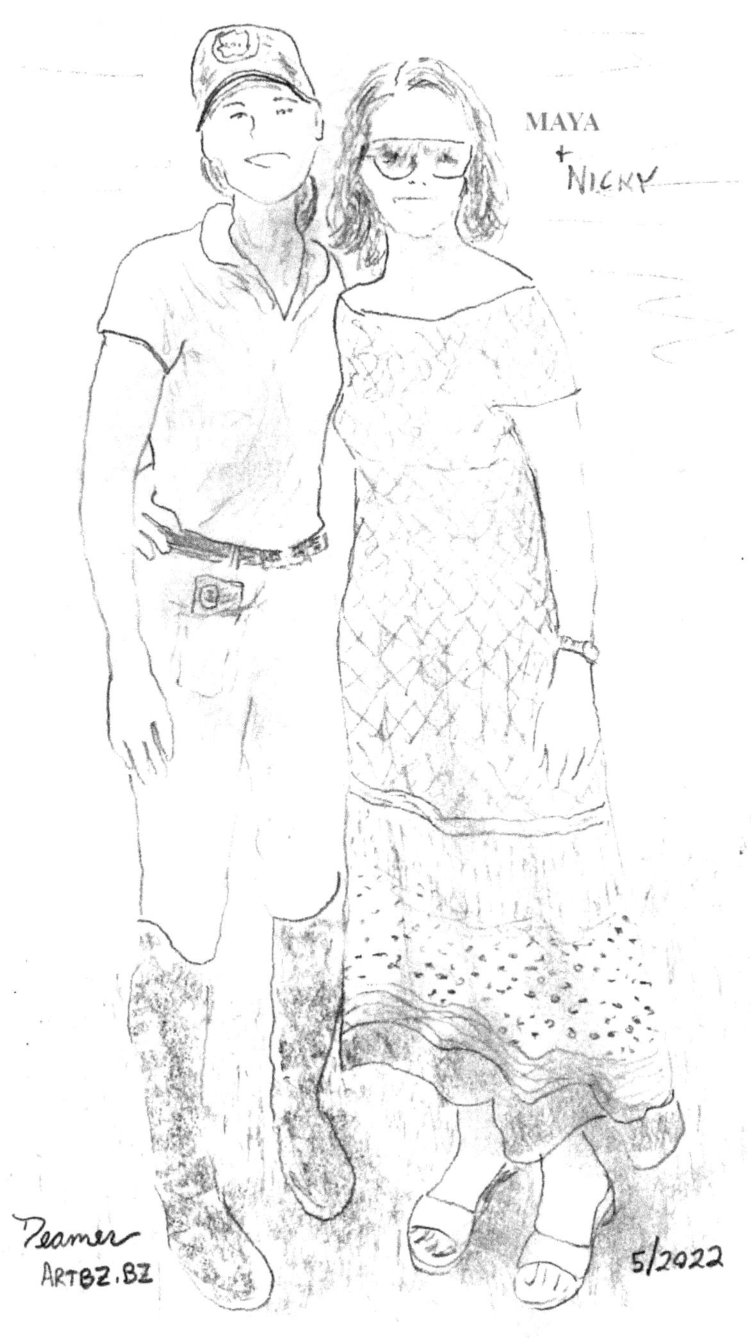
MAYA
+ NICKY
Deamer
ARTBZ.BZ
5/2022

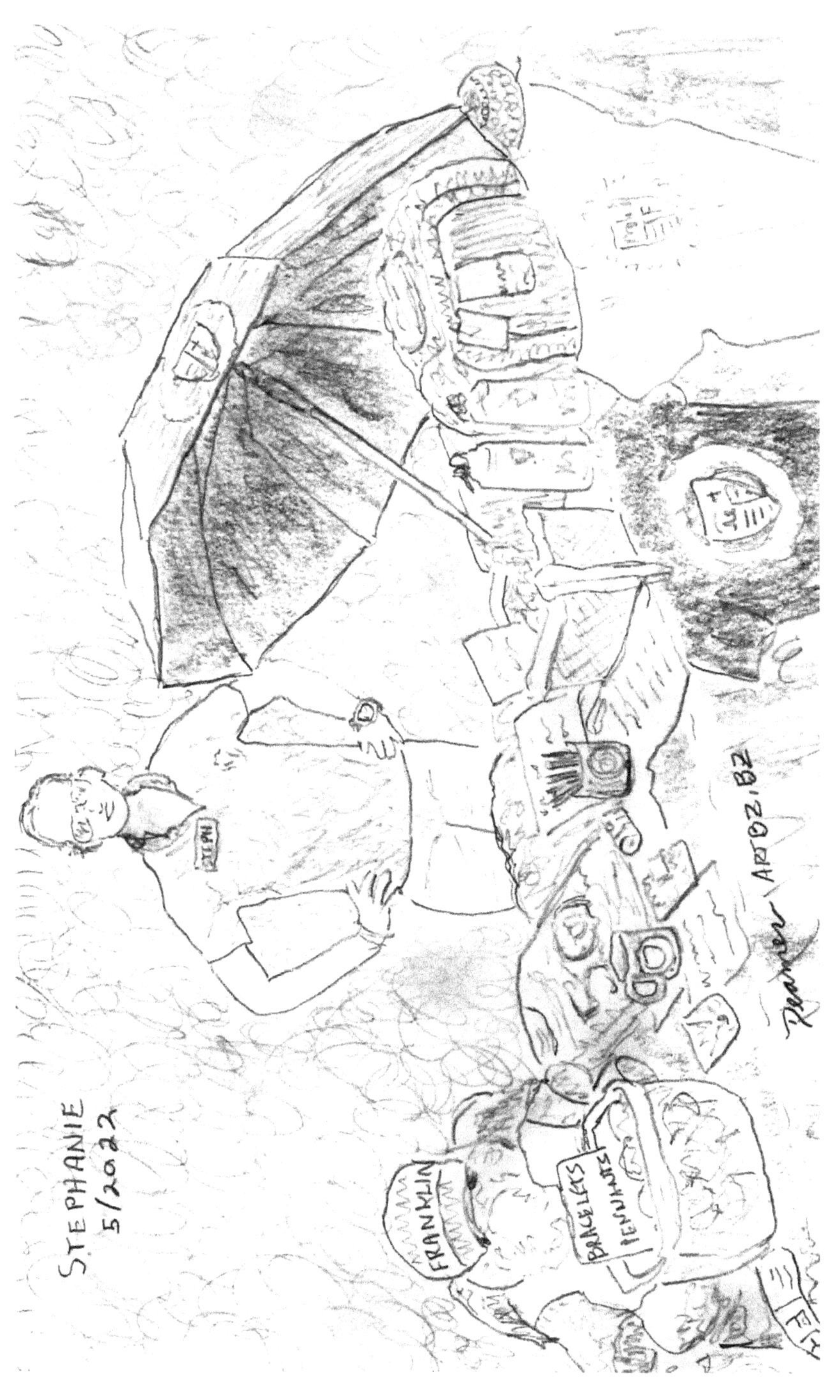
STEPHANIE 5/2022
INDIA
FRANKLIN
BRACELETS
PENDANTS
Pearce AP 02, B2

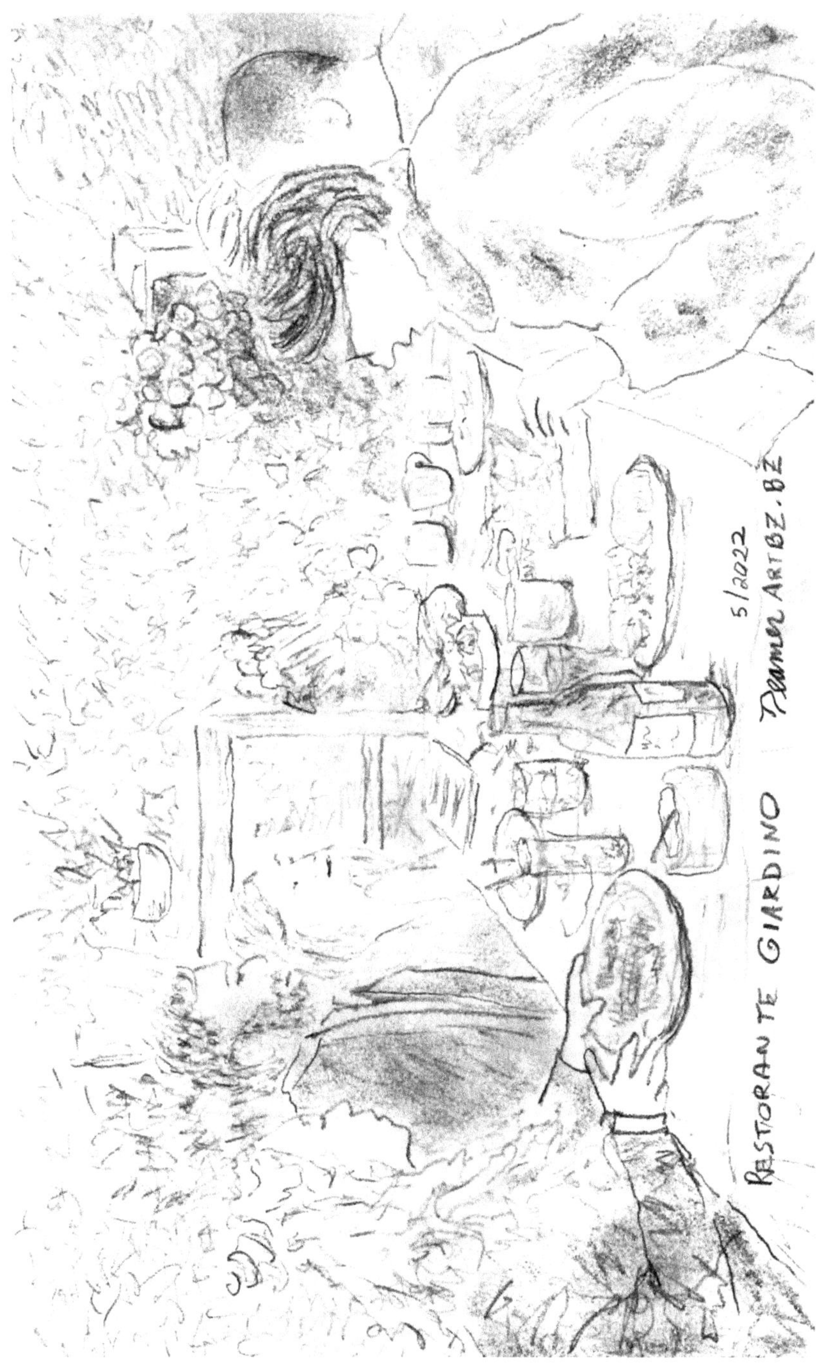
5/2022
Damen Artbz.bz
Ristorante Giardino

PARADISO DOCK

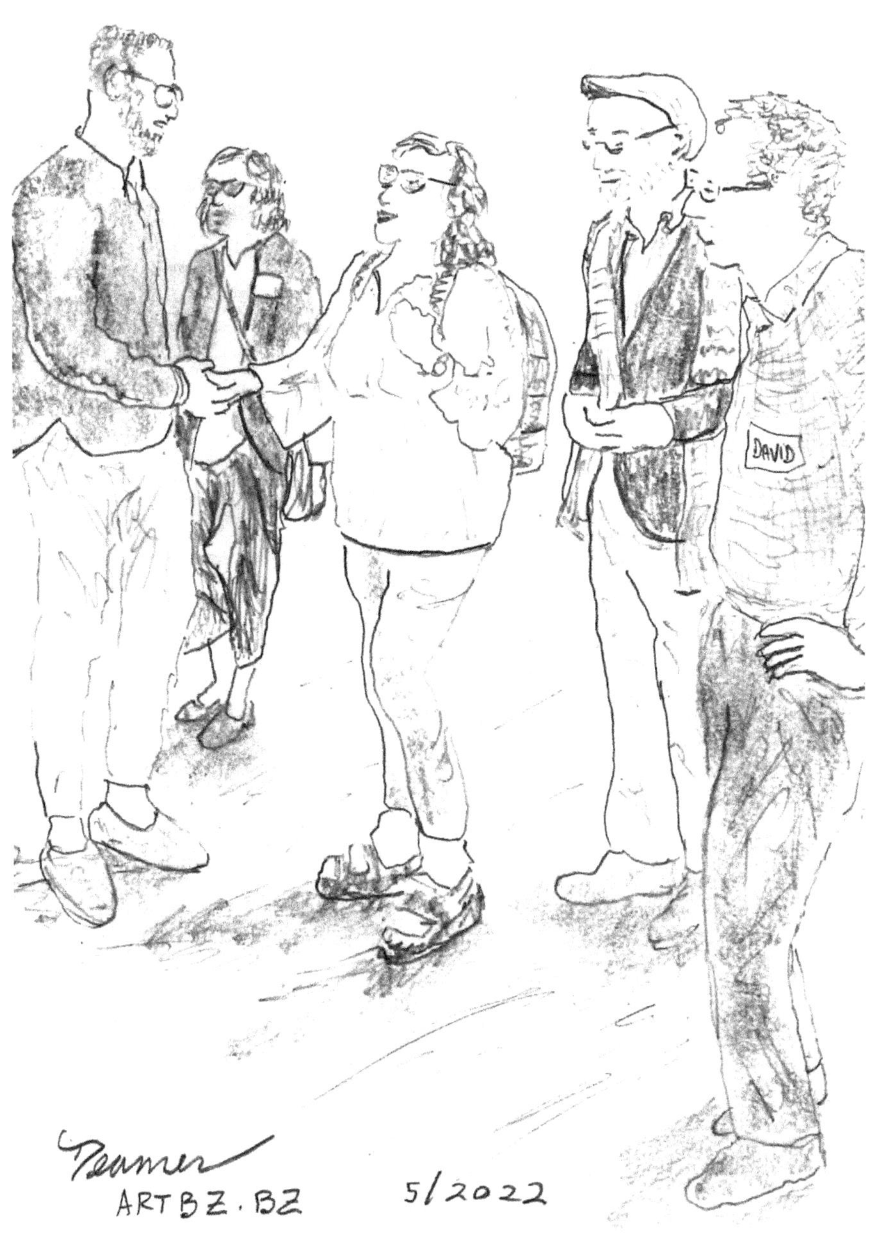

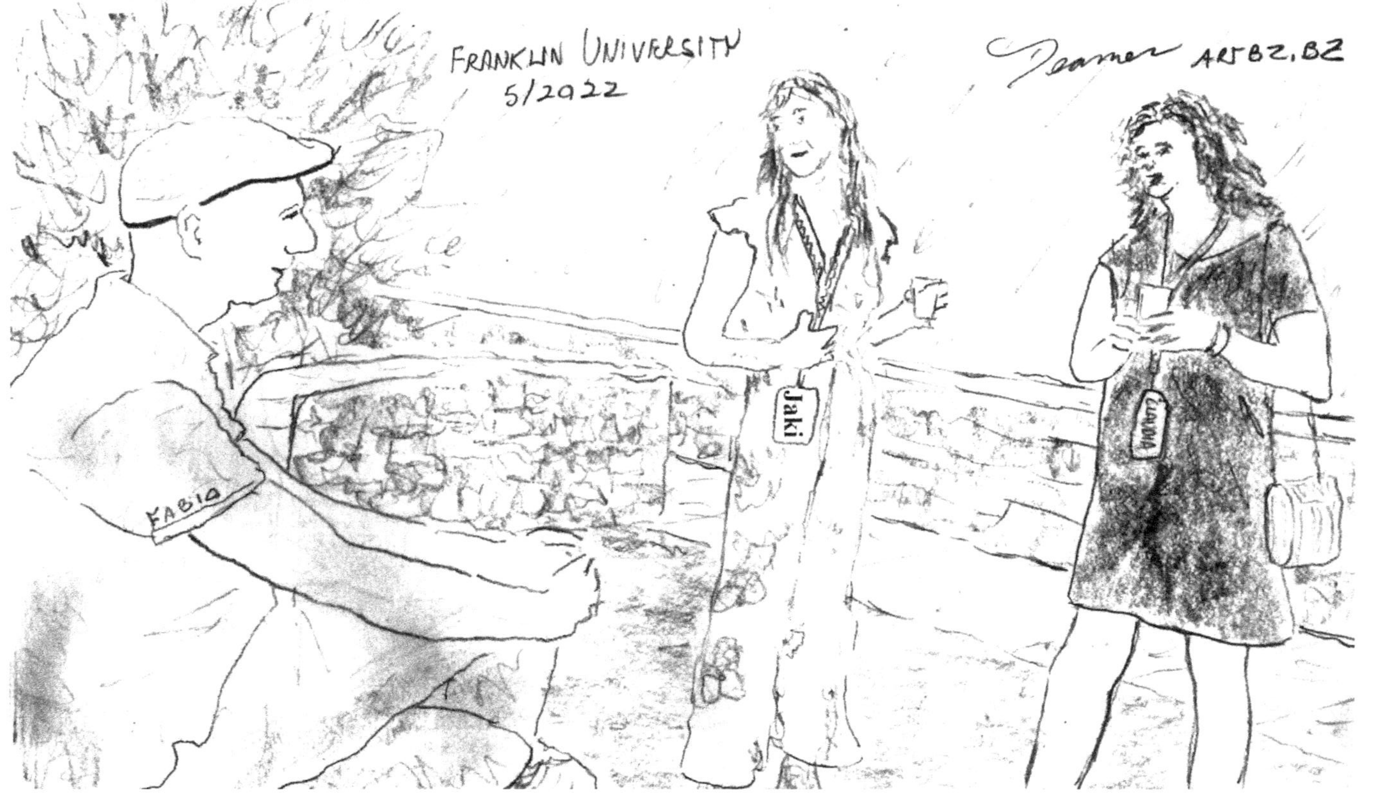
FRANKLIN UNIVERSITY
5/2022
Deamer ART 82.82
Jaki
CLAUDIA
FABIO

96

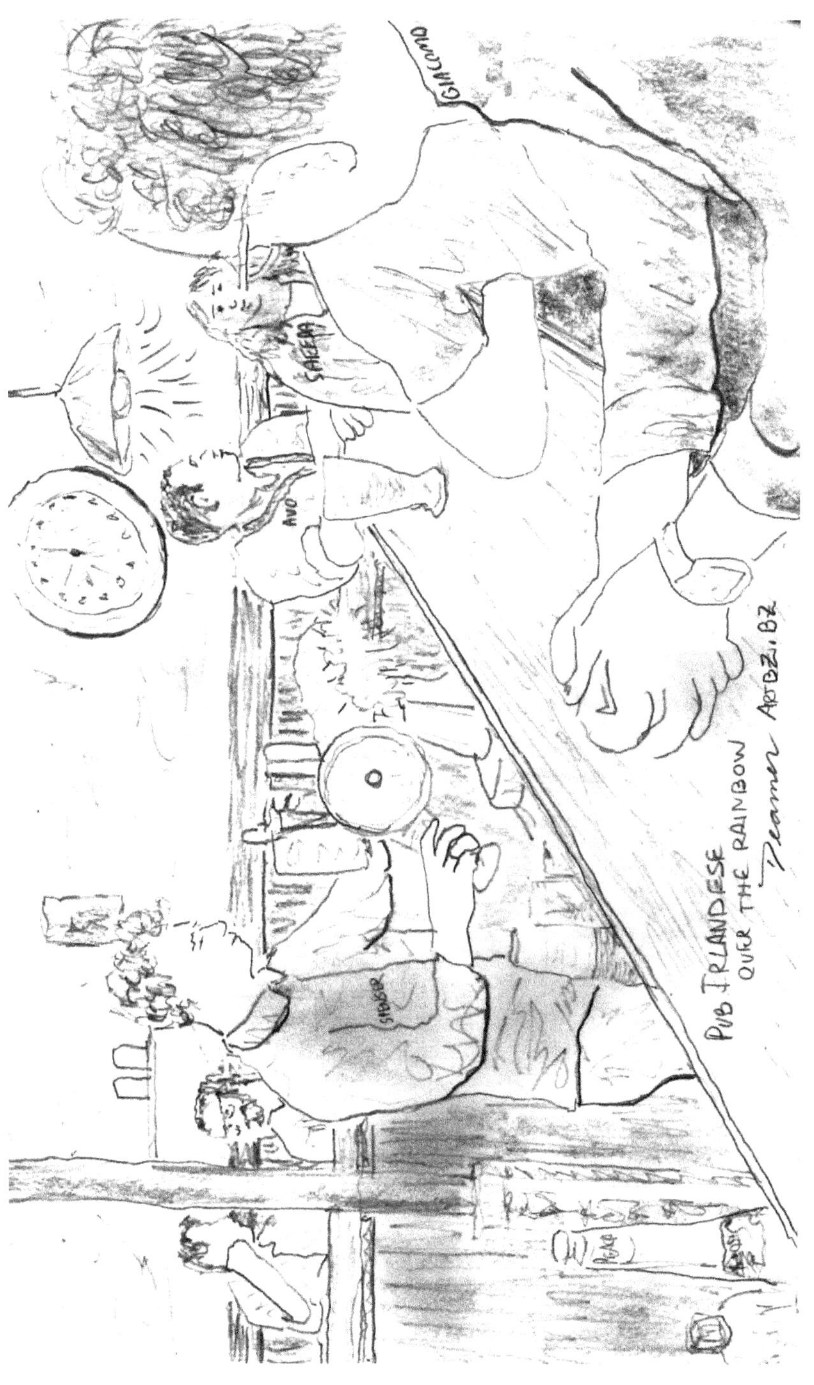
GIACOMO
SABENA
AVO
SHAVER
PUB IRLANDESE
OVER THE RAINBOW
Reamer Apr 02.02

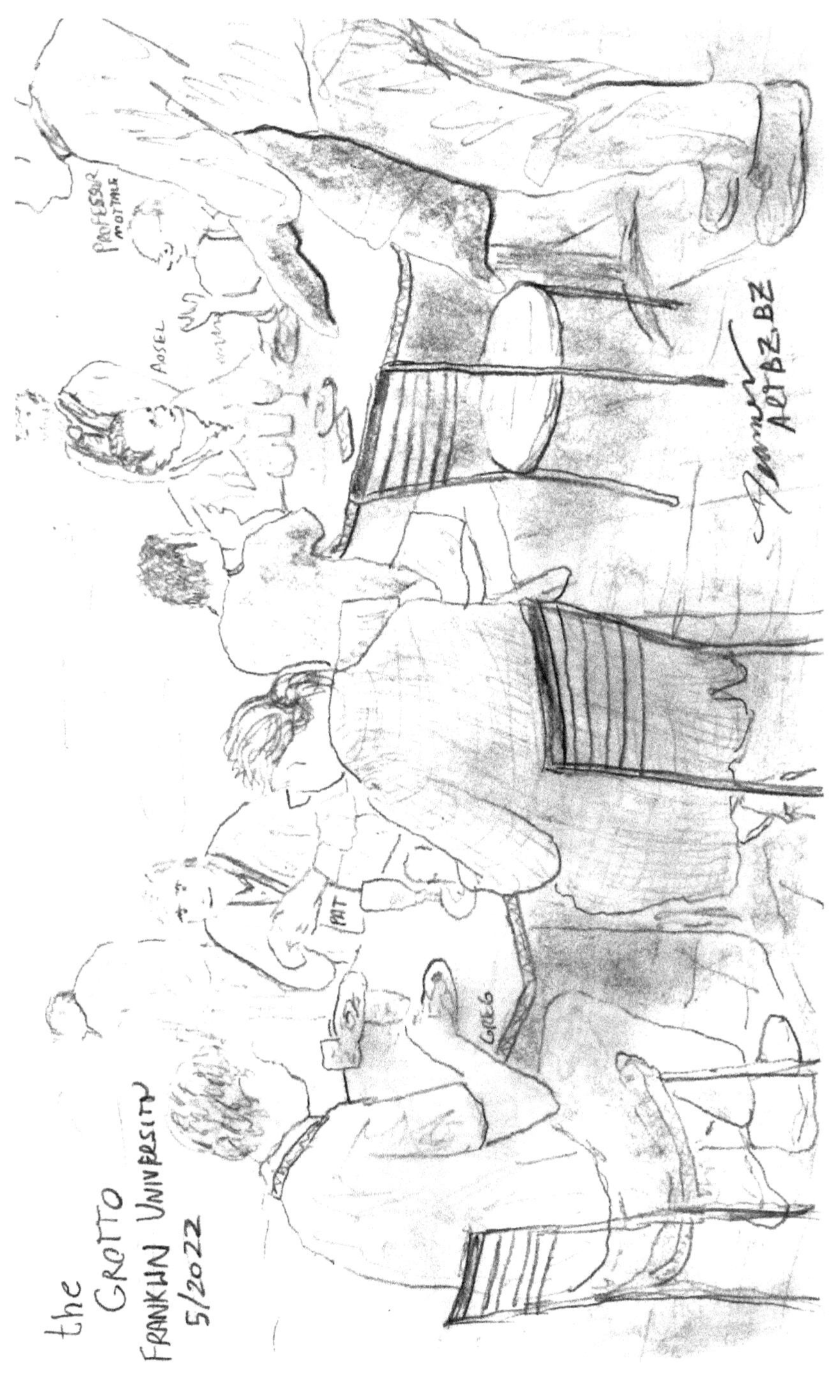
PROFESSOR
MOTTALE
AOSEL
PAT
GREG
the
GROTTO
FRANKLIN UNIVERSITY
5/2022

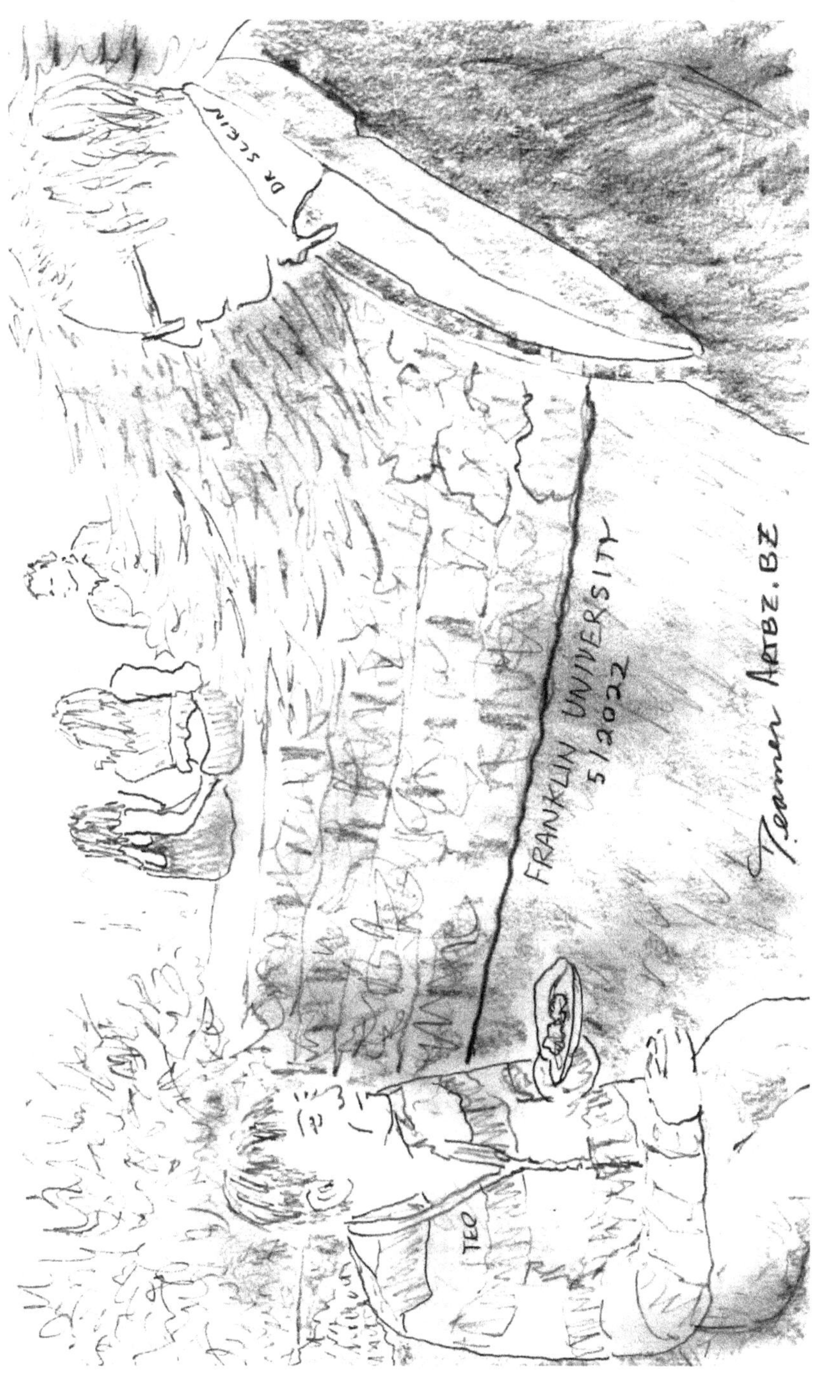
DR SLEIN
FRANKLIN UNIVERSITY
5/2022
Teamen AABZ.BZ
TEO

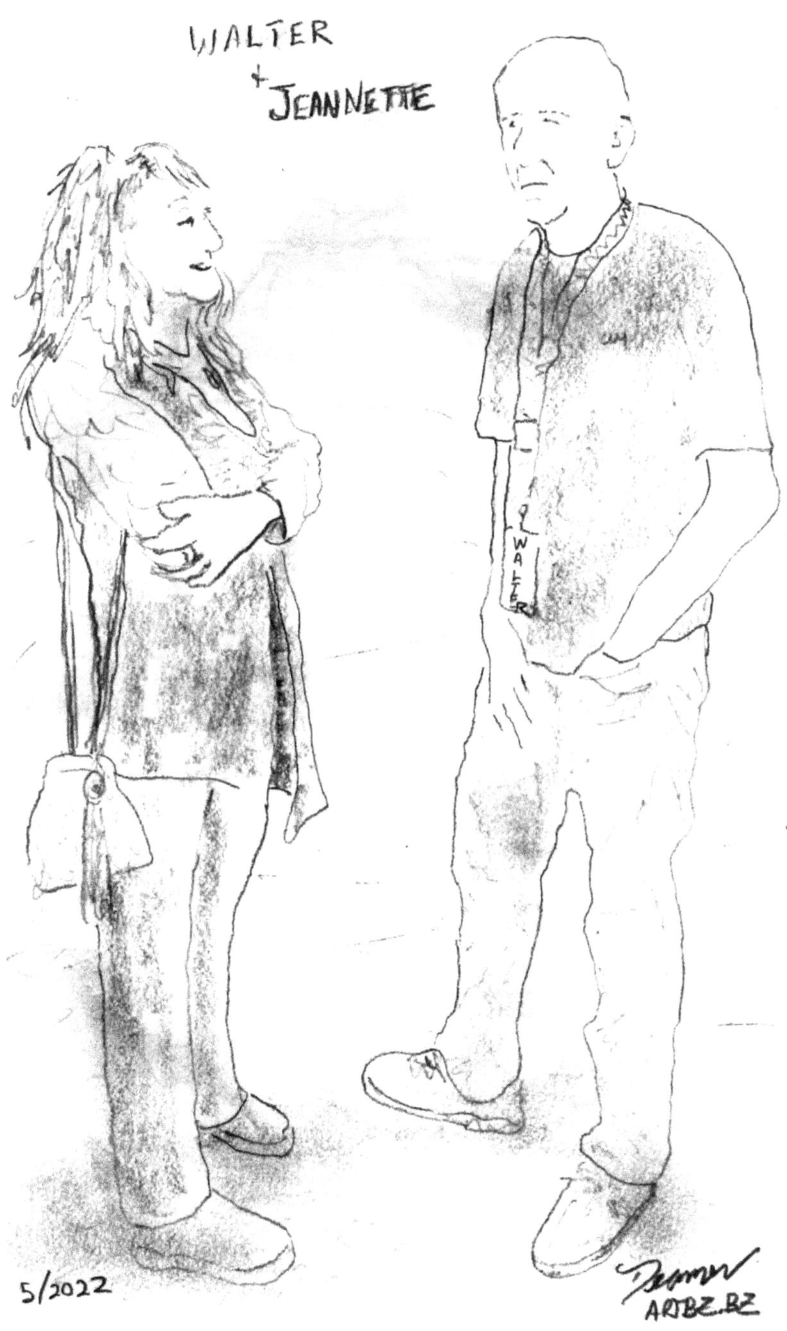

WALTER
& JEANNETTE
WALTER
5/2022
ARTBZ.BZ

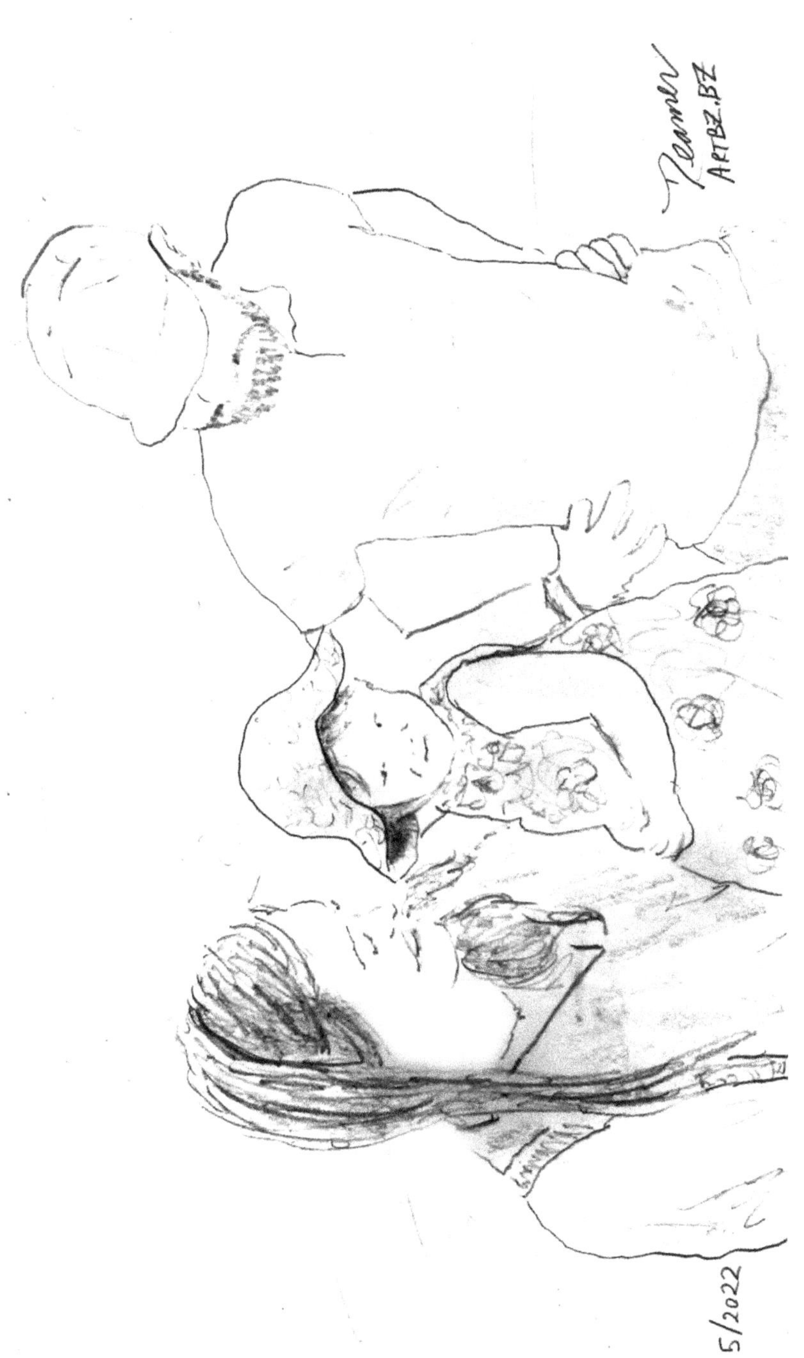
Reamer
ArtBZ.BZ
5/2022

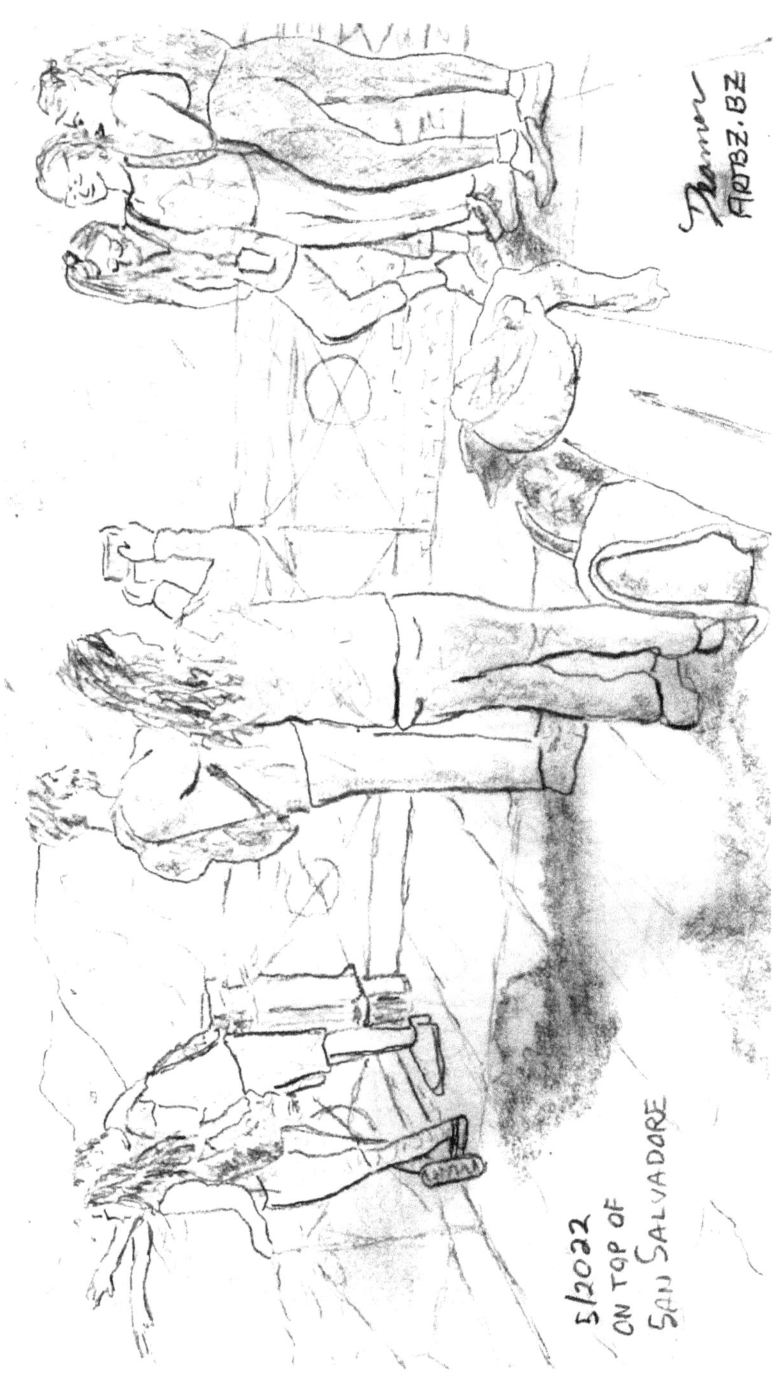
5/2022
ON TOP OF
SAN SALVADORE
ARTBZ.BZ

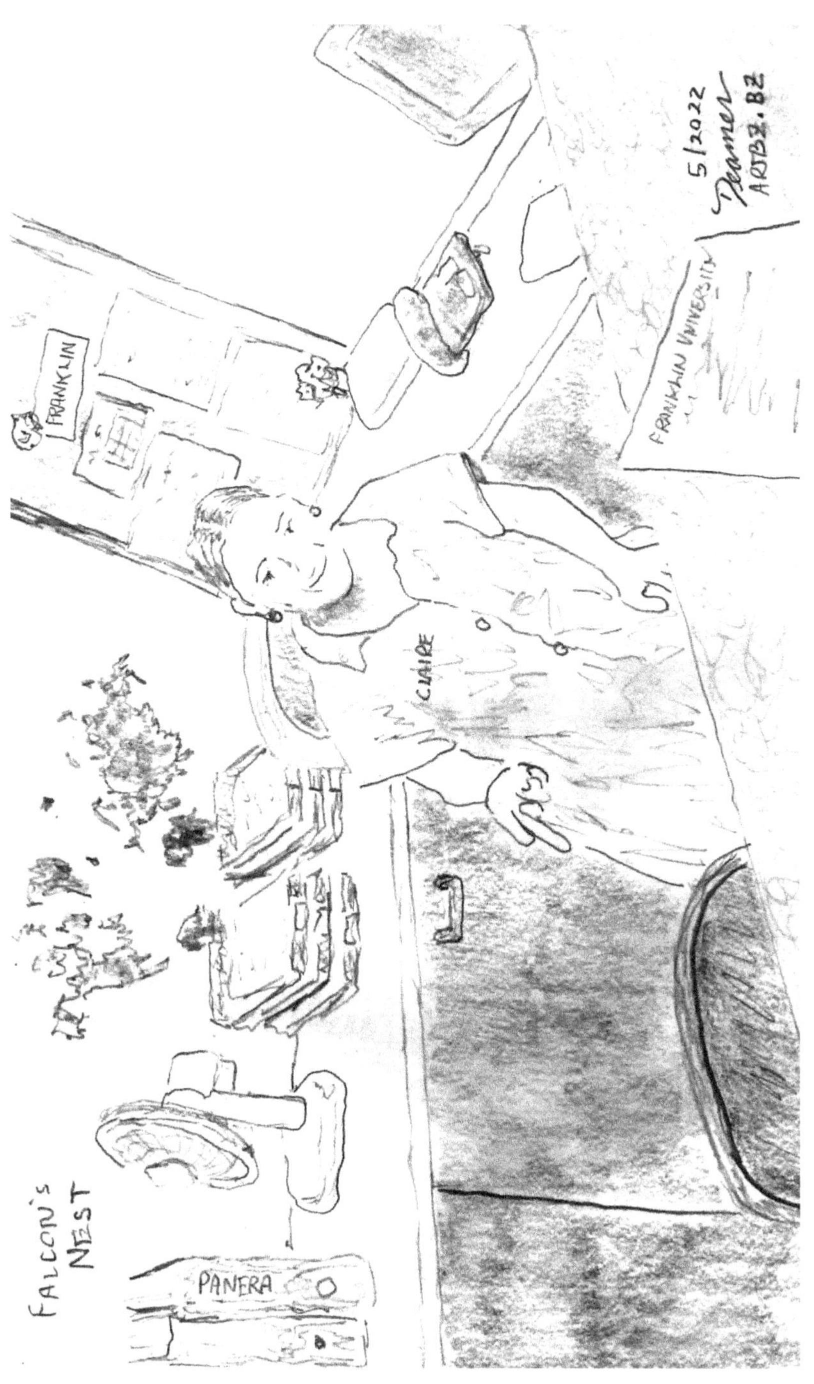
FRANKLIN
FRANKLIN UNIVERSITY
5/2022
ARTS2.B2
CLAIRE
FALCON'S NEST
PANERA

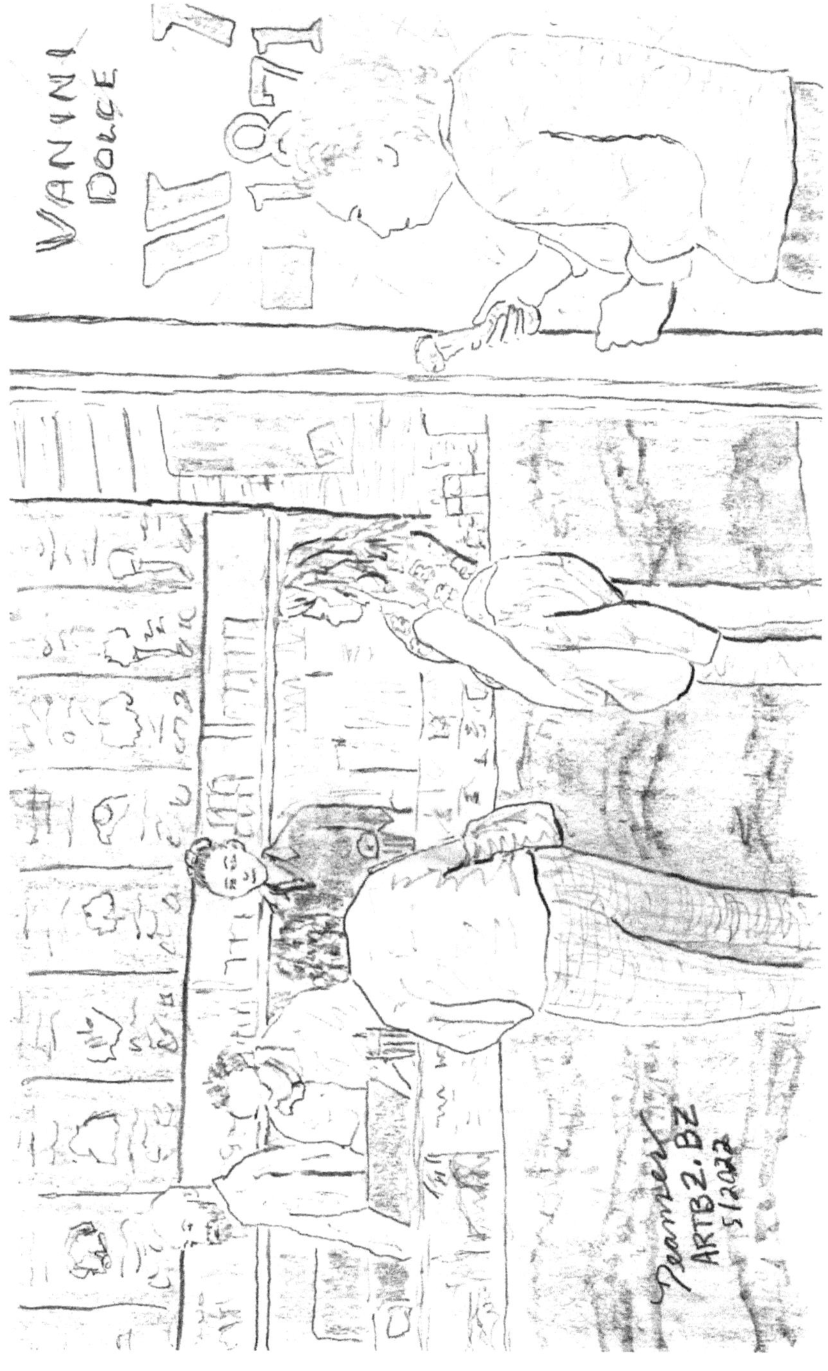

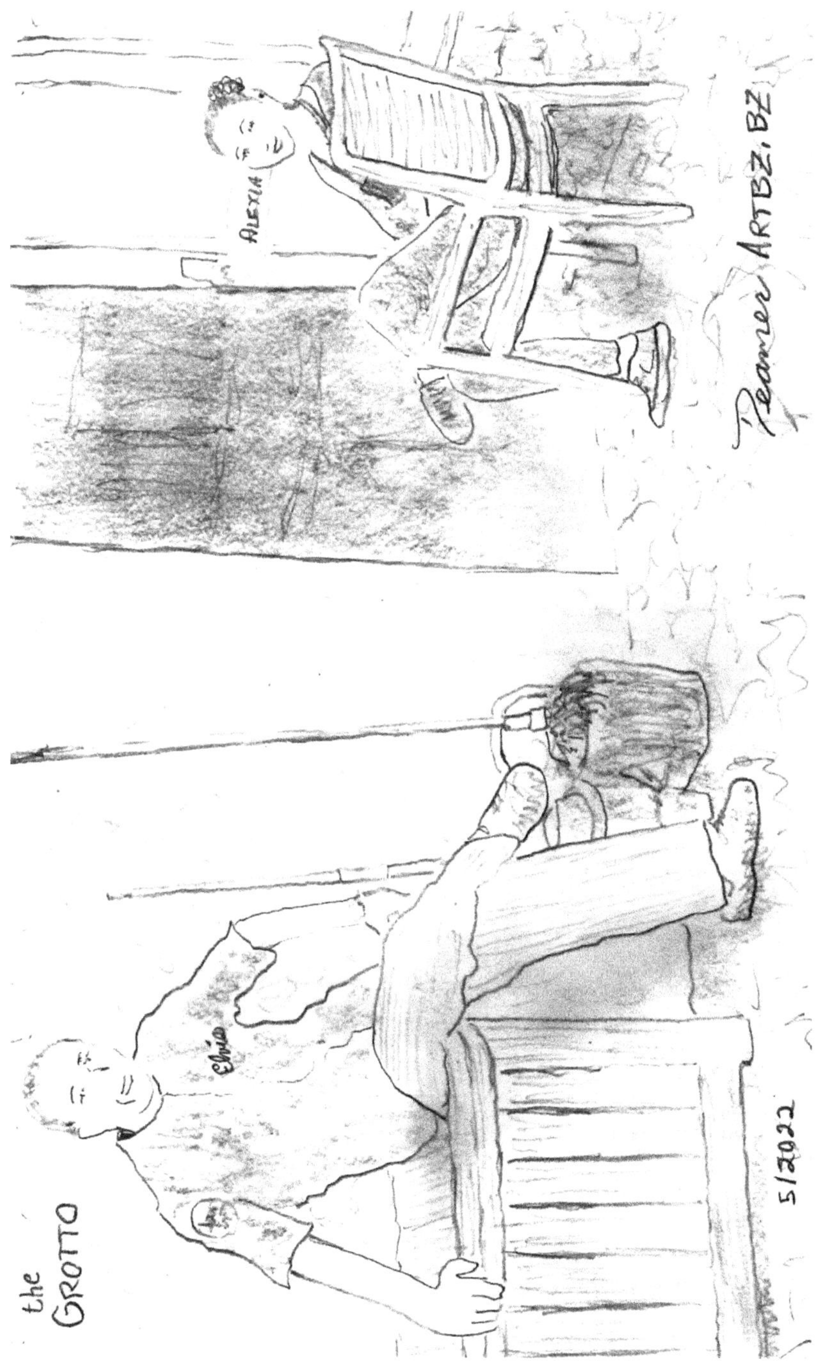
ALEXIA
Pearces ARTBZ, BZ
the GROTTO
Elvis
5/30/22

114

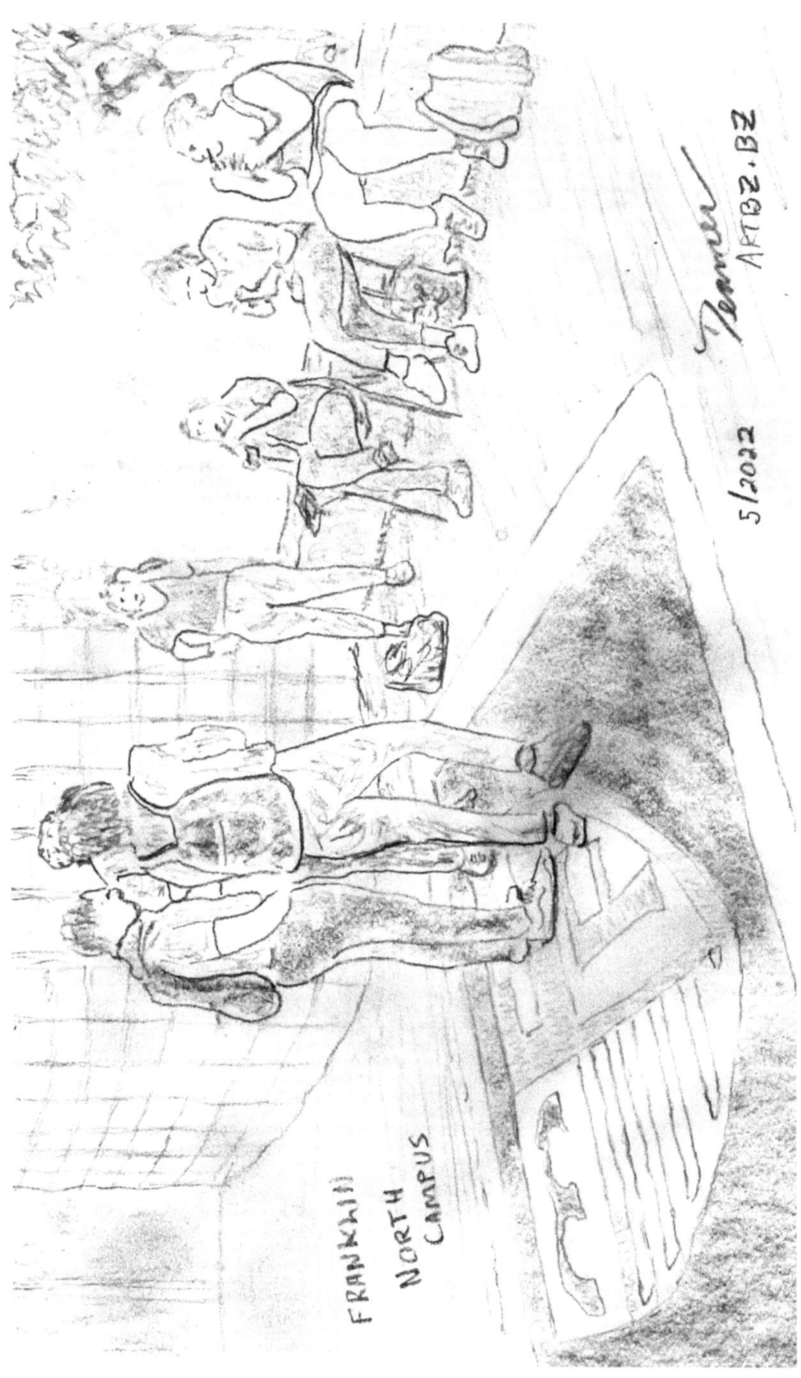
FRANKLIN
NORTH
CAMPUS
5/2022
ART82.BZ

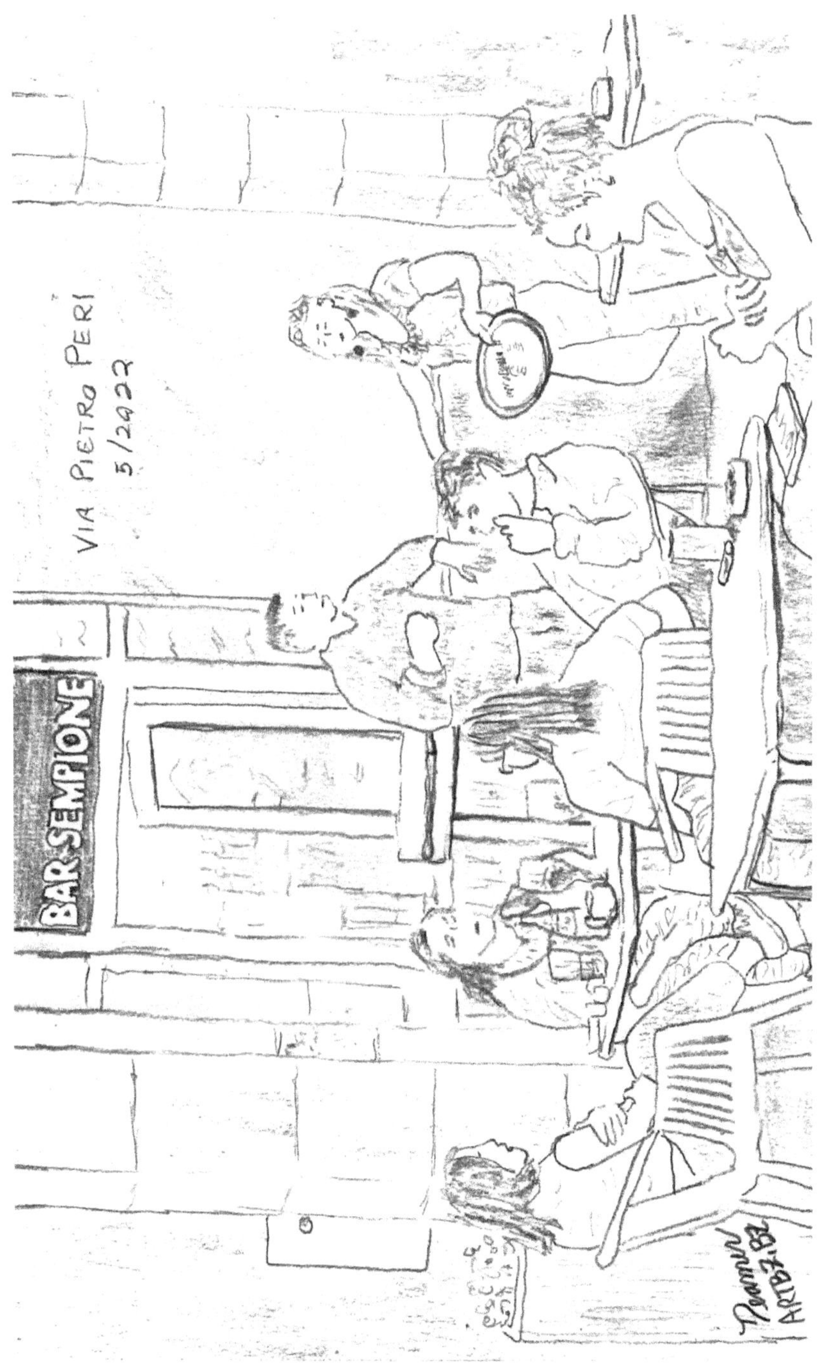
BAR SEMPIONE
VIA PIETRO PERI 5/24/22

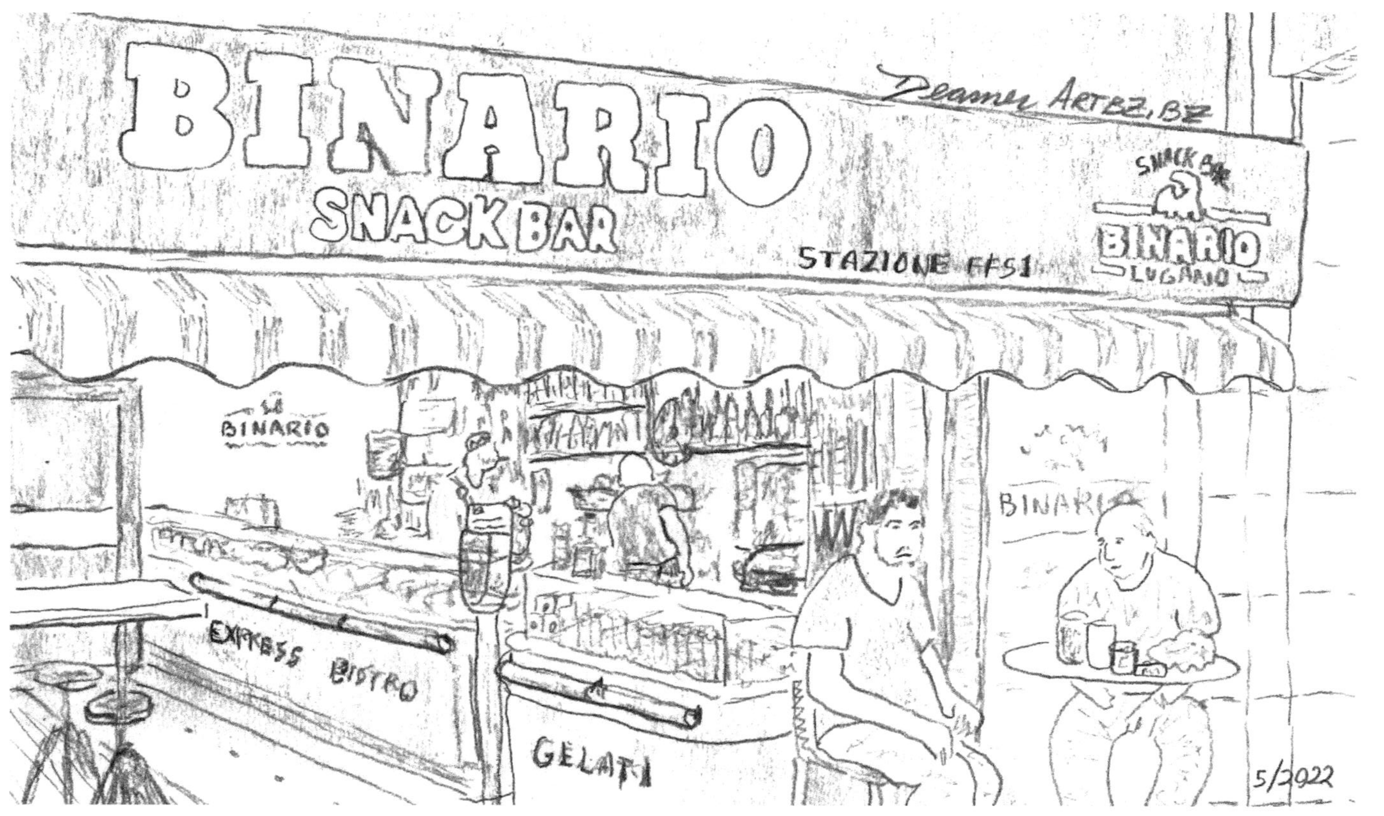
BINARIO
SNACK BAR
Deamu Artbz, Bz
SNACK BAR
BINARIO
LUGANO
STAZIONE FFS1
BINARIO
BINARIO
EXPRESS BISTRO
GELATI
5/2022

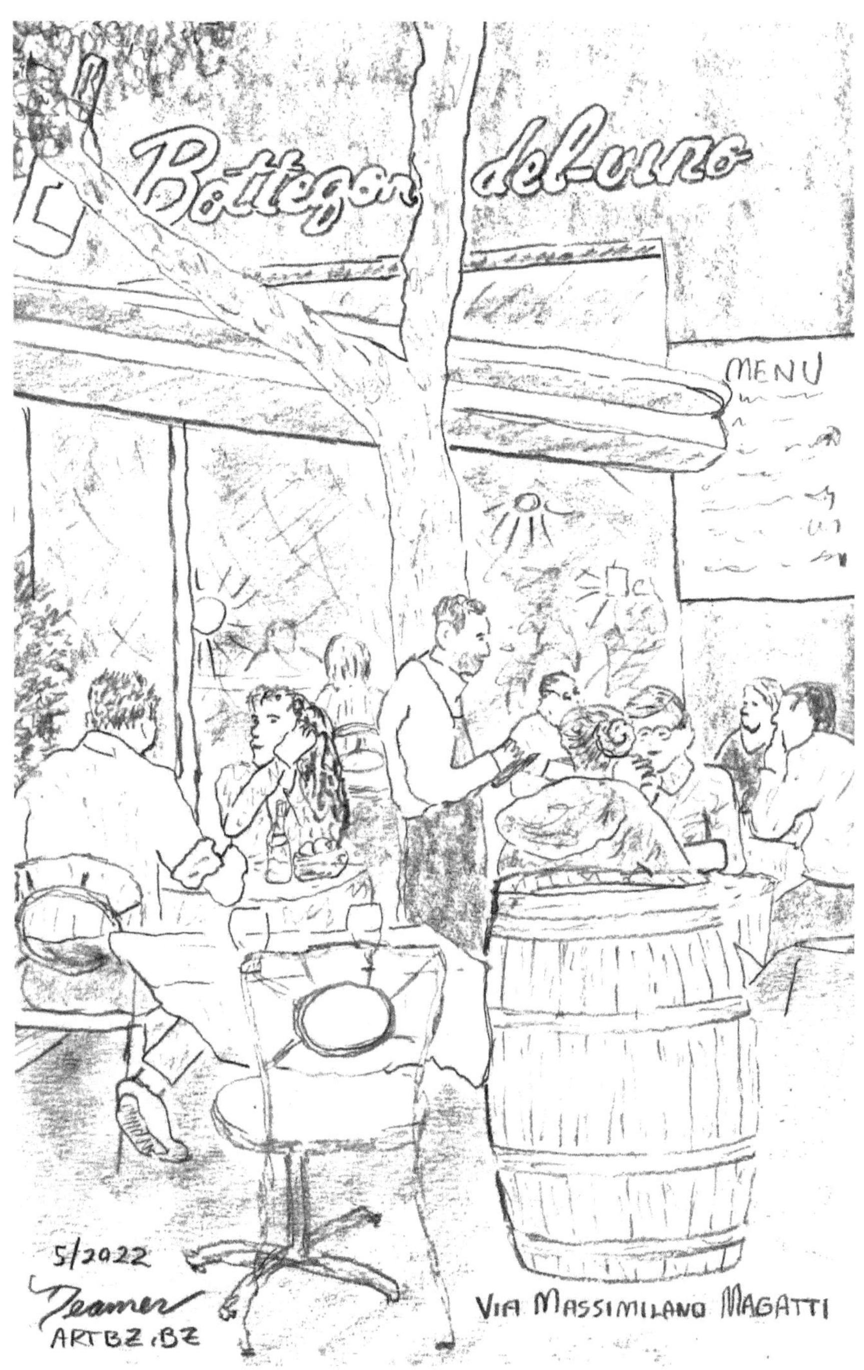
Bottega del vino
MENU
5/2022
Teamer
ARTBZ.BZ
VIA MASSIMILANO MAGATTI

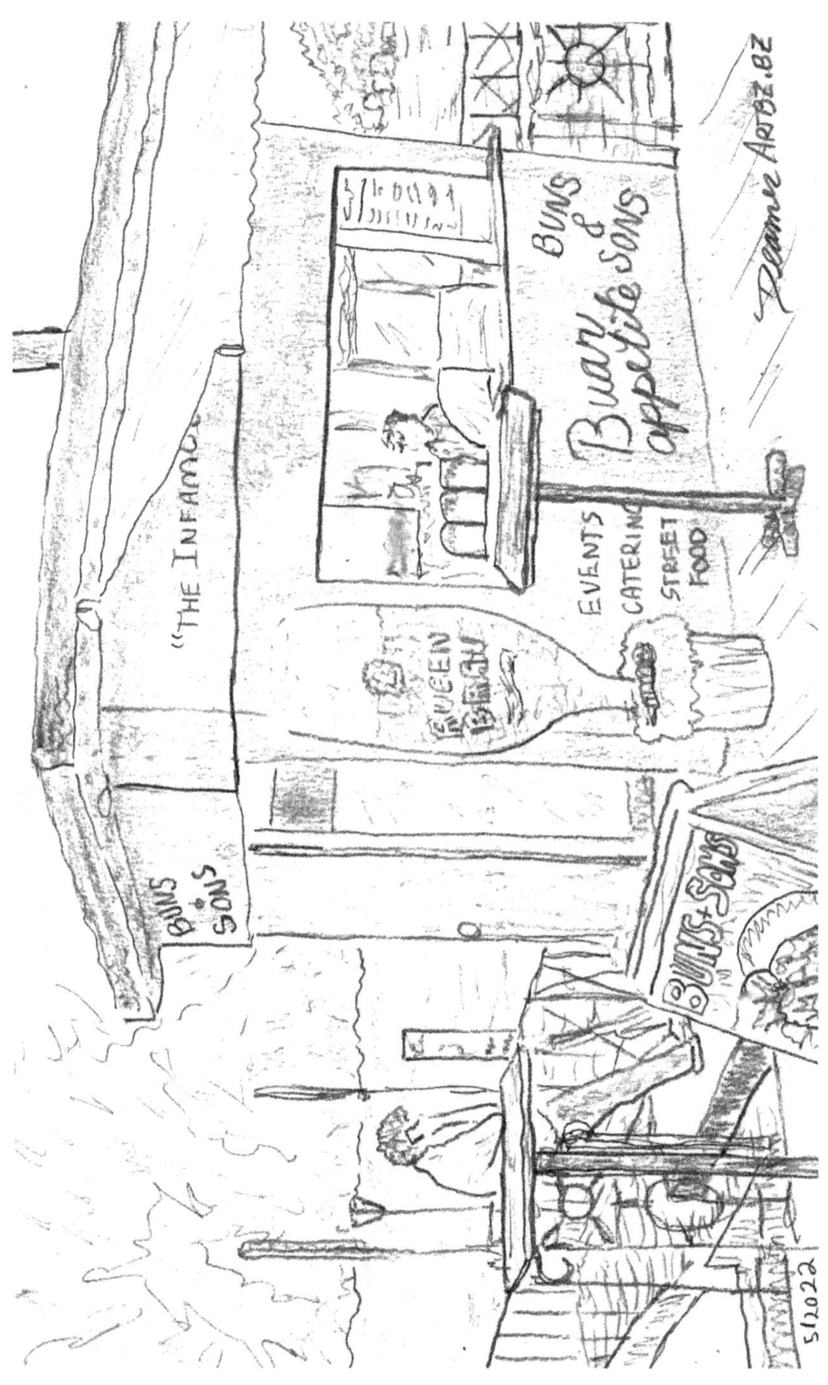
"THE INFAMOUS
BUNS & SONS
BUNS & appetito SONS
EVENTS
CATERING
STREET FOOD
QUEEN BROU
BUNS + SONS
Dramir ArtBz.Bz
5.10.22

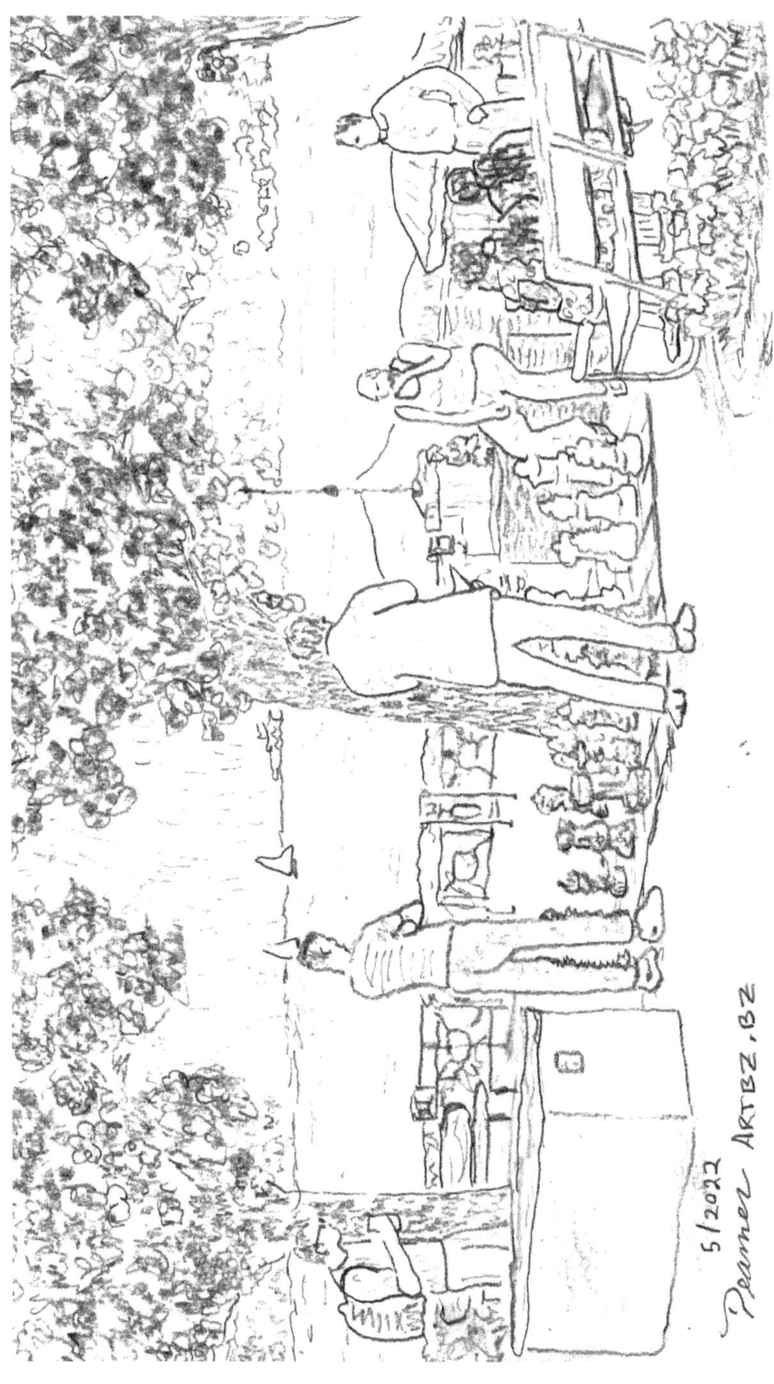
5/2022
Posner ARTBZ.BZ

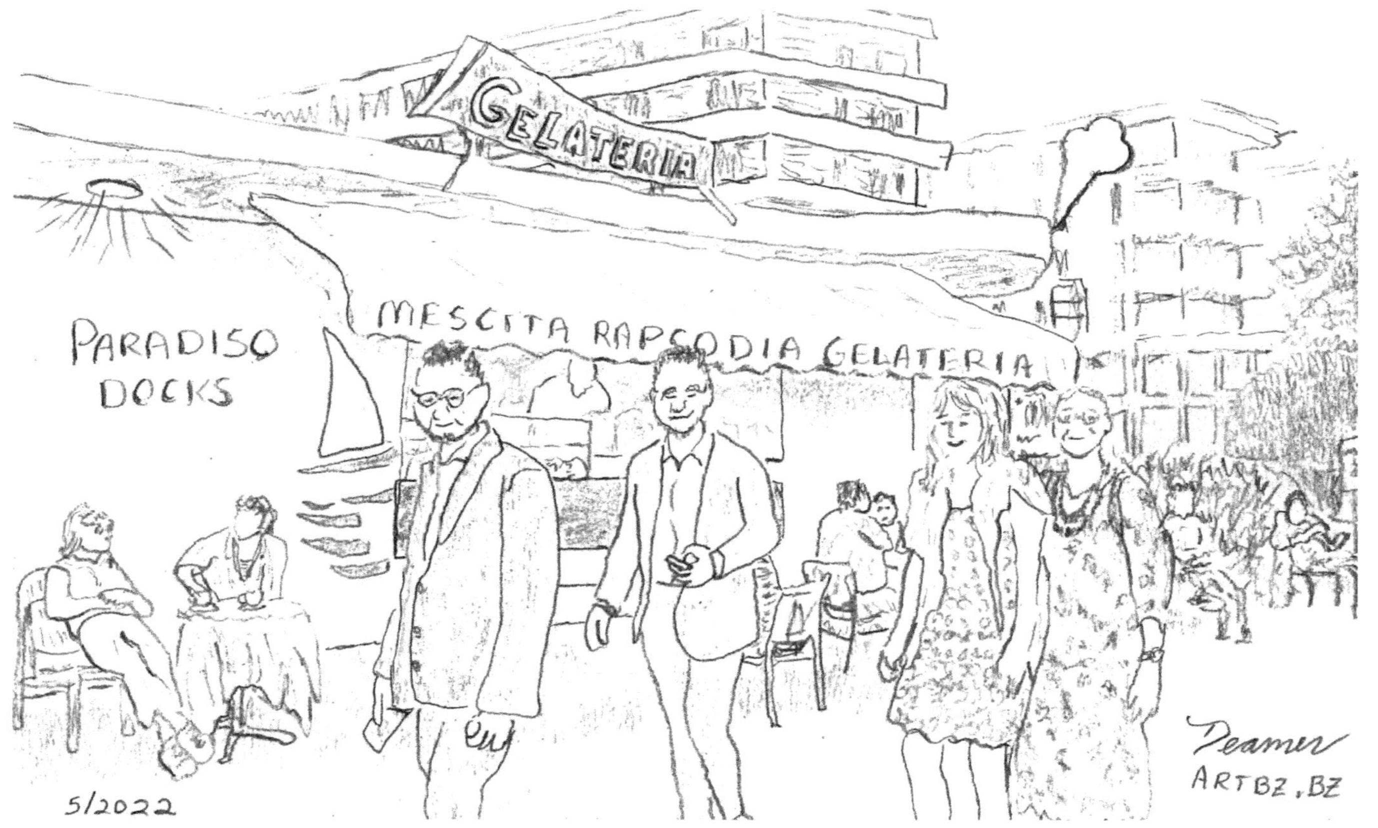
GELATERIA
MESCITA RAPSODIA GELATERIA
PARADISO DOCKS
Deamer
ArtBz.Bz
5/2022

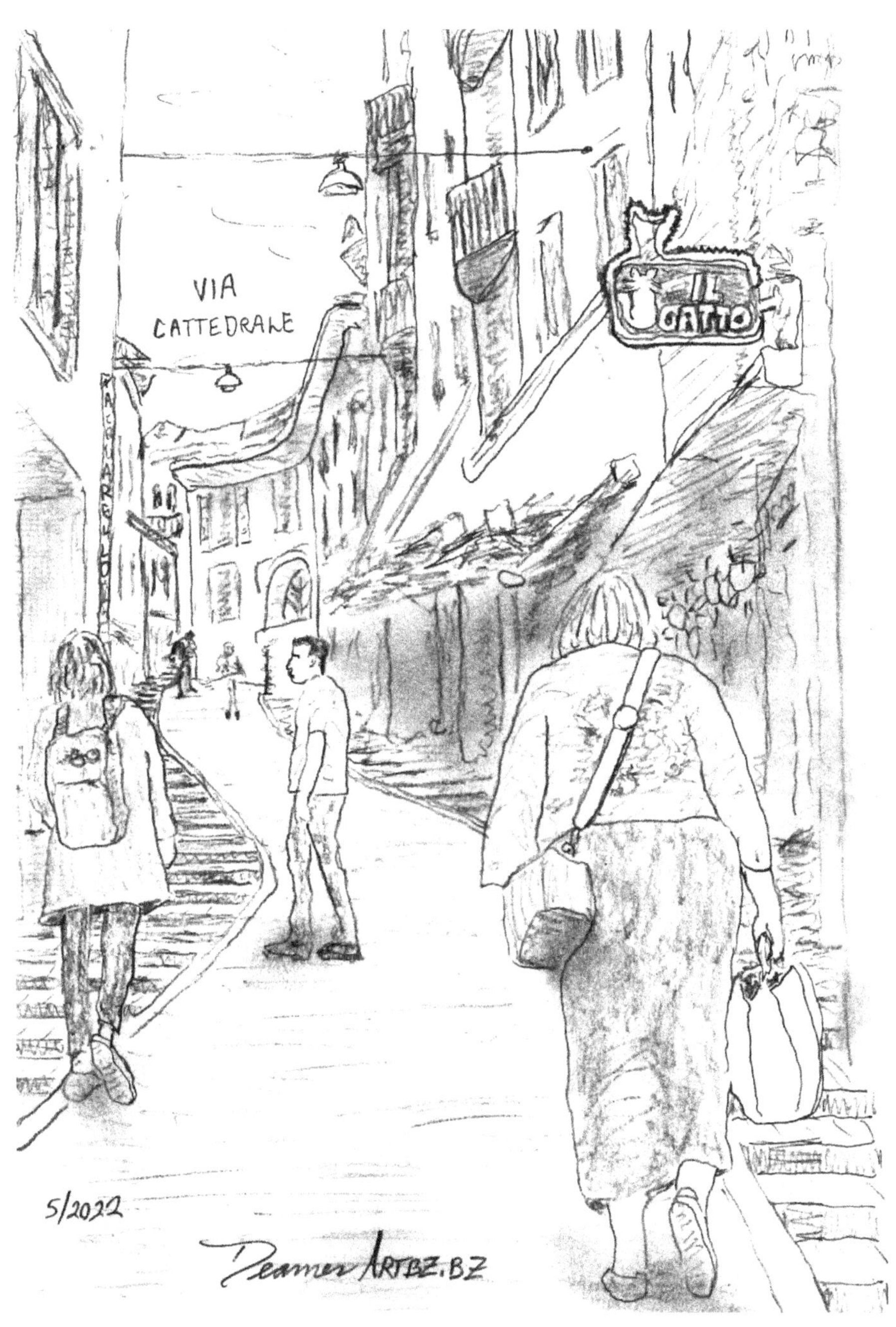
VIA
CATTEDRALE
IL GATTO
ACQUARELLO
5/2022
Deamer ARTBZ.BZ

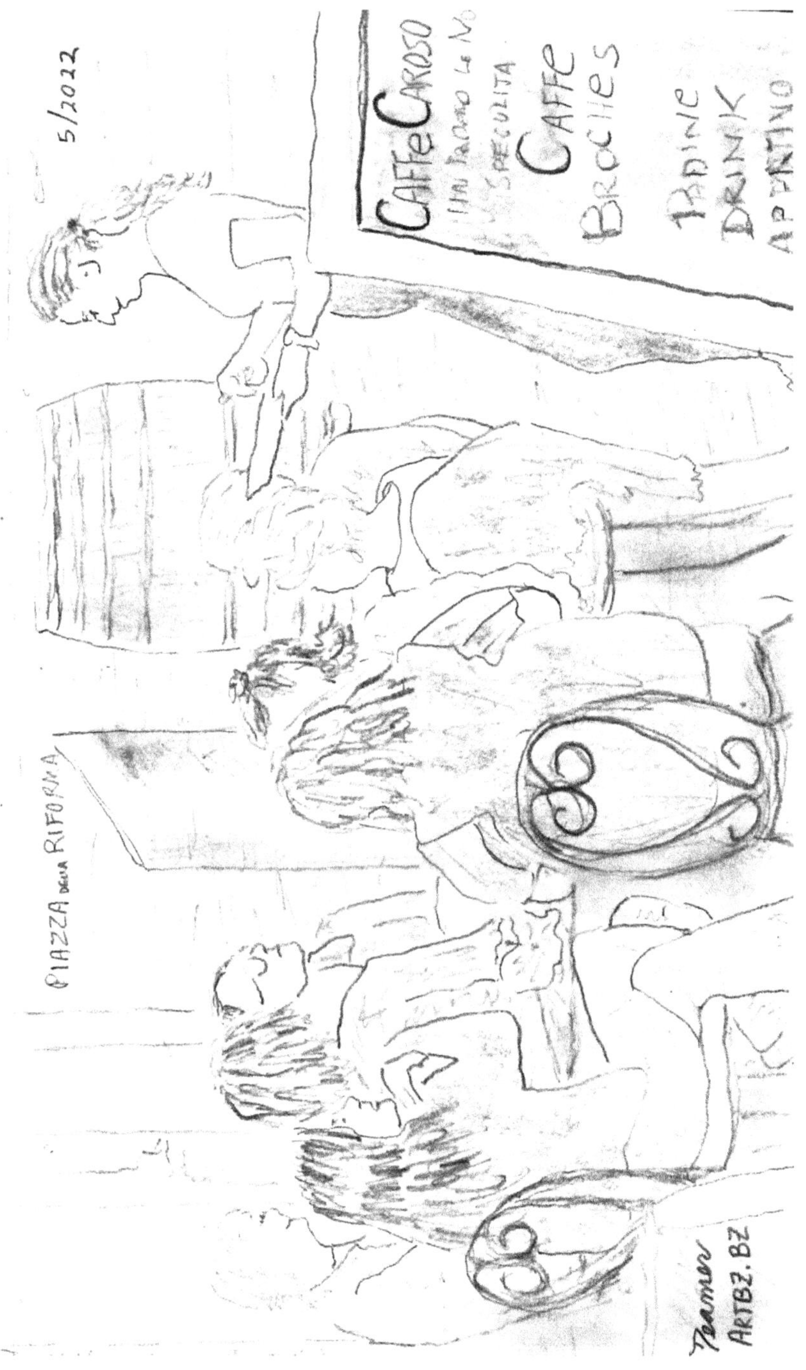
5/2022
CAFFE CAROSO
Un bagno le No
SPECIALITA
CAFFE BROCHES
PANINI
DRINK
APERTIVO
PIAZZA della RIFORMA
Teamus
ARTBZ.BZ

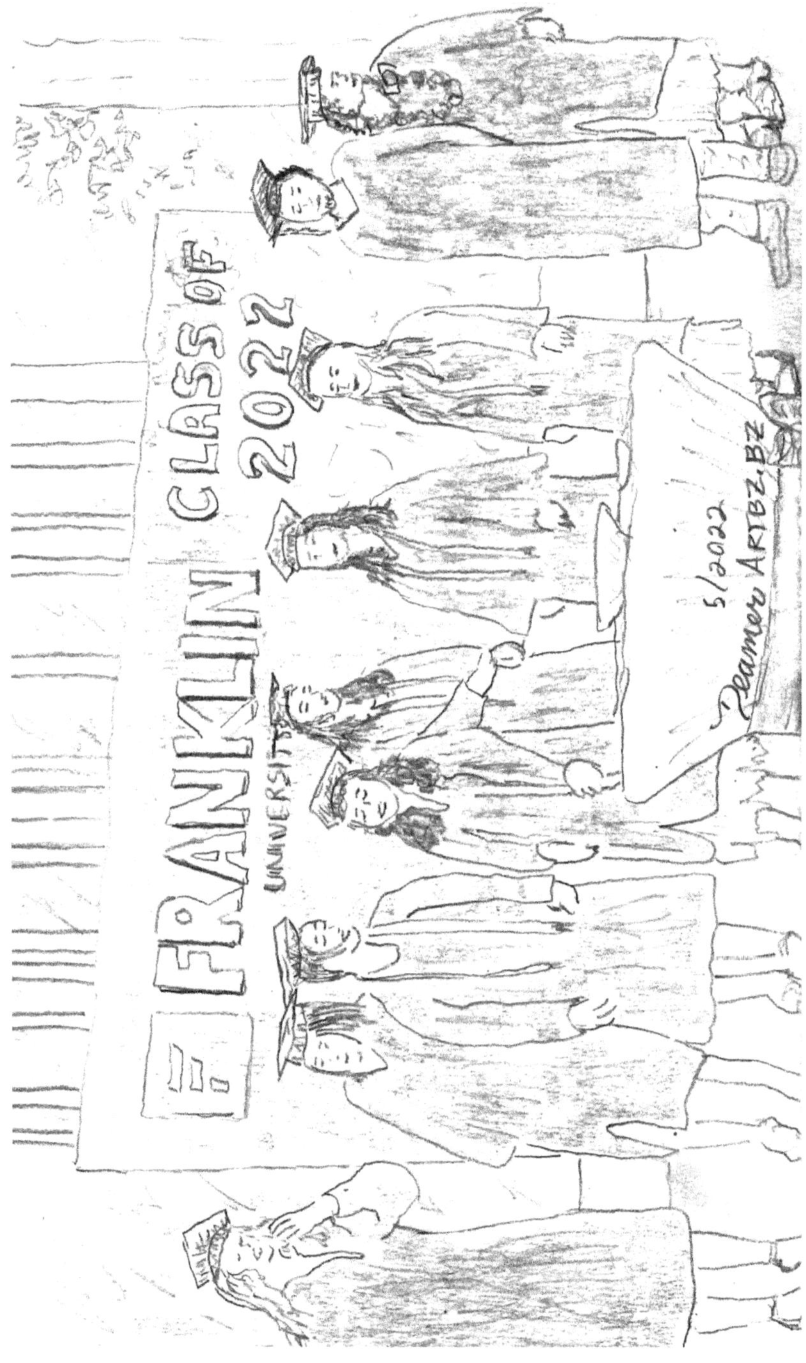
FRANKLIN UNIVERSITY
CLASS OF 2022
5/2022
Deamer ARTBZ.BZ

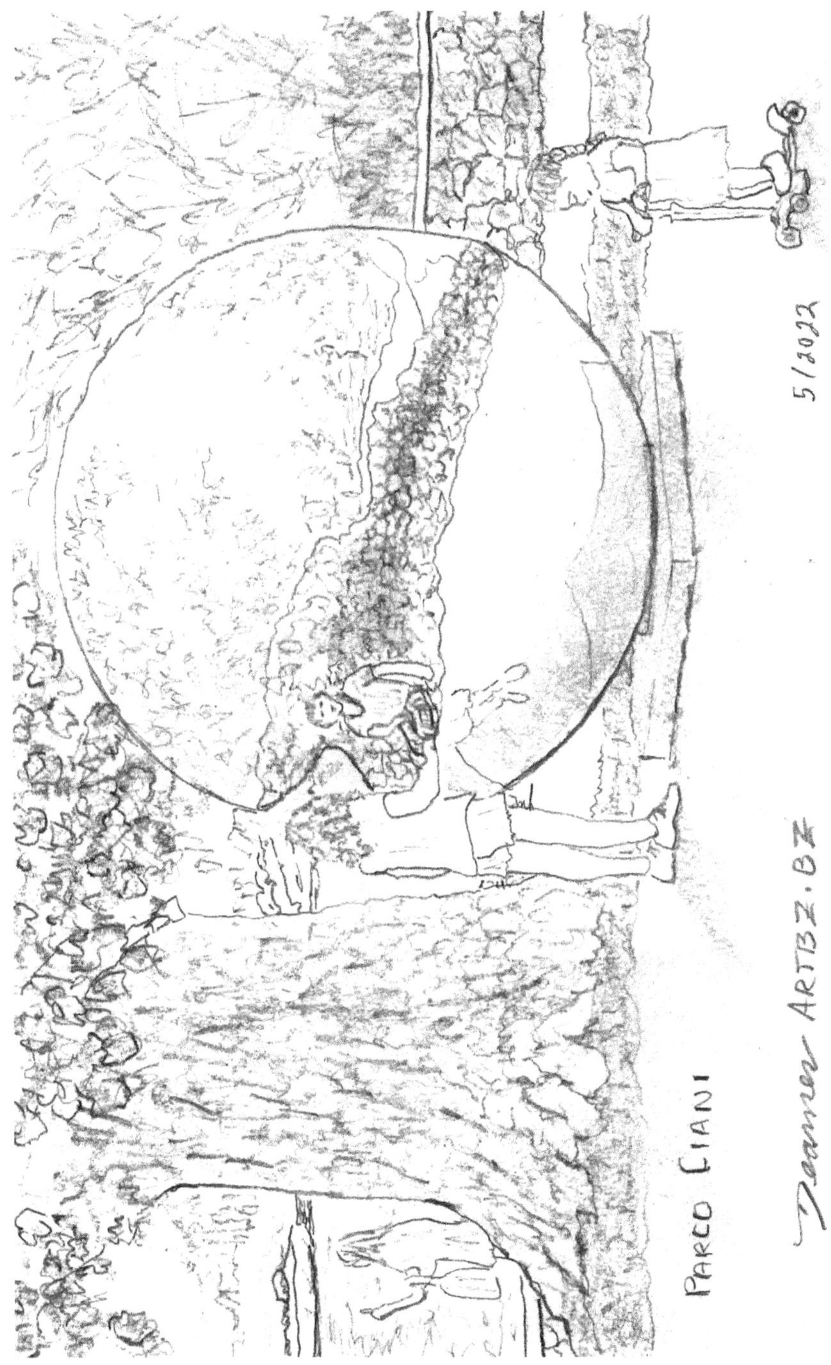
PARCO CIANI
5/2022
Deanna ARTBZ.BZ

137

Spaghetti Store   CAMPARI
Spaghetti Store
TAGLIOLINI FRESCO
DA OGGI
Spaghetti store
VI OFFRE
UNA GUSTOSA
NOVITA
VENITE
A PROVARE
la Vera
Pizza
napoletana
5/2022   PIAZZA RIZIERO REZZONICA
Deanna ARTBZ.BZ

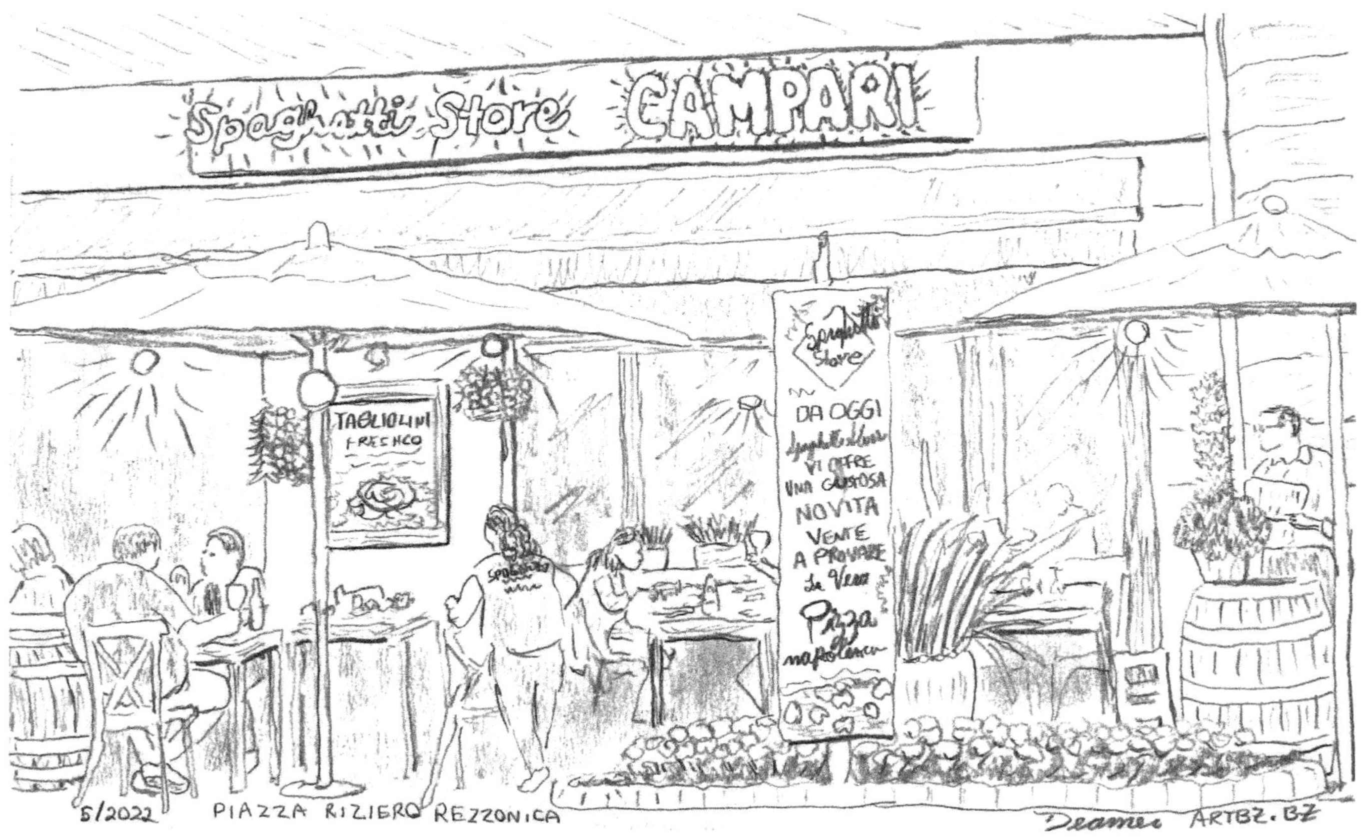

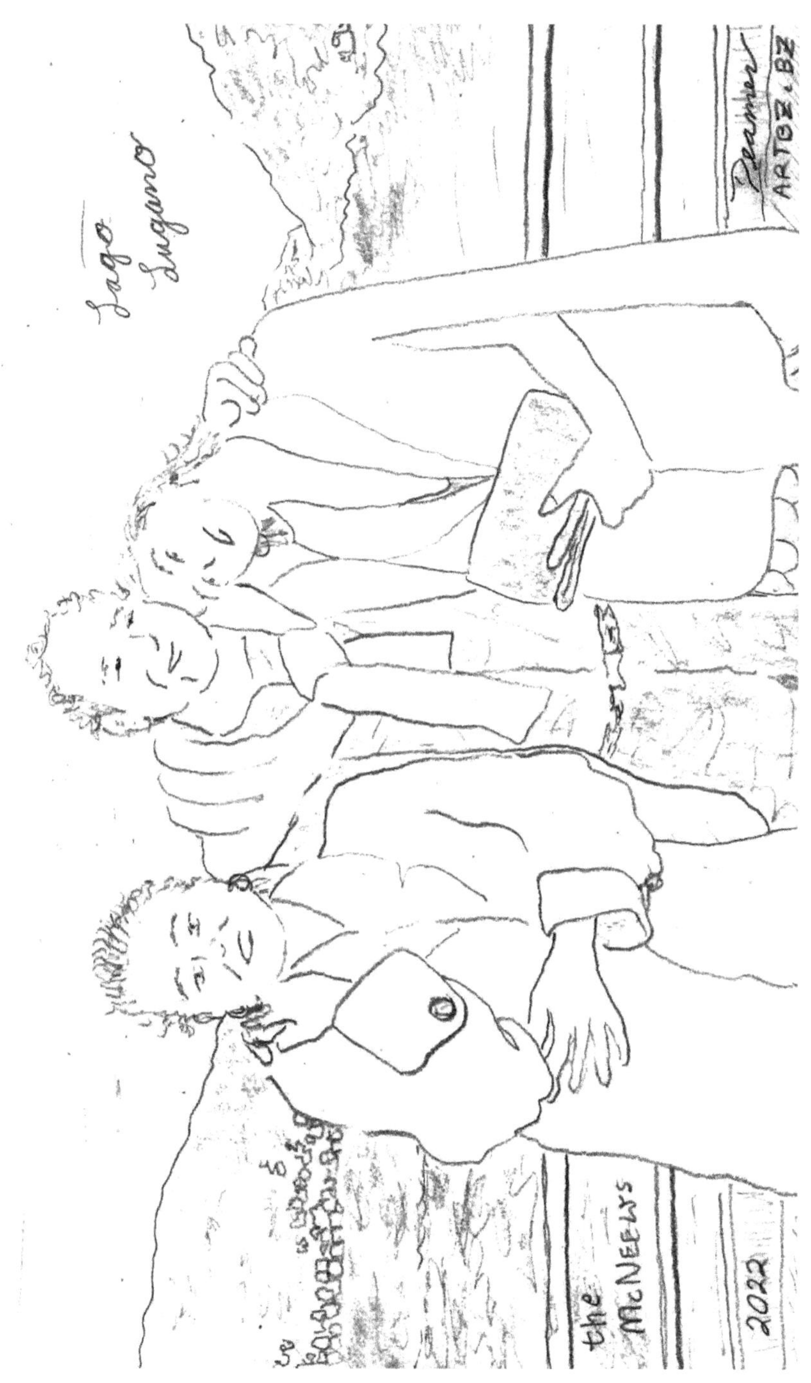
Lago
Lugano
ARTGZ.BZ
the
McNeelys
2022

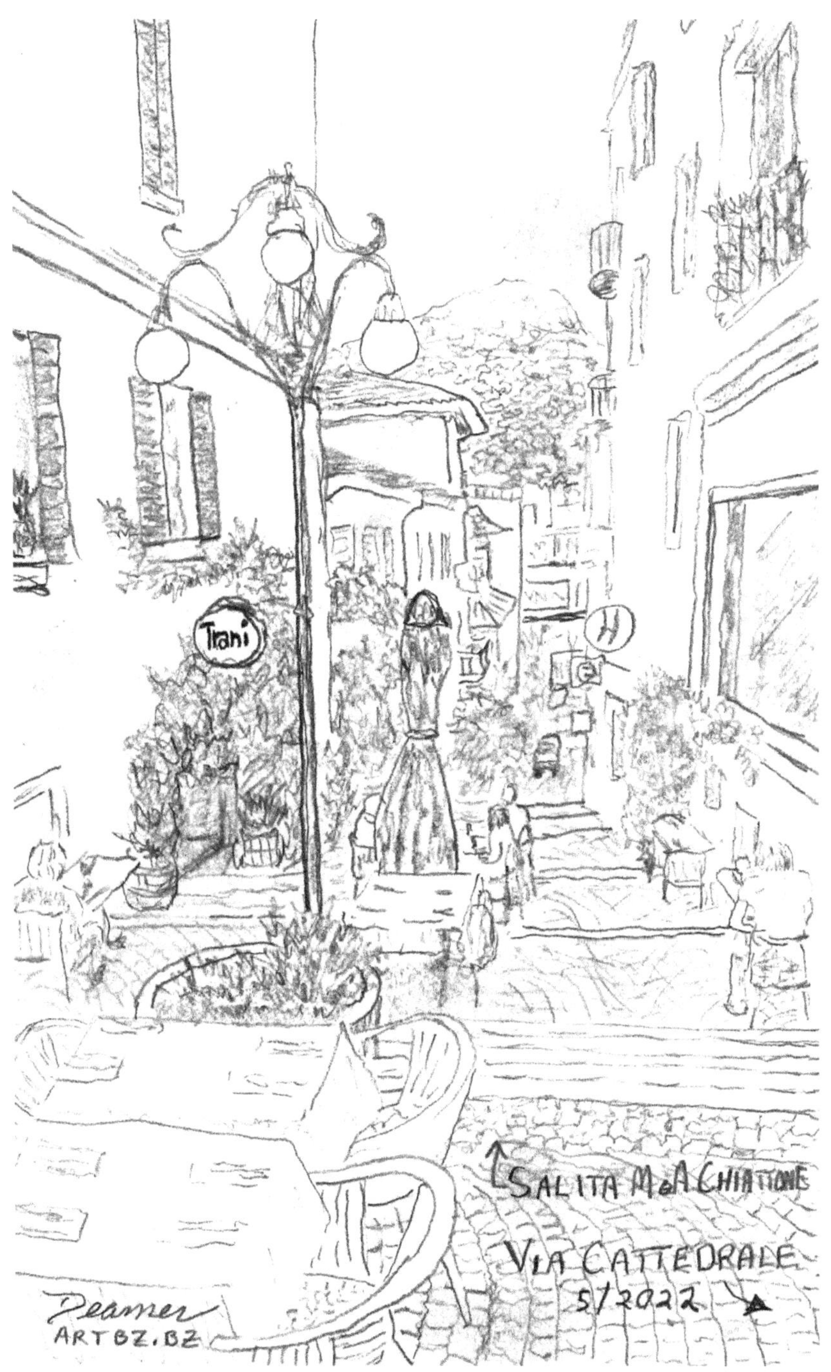
Trani
SALITA MaA ChiATTONE
VIA CATTEDRALE
5/2022
Deamer
ARTBZ.BZ

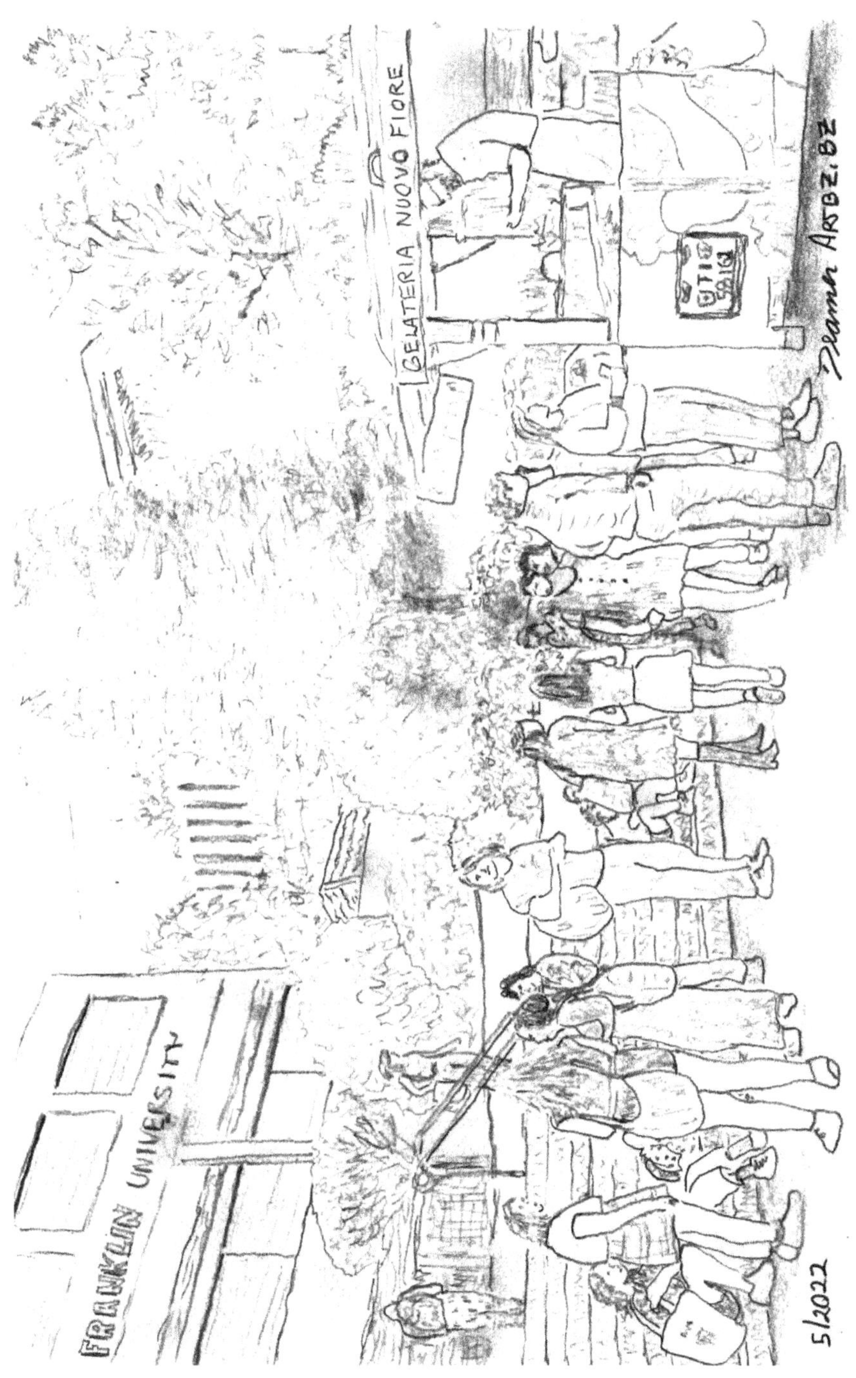
GELATERIA NUOVO FIORE
FRANKLIN UNIVERSITY
5/2022

PONTE TRESA ITALY

144

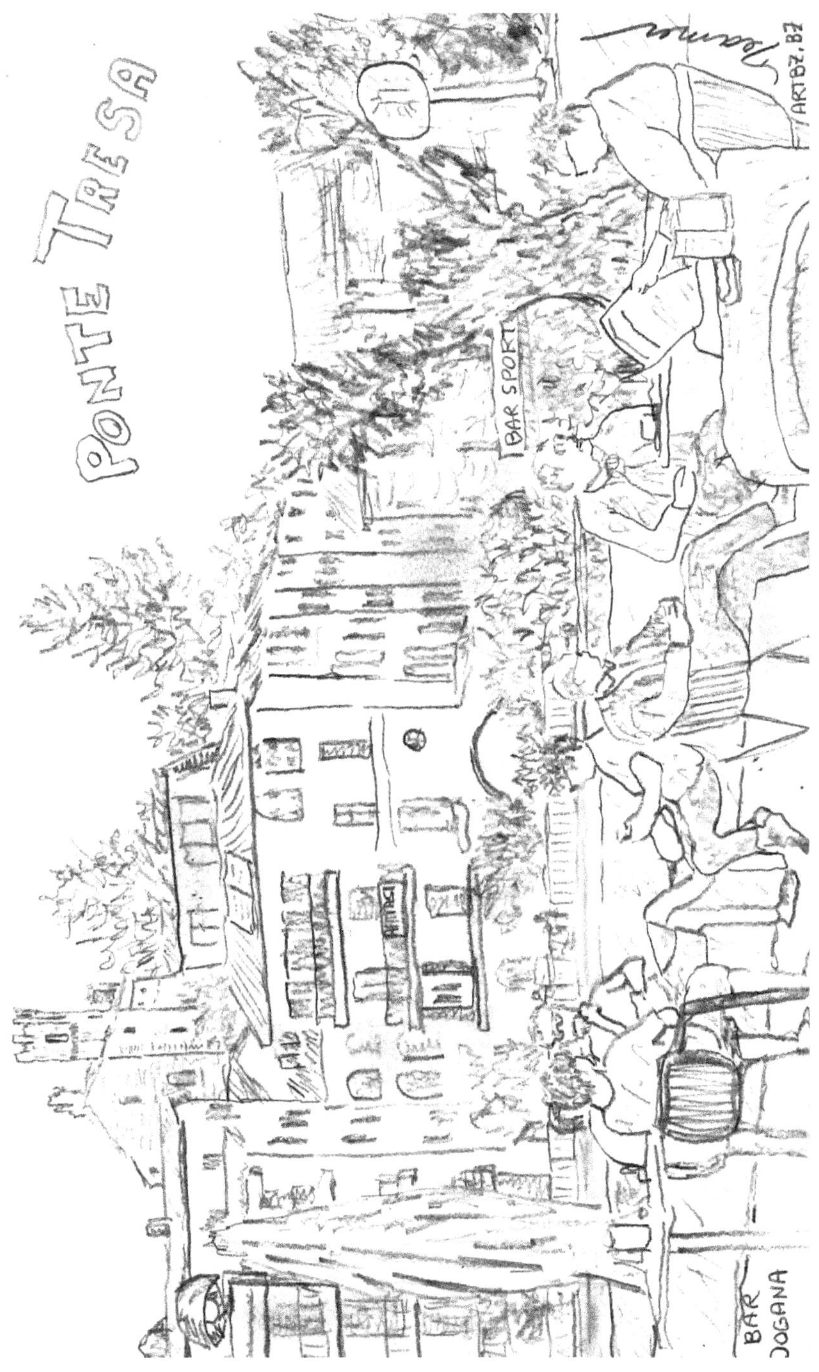
PONTE TRESA
BAR SPORT
BAR DOGANA

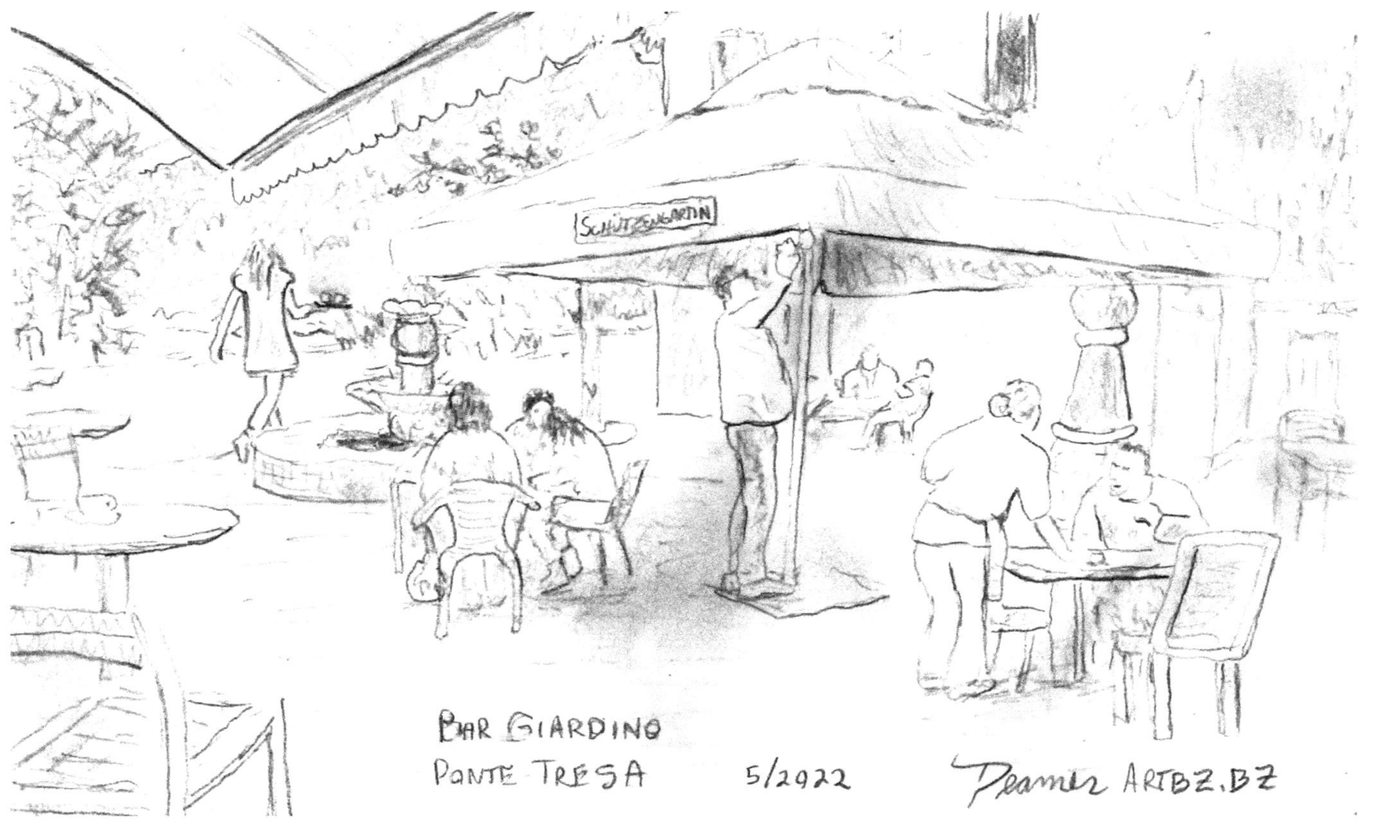
SCHÜTZENGARTN
Bar Giardino
Ponte Tresa   5/2022   Deamer ARTBZ.BZ

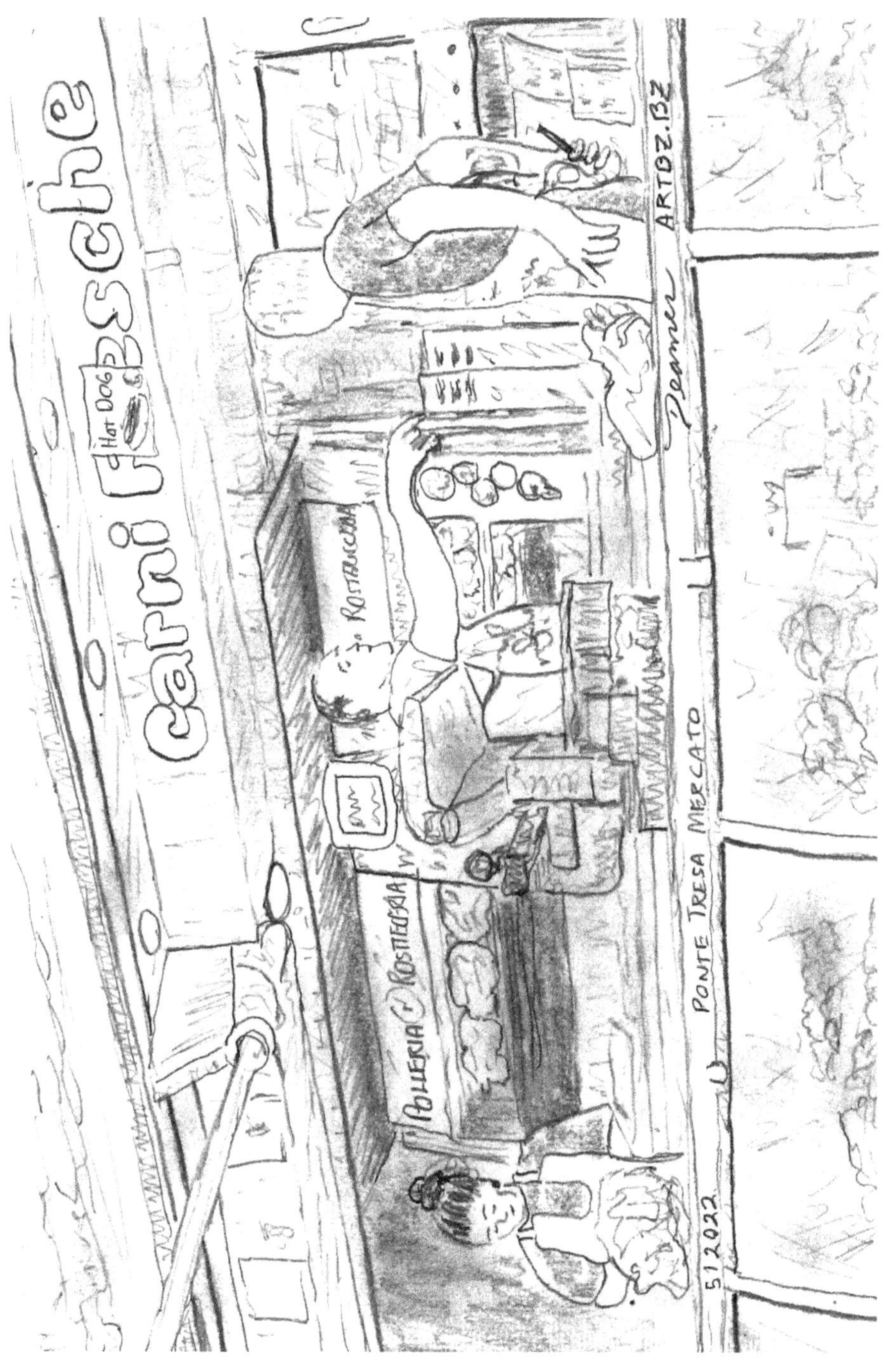
Carni Tedesche
Hot Dog
Rosticceria
Polleria Rosticceria
Ponte Tresa Mercato
Jeanne
ART02.132
5.12.022

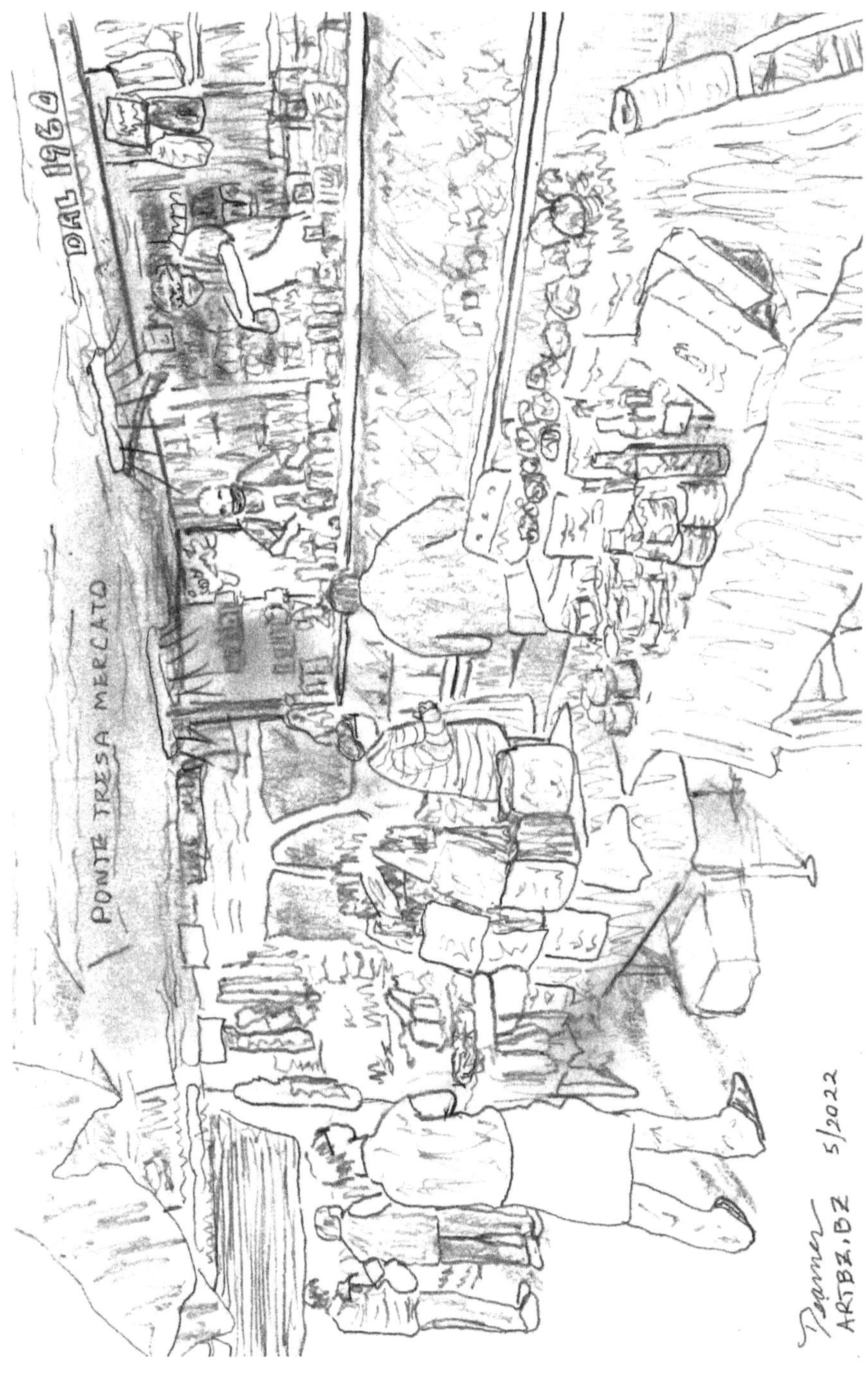
DAL 1960
PONTE TRESA MERCATO
ARTBZ.BZ   5/2022

152

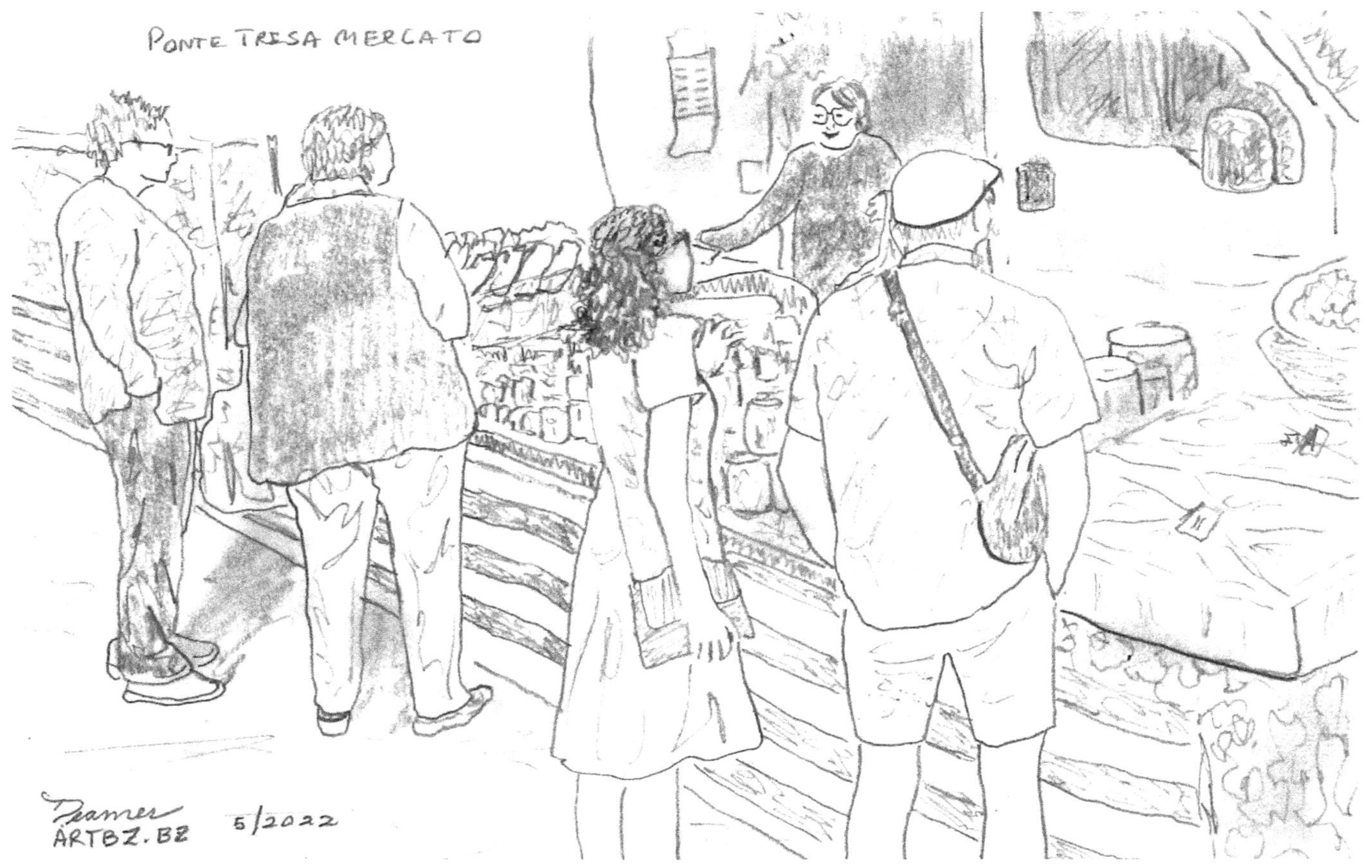
PONTE TRESA MERCATO
Jeanne
ARTBZ.BZ   5/2022

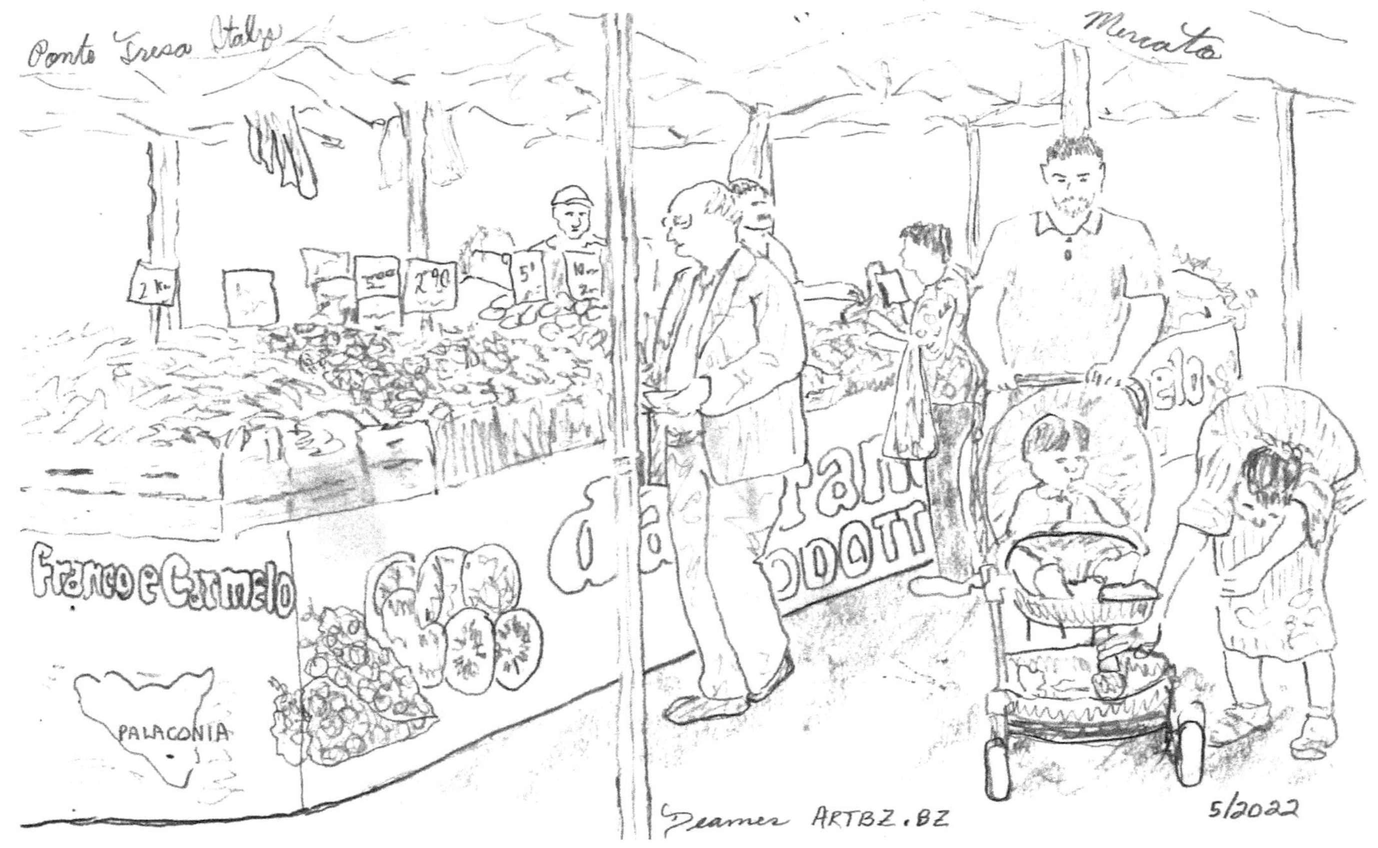

Ponte Tresa Italy
Mercato
Franco e Carmelo
PALAGONIA
Dreamer ARTBZ.BZ
5/2022

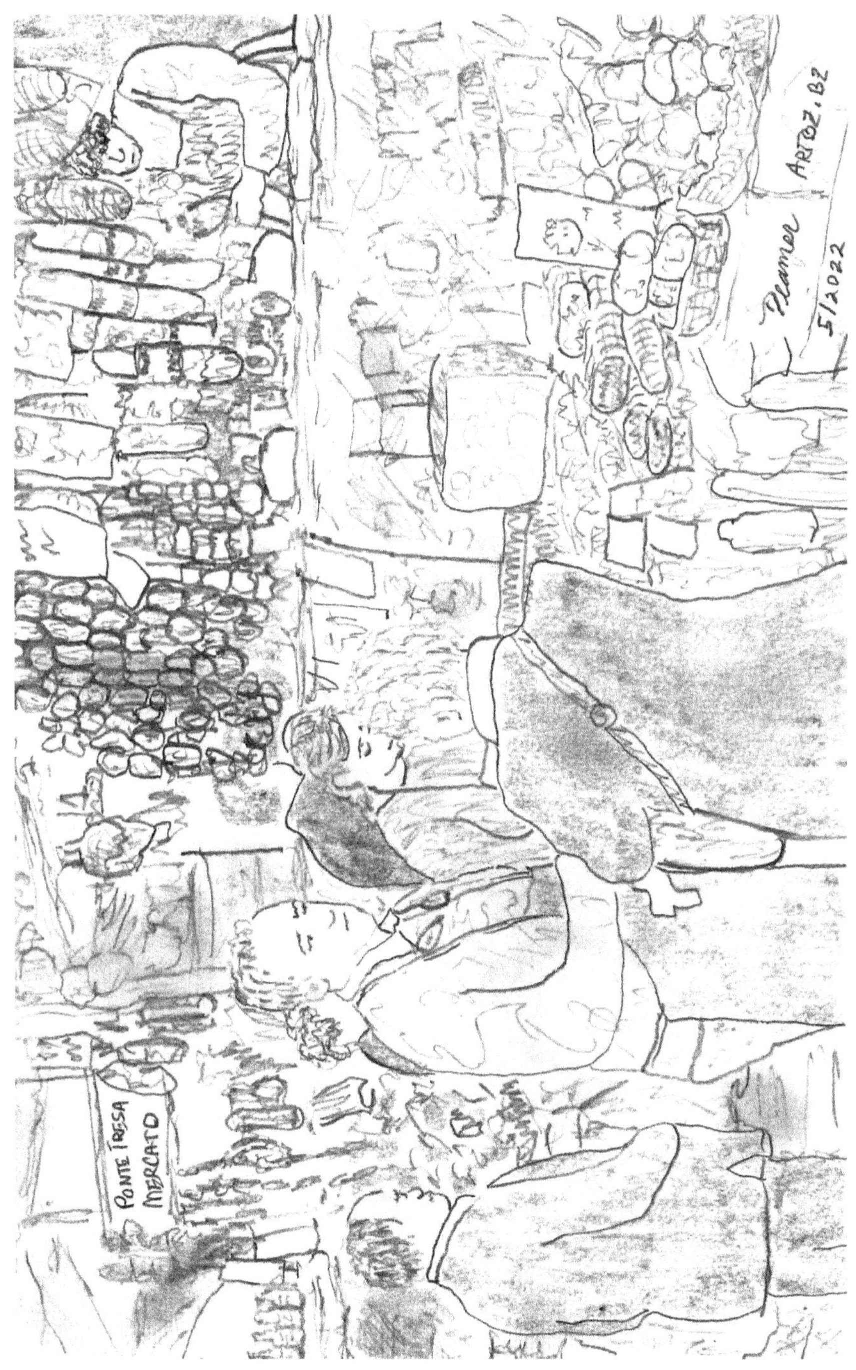
PONTE TRESA
MERCATO

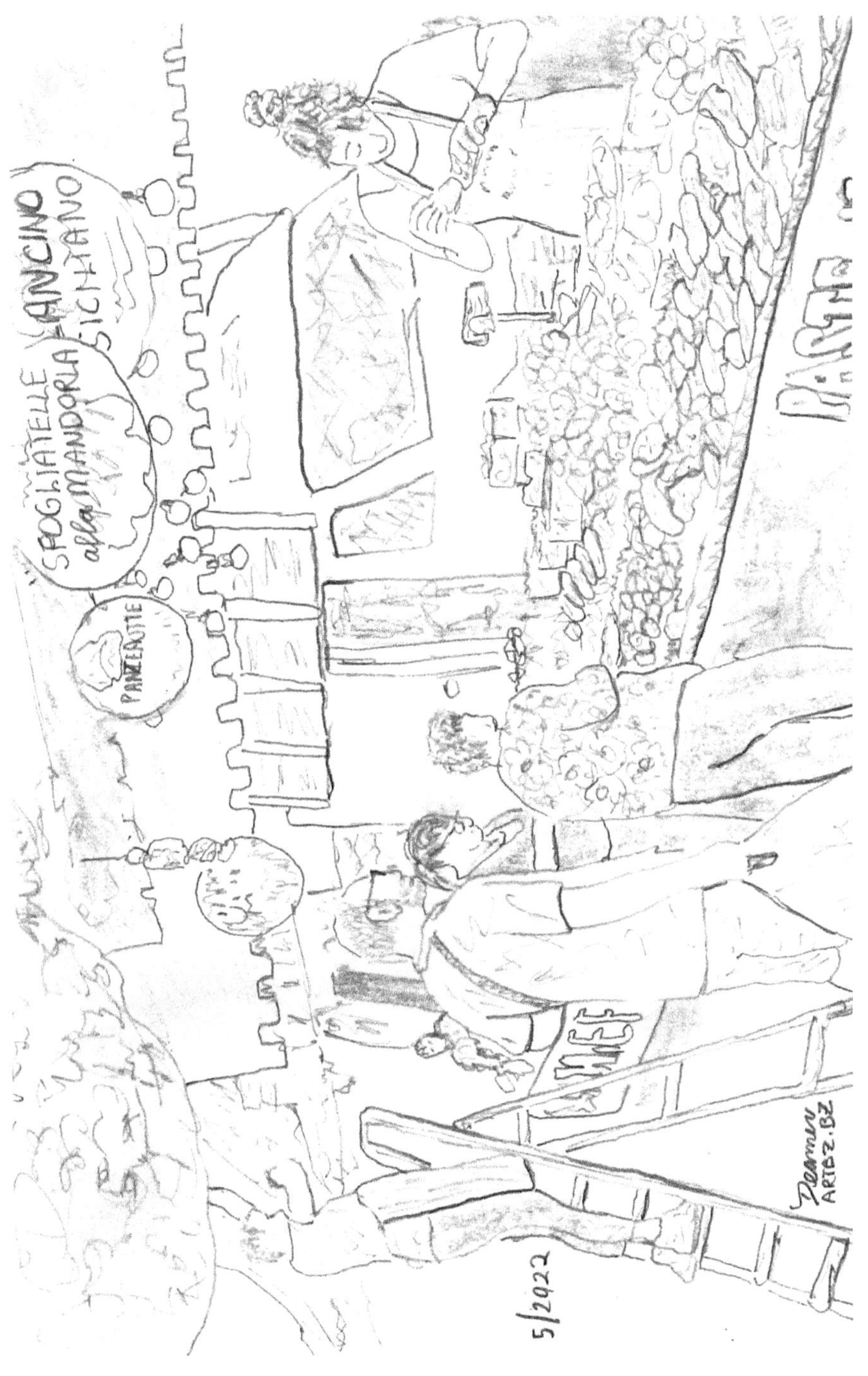
SPAGLIATELLE alla MANDORLA
PANCINO
SCHIAVO
PANZEROTTE
PASTA
5/29/22
Dearmin
ARTez.BZ

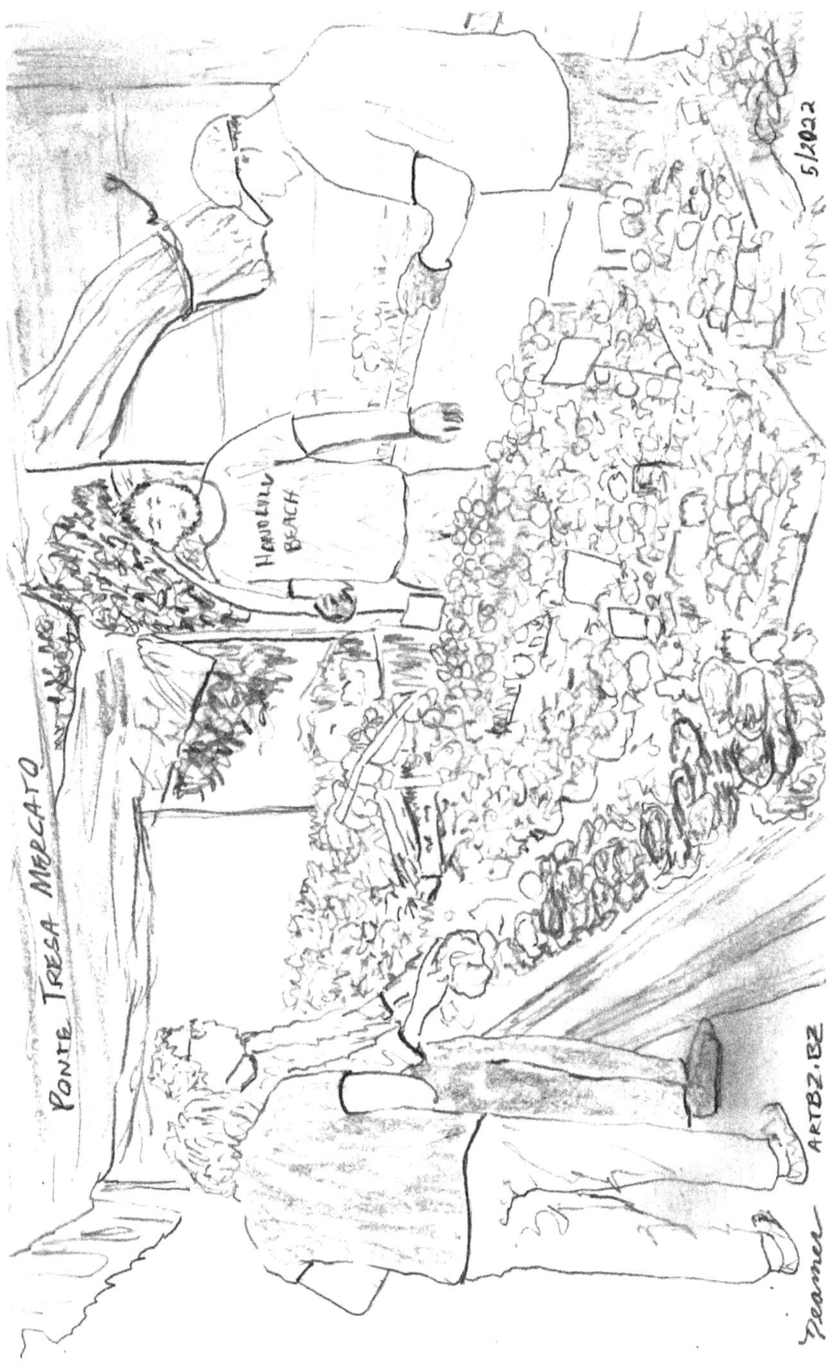
PONTE TRESA MERCATO
HEAVENLY BEACH
5/2022
ARTB2.B2

MILAN ITALY

Owning and Living a Café

My life as a café owner is a living oxymoron. Each day is filled with opposites. My business would crumble like toasted bread, if I didn't go through the daily routines that make the everything function. On the other hand, what keeps me in business is all my efforts to ignore these details and concentrate on those I serve. I became a café owner after eliminating several other pursuits. You could say that I found ways to make money, but I had not found a way to make a life. Here, in my part of Italy, our regulars are like family. I know their habits and they know mine. I understand that the local café isn't always like this. My American friend tried to explain the commerce efficiency of a coffee house like a Starbucks, but I just couldn't understand it. Not that serving tourists isn't a big part of my business. But I treat them just like they are part of my extended family. When it comes to café talk, I have learned enough additional languages to converse with my visitors. This is quite fun for me, not to mention that I feel a gratitude for connecting with the rest of the world. Even if it is over a small bite and that heavenly combination of coffee and milk. In the early days, when I was struggling to deal with the oxymoron of running a café, I would feel a pain at the end of each day. All to often I felt I hadn't gotten things right. Eventually, I learned to enjoy the contrast of performing the routines and serving with a smile. Like my morning washing of the shop glass front. It's a routine which could be considered a time-consuming task. But I've come to really enjoy the process and the result. While I wash the window to my world, I have my back to Via Dante, a street filled with walkers and bike riders. As my squeegee gives them a clear view into my place, I get to watch them pass by in the reflections. This has become a great joy to witness each morning. I not only feel that my task is inviting those who pass inside, I feel like I am also a part of their daily routine. Hmm, inviting in and viewing reflections, kind of an oxymoron of its own, don't you think?

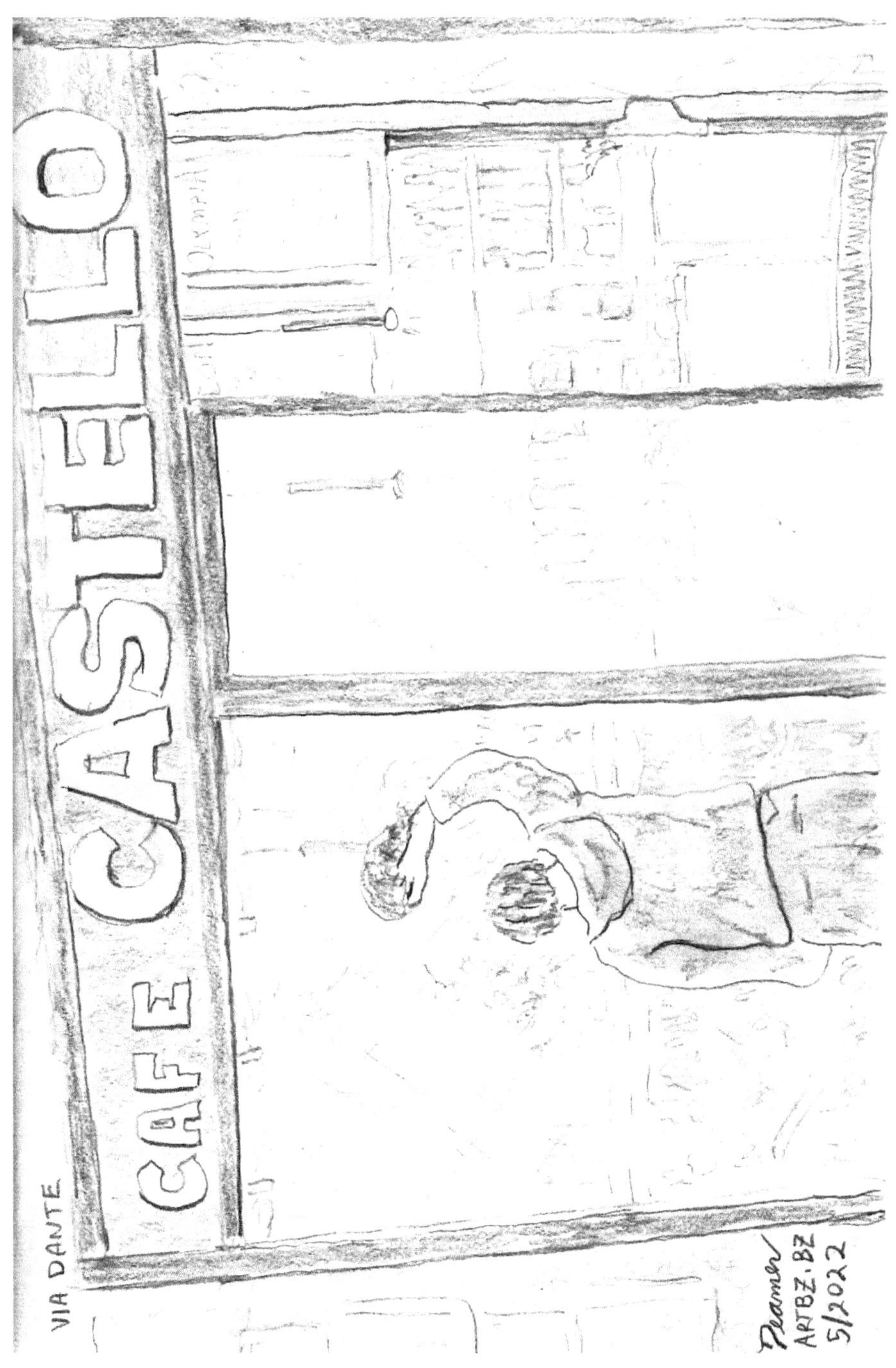

VIA DANTE
CASTELLO
CAFE CASTELLO
Pramer
ARTBZ.BZ
5/2022

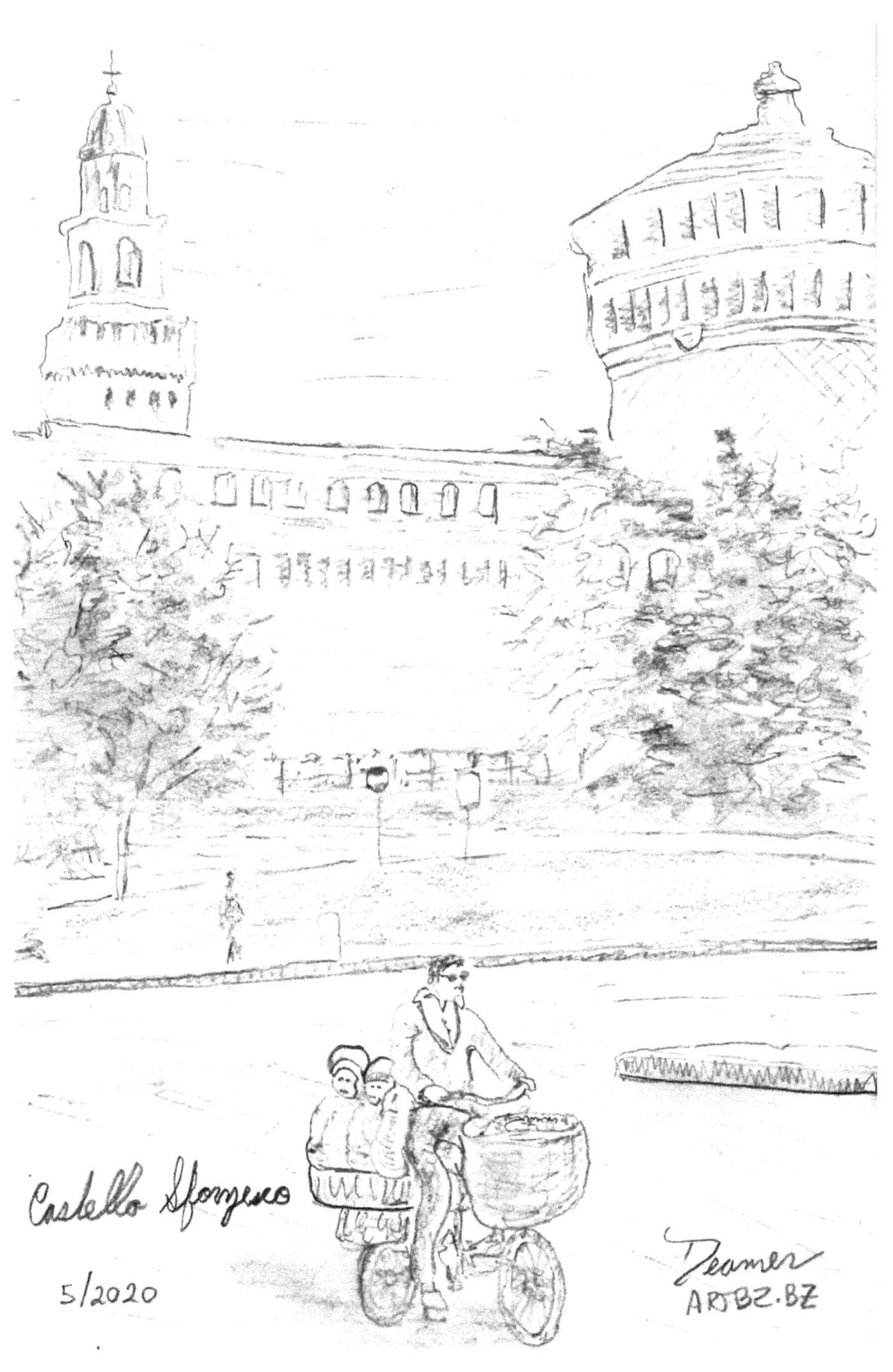
Castello Sforzesco
5/2020
Deamer
ARJBZ.BZ

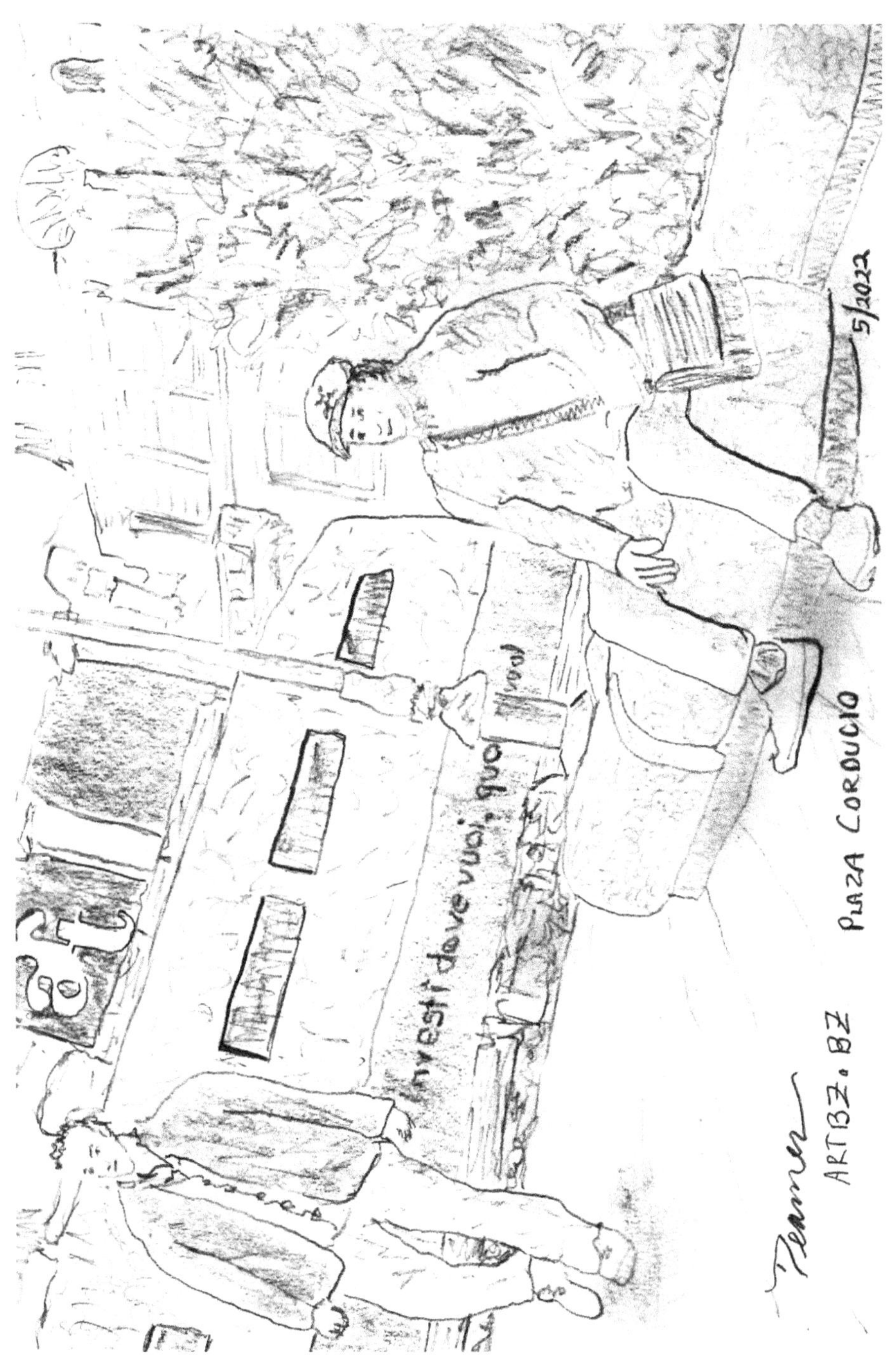
Investi dove vuoi, qui
ART82, BZ
PLAZA CORDUCIO
5/2022

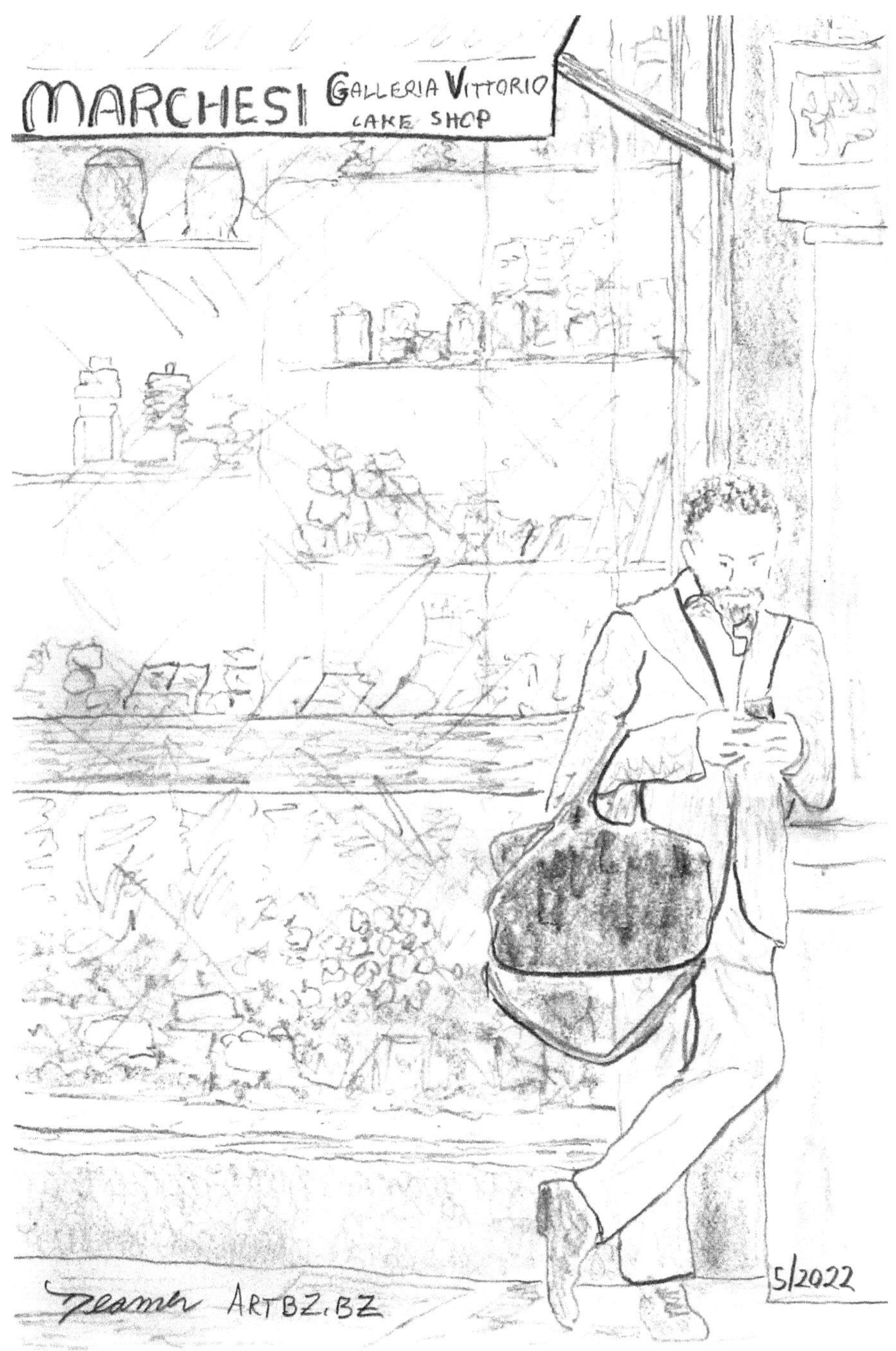
MARCHESI
GALLERIA VITTORIO
CAKE SHOP
Deamer ARTBZ.BZ
5/2022

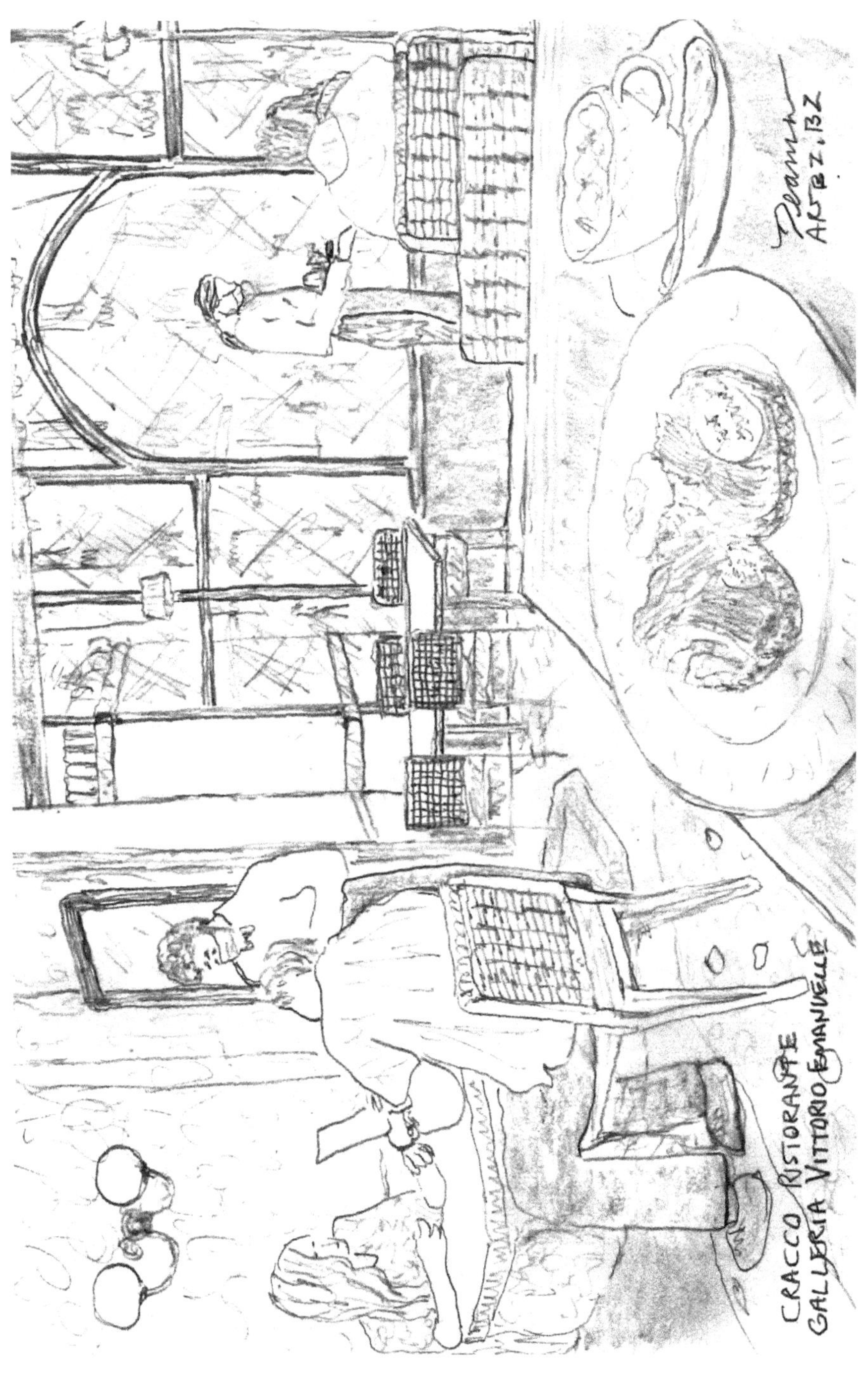
CRACCO RISTORANTE
GALLERIA VITTORIO EMANUELE

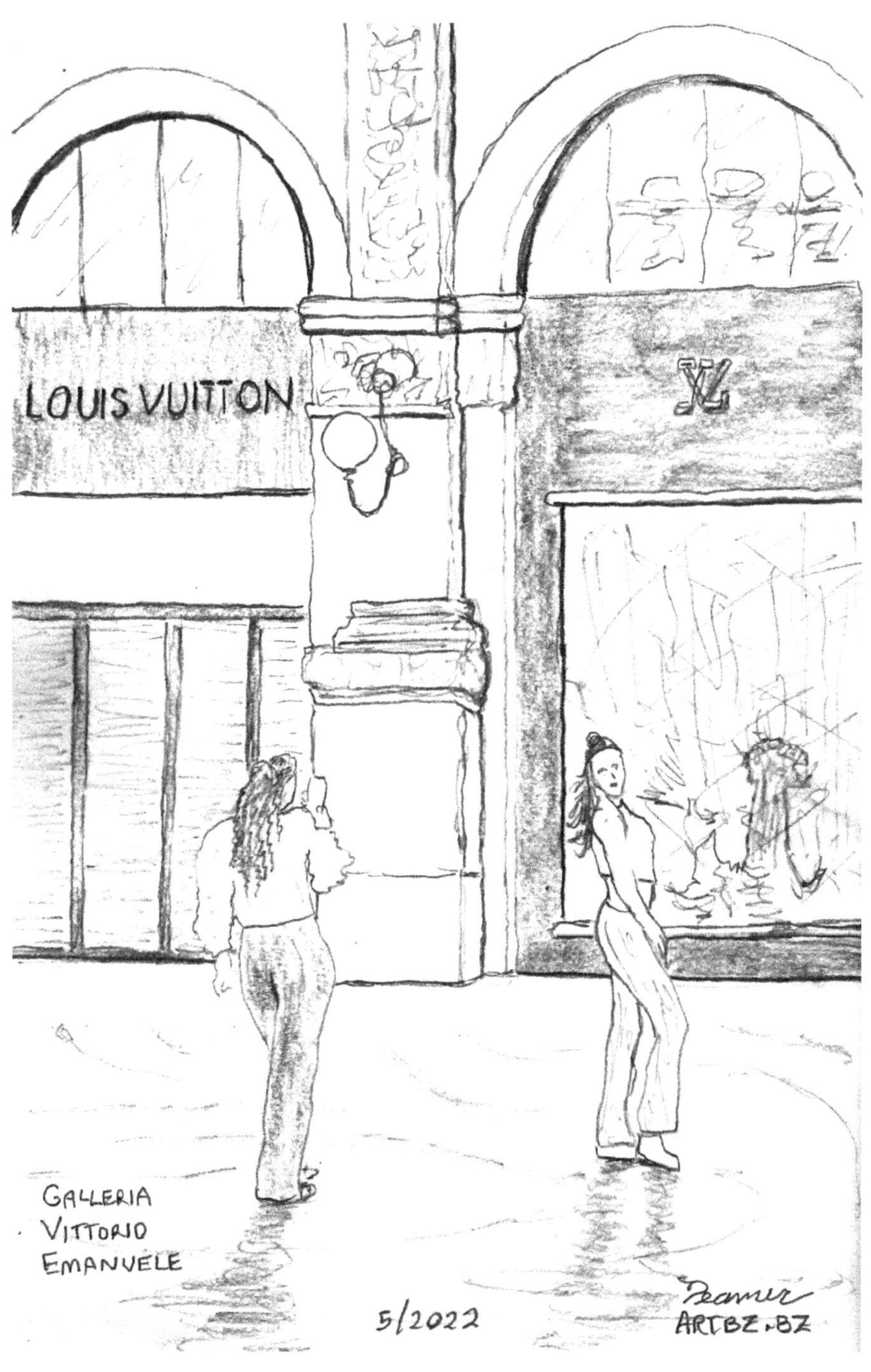
LOUIS VUITTON
GALLERIA
VITTORIO
EMANVELE
5/2022
ARTBZ.BZ

Sonoma California SIFF Sonoma International Film Festival

Enjoying the Sonoma Film Festival

The Annual Sonoma Film Festival has become a highlight of our year, every year. Those days that drag at work or when the kids call with their problems, are easier to handle when the calendar is getting closer to March. I think this is our twentieth year attending. I still think fondly of the early years when it felt like we were sneaking into a little community party. Now it feels more like we are part of something that is inviting the world to 'our' little town. Even though my husband and I live a couple of hours away, coming annually to this event has made Sonoma feel like our village too. Though, I suppose part of the attraction is that it is familiar but not so close that we associate it with normal life. No, having it as a getaway makes it that more special. It has become a place where we leave behind the day-to-day and live an adventure. Not only are there the latest local wines to taste and menus to explore, the festival brings the world to us in the art of film. There is that whole insider feeling of seeing films before they have been distributed to the rest of the world—to being on the front lines of their unveiling. There is also that thrill of enjoying the shorts, movies that may never get a large audience, yet we get to see them and often meet those behind the making of them. We love the whole experience. The festival has been a part of Sonoma so long that the culture of film has joined the existing practically religious passion for great wine and food. It is such a pleasure to catch a couple of films and then discuss them at one of the wonderful Sonoma restaurants. It doesn't get much better than enjoying the local food and wine, while discussing a film that just tickled are brains and hearts. Like on this night, when the always fun bartender Candice and a gentleman sitting at the bar beside us, discussed the film 'Mr. Blake at Your Service.' I have always enjoyed John Malkovich, he just has that certain something that pulls you into his film appearances. How fun to experience him speaking French in a story of countryside France. After dinner we are headed to see a documentary of the life and influence of Cindy Lauper, 'Let the Canary Sing.'

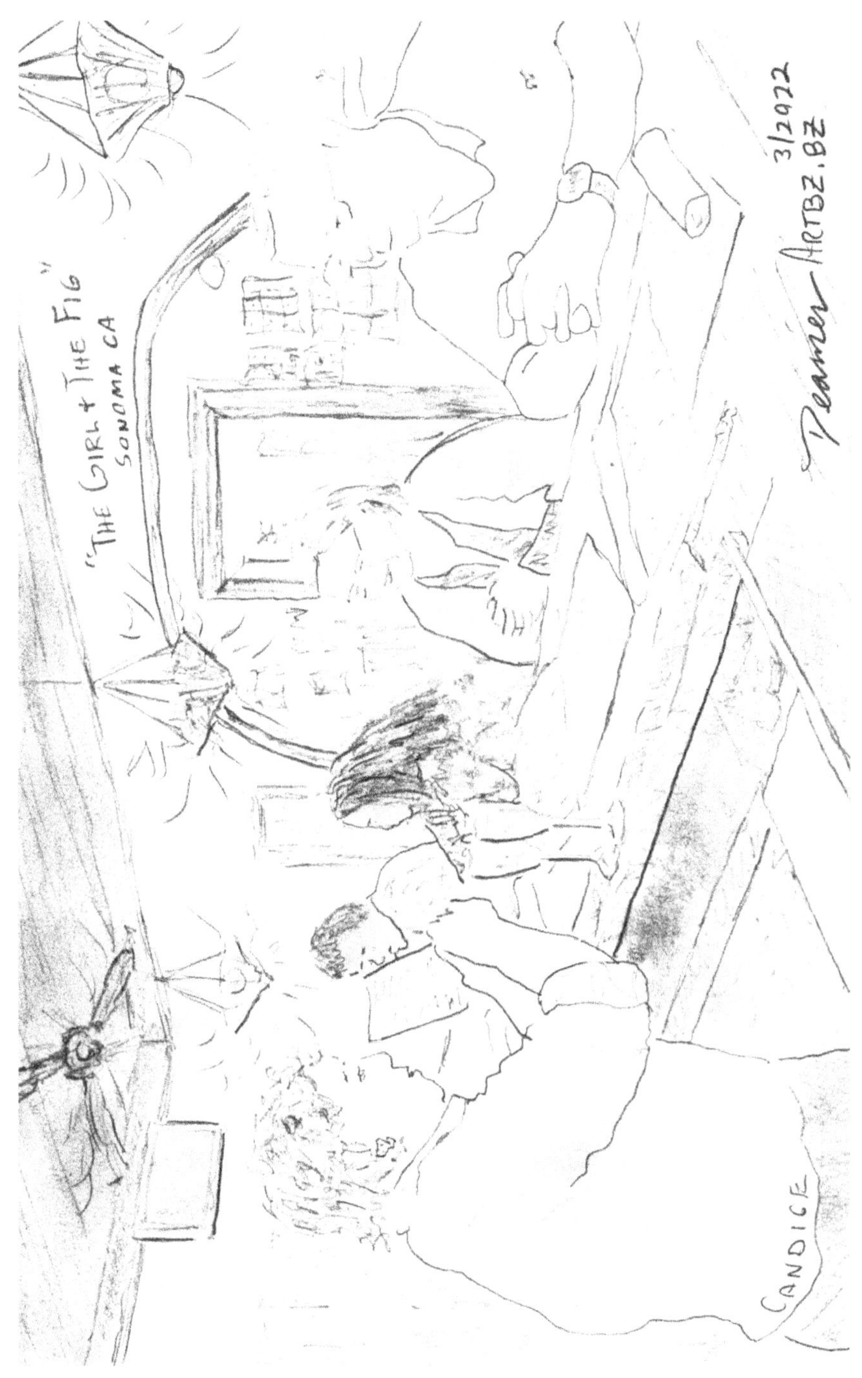
"THE GIRL + THE FIG"
SONOMA CA
CANDICE
Reamer ARTBZ.BZ
3/2922

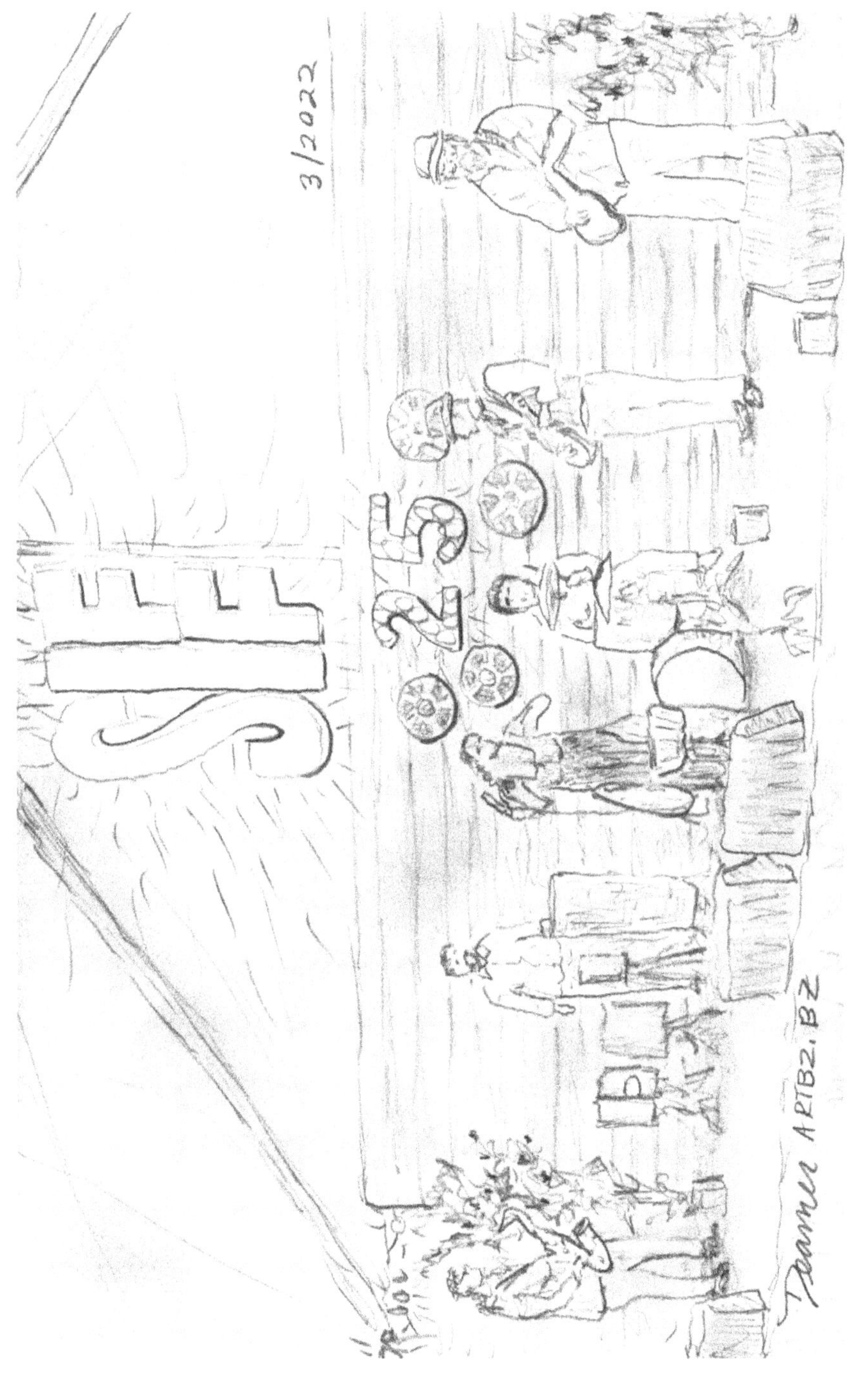

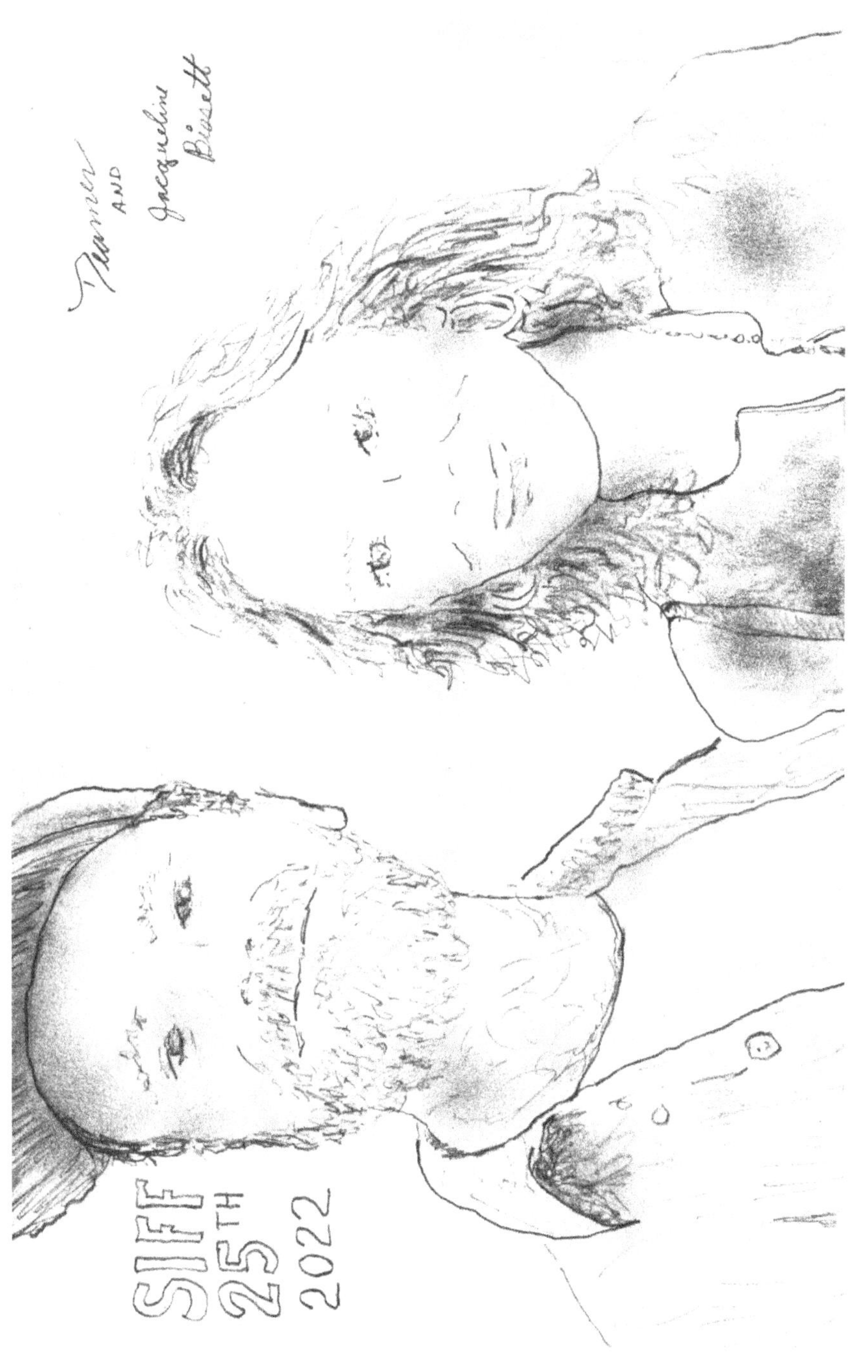
Warren
AND
Jacqueline
Bisett
SIFF
25TH
2022

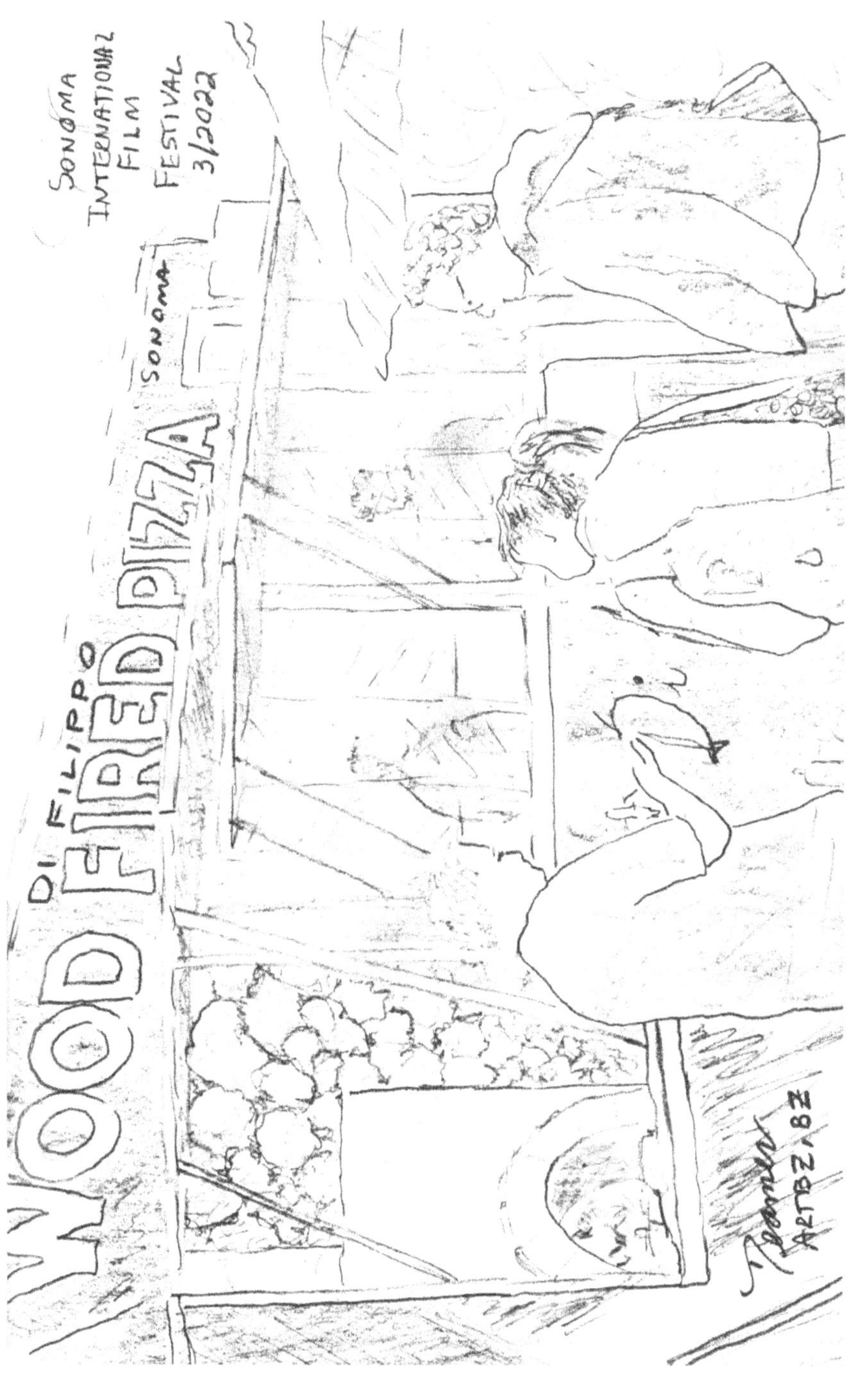

WOOD FIRED PIZZA
DI FILIPPO
Sonoma
SONOMA
INTERNATIONAL
FILM
FESTIVAL 3/2022

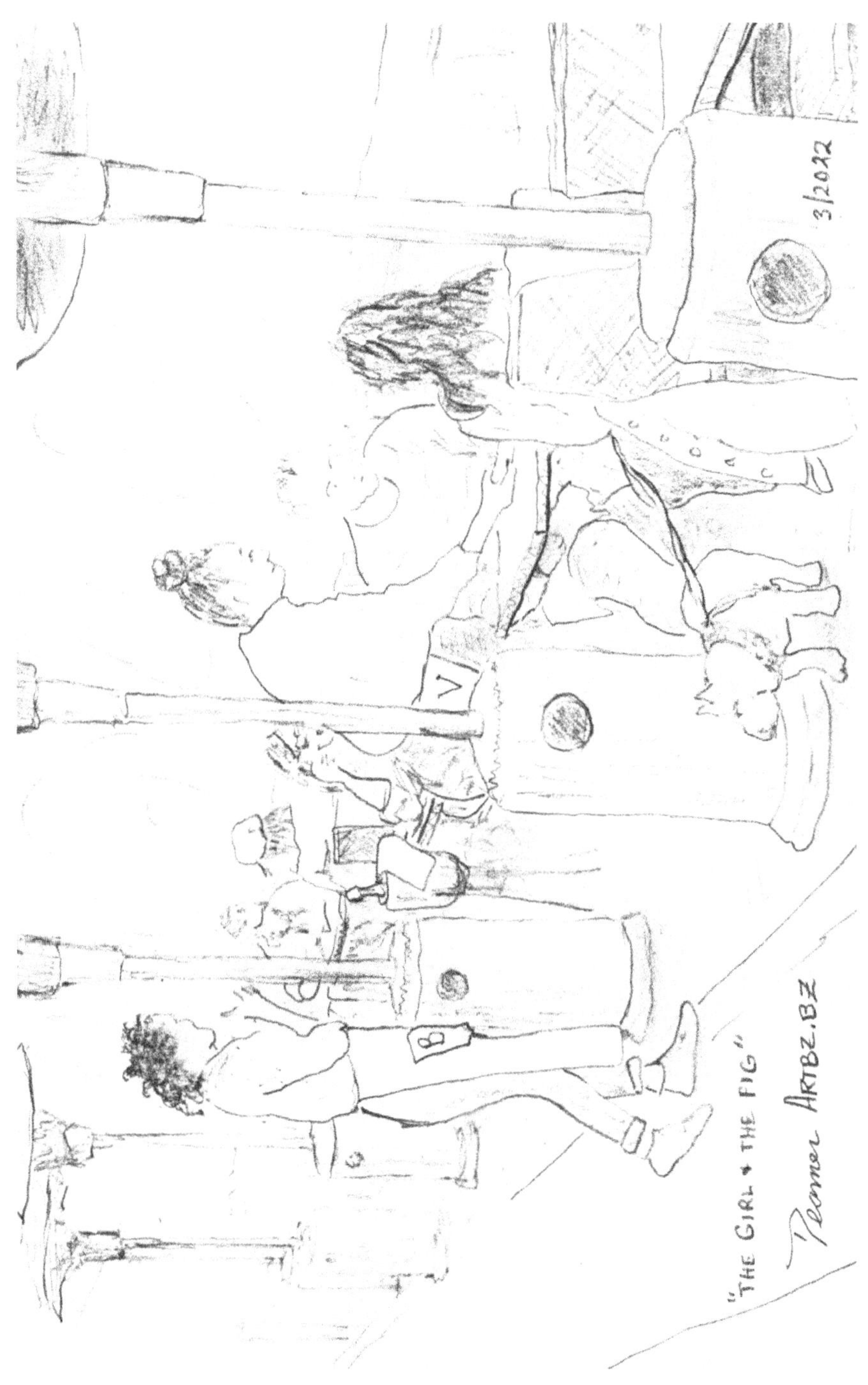
"THE GIRL & THE FIG"
Reamer ARTBZ.BZ
3/2022

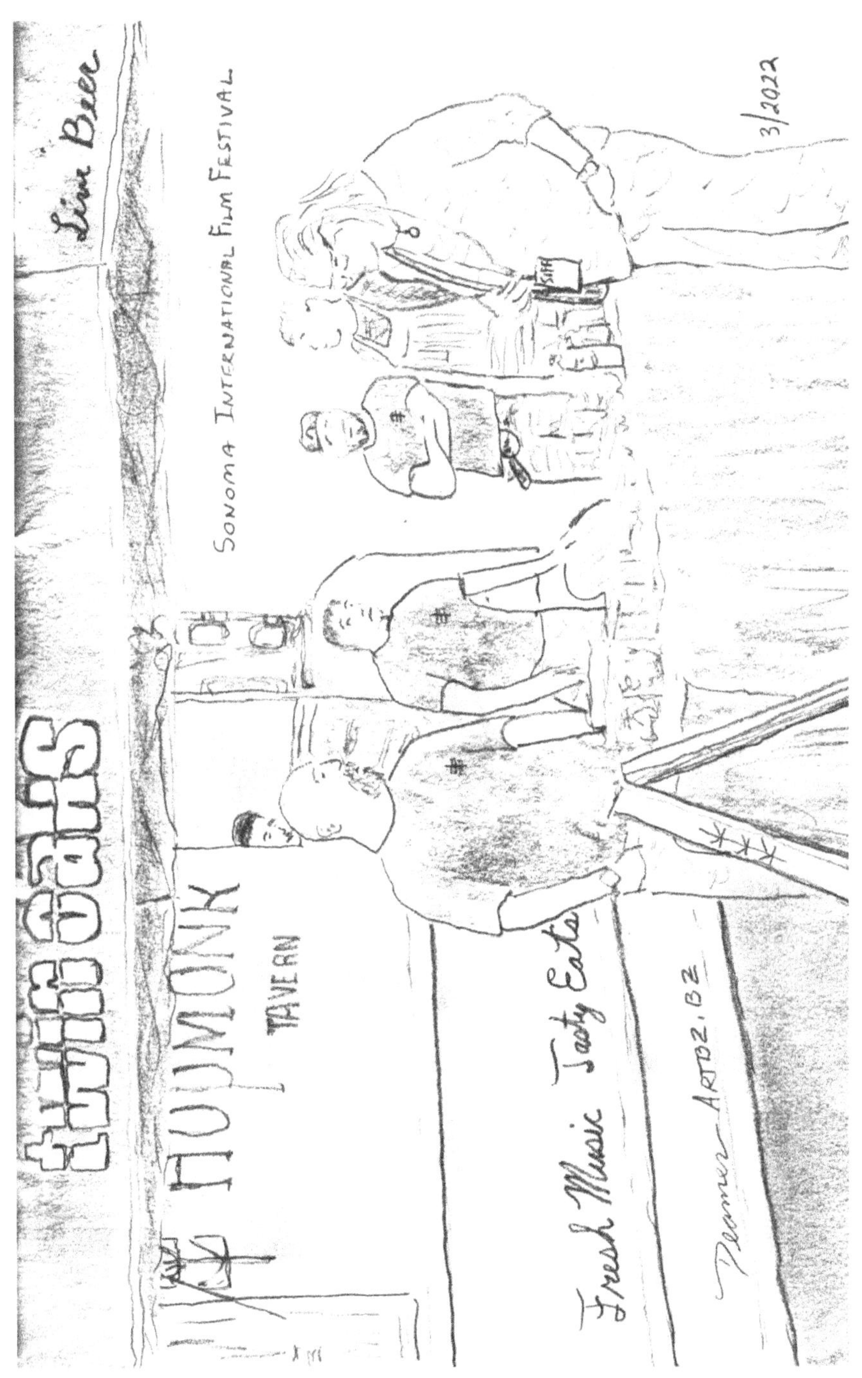

twin oaks
Live Beer
HOPMONK
TAVERN
SONOMA INTERNATIONAL FILM FESTIVAL
Fresh Music Tasty Eats
Deamer ART02.B2
3/2022

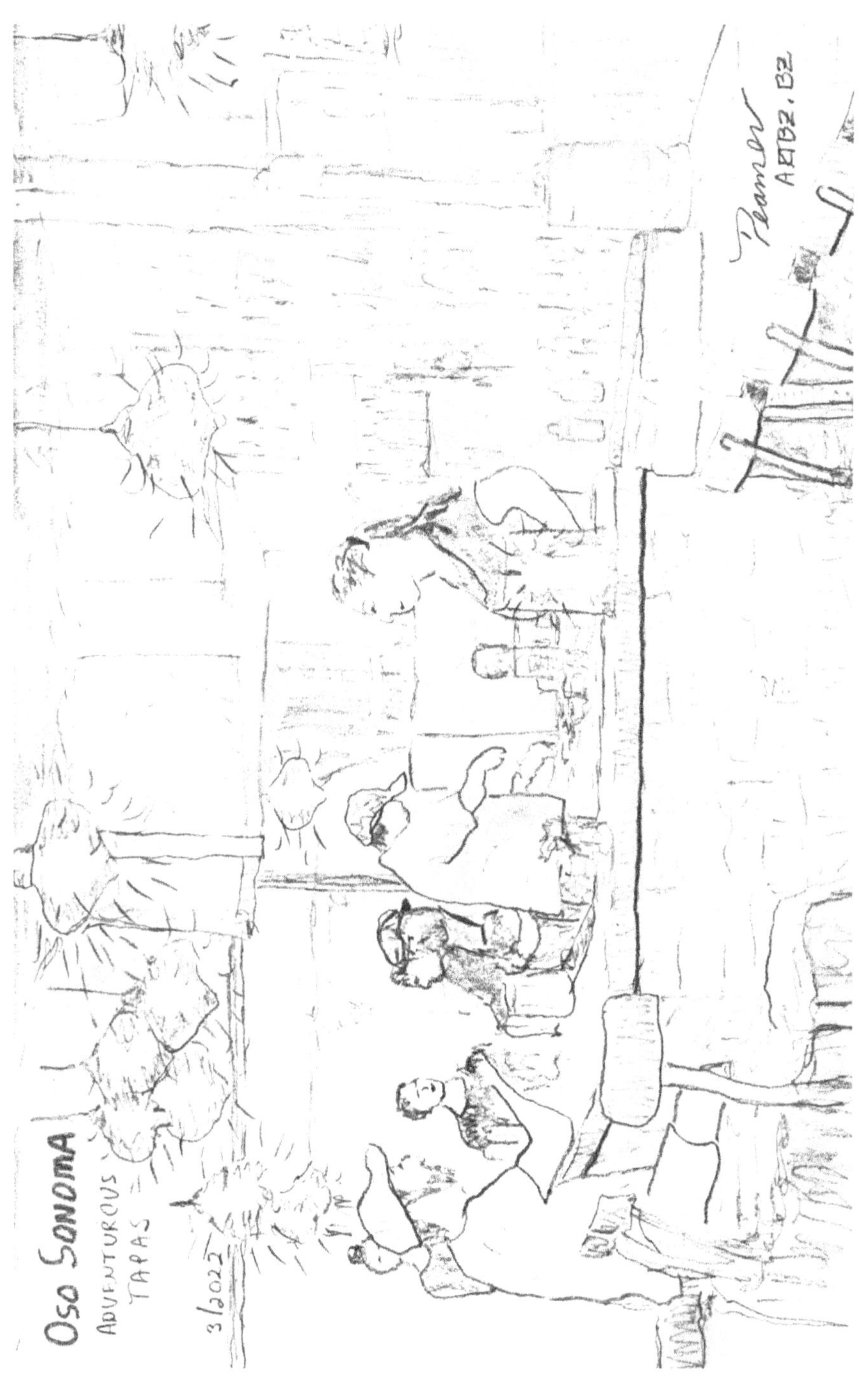
Oso Sonoma
Adventurous Tapas
3/2022
Reamer
ARTB2.B2

188

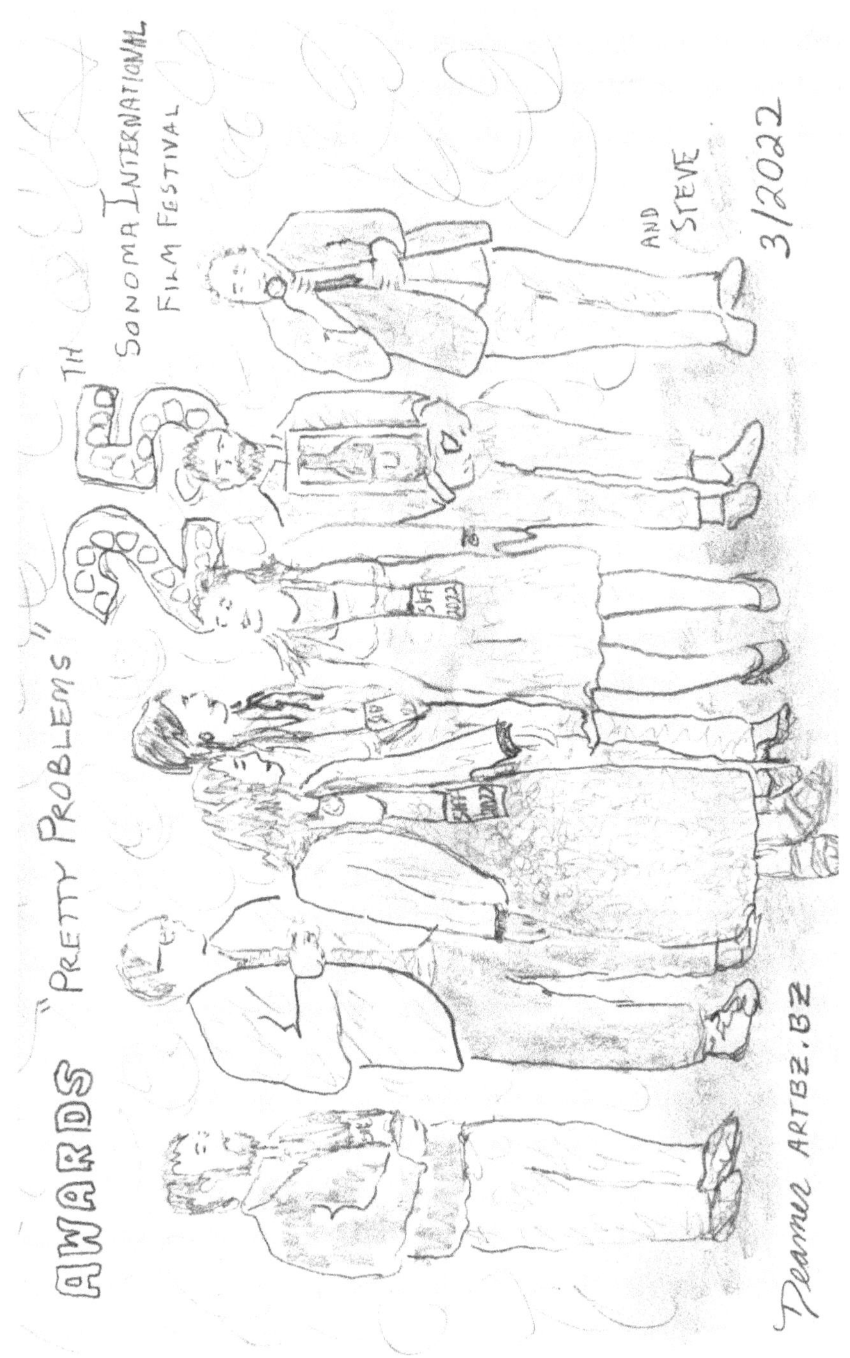
AWARDS "PRETTY PROBLEMS"
25TH SONOMA INTERNATIONAL FILM FESTIVAL
AND STEVE
3/2022
Deamer ARTBZ.BZ

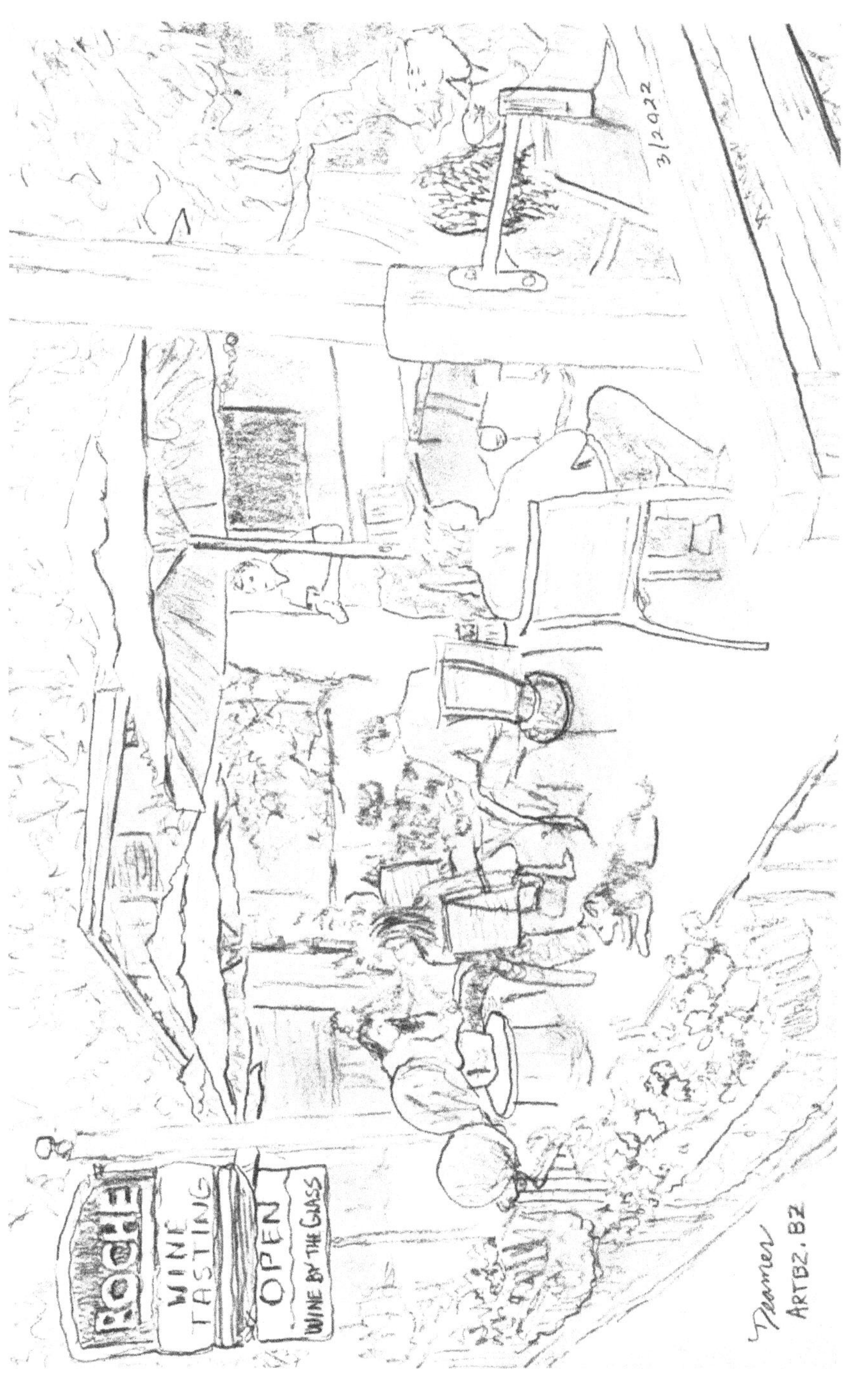
ROCHE
WINE TASTING
OPEN
WINE BY THE GLASS
3/2022

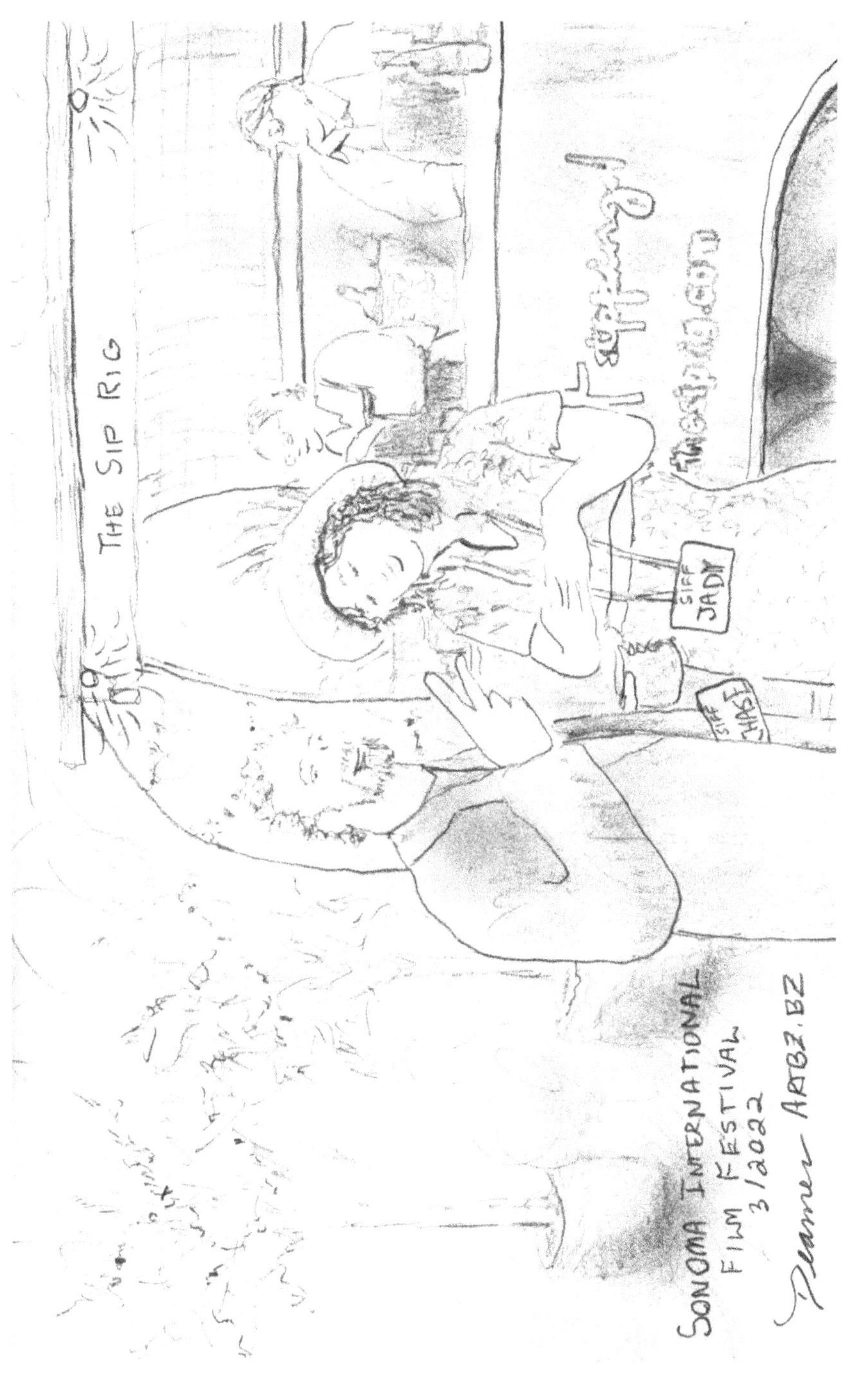
THE SIP RIG
SIFF JADY
SIFF CHASE
SONOMA INTERNATIONAL
FILM FESTIVAL 3/2022
Plamer ARTBZ.BZ

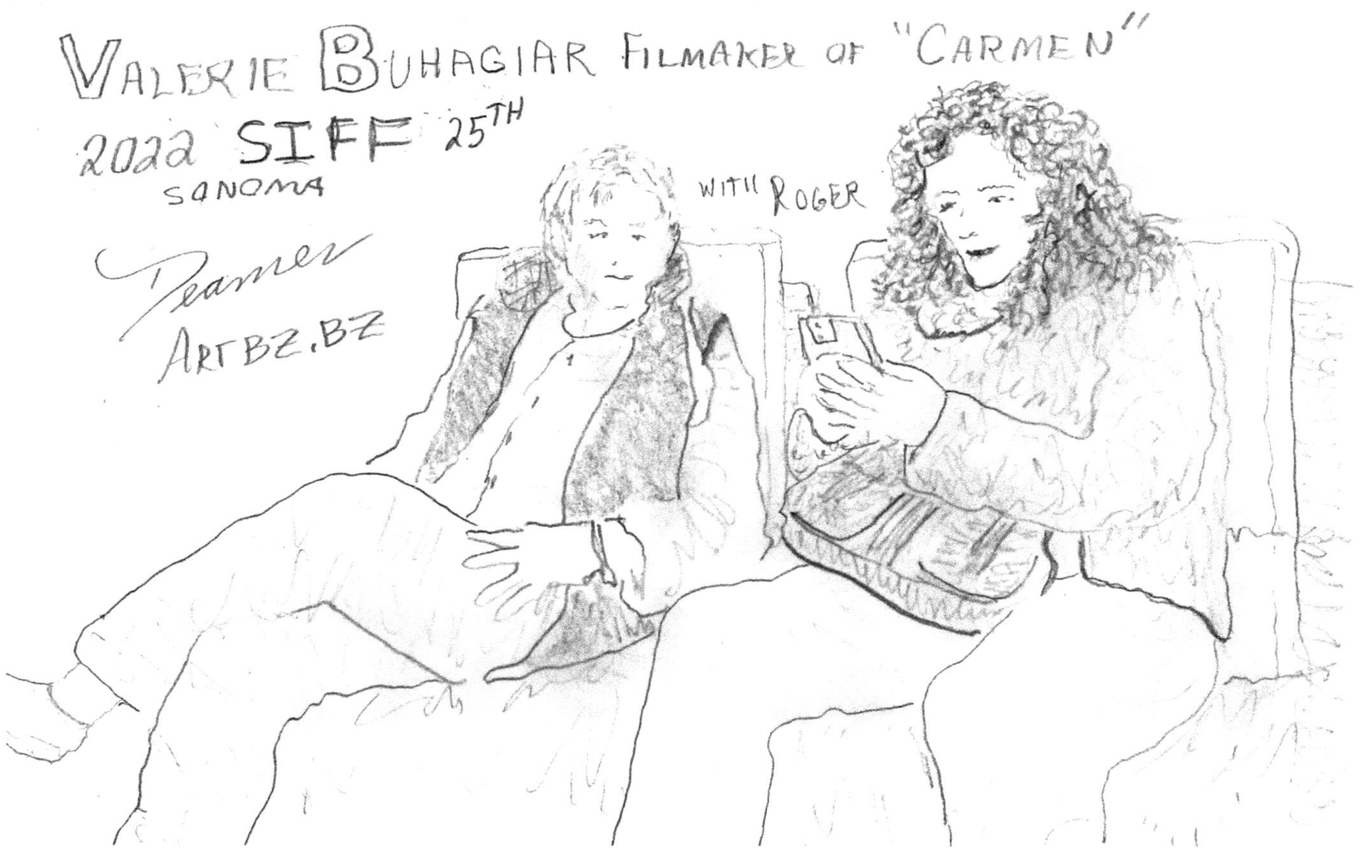
VALERIE BUHAGIAR FILMAKER of "CARMEN"
2022 SIFF 25TH
SONOMA
WITH ROGER
Jeanne
ArtBz.Bz

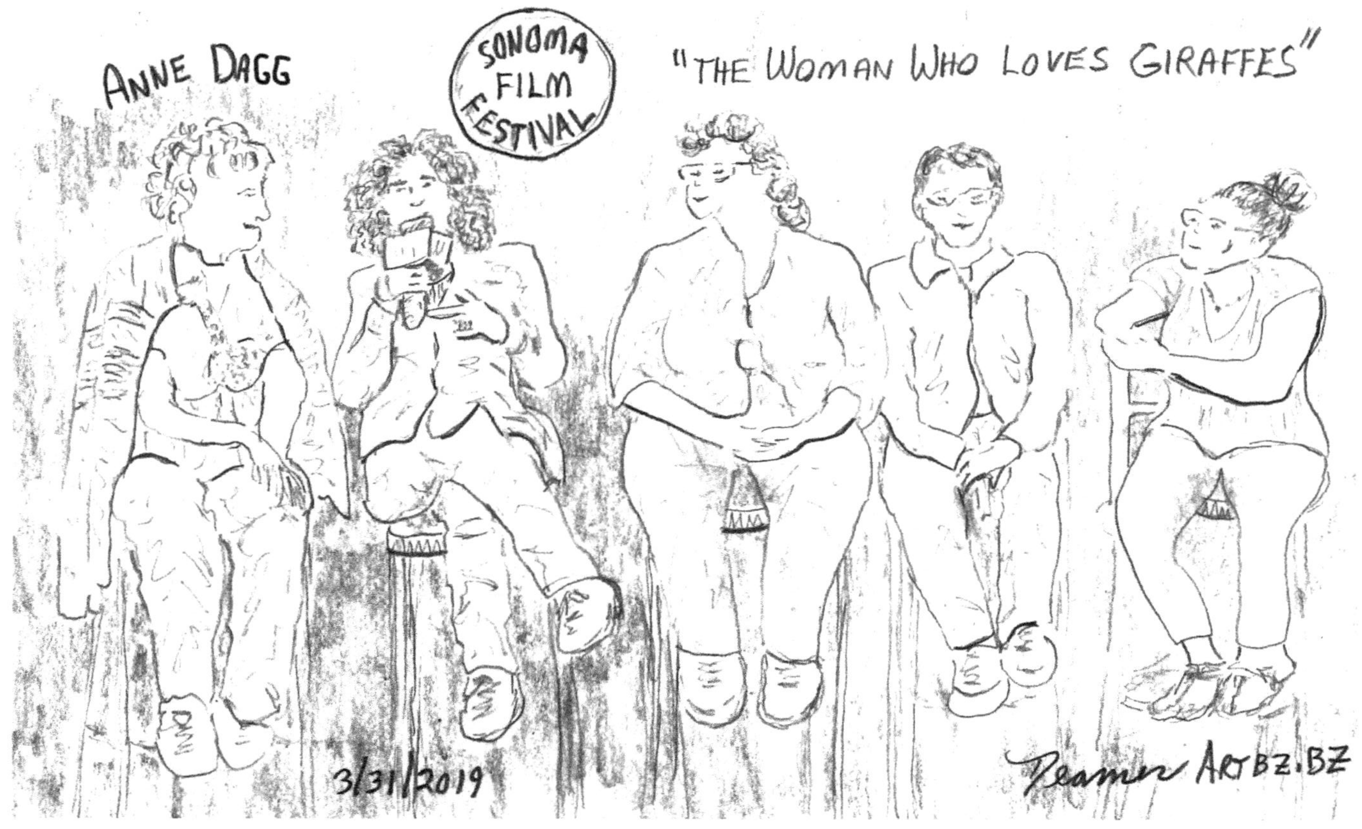
ANNE DAGG
SONOMA FILM FESTIVAL
"THE WOMAN WHO LOVES GIRAFFES"
3/31/2019
Reamer ARTBZ.BZ

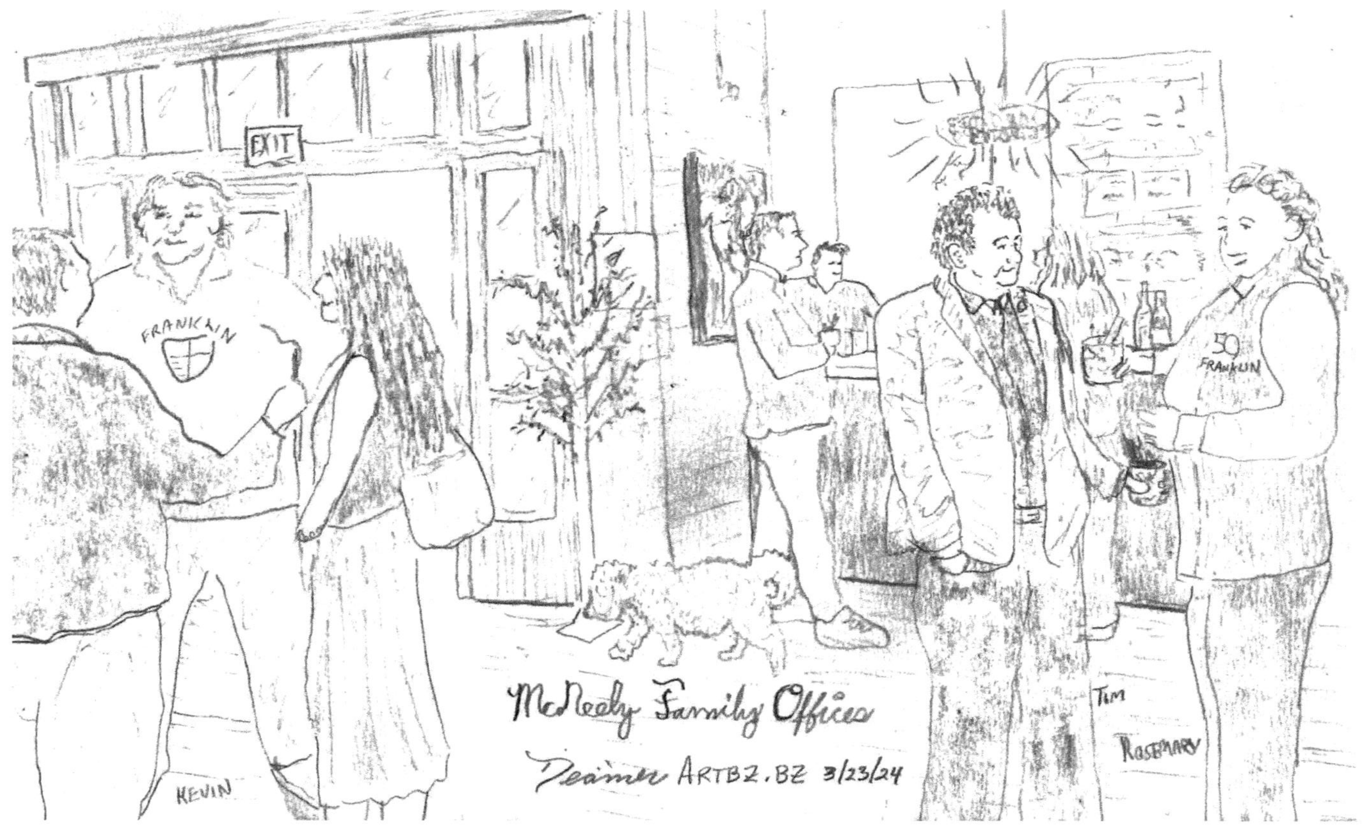
EXIT
FRANKLIN
KEVIN
McNeely Family Offices
Feature ARTBZ.BZ 3/23/24
FRANKLIN
Tim
ROSEMARY

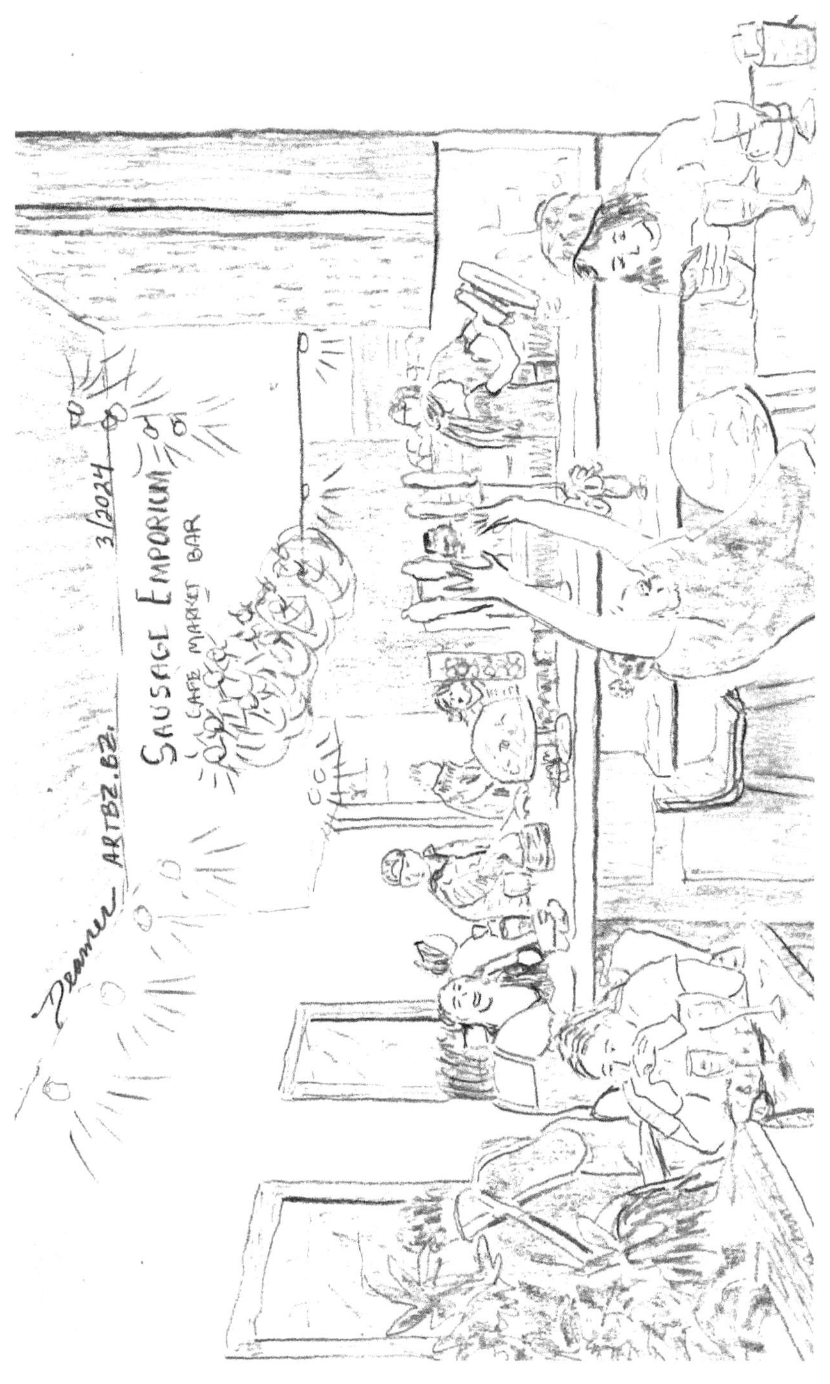
SAUSAGE EMPORIUM
CAFE MARKET BAR
Deamer ARTB2.B2.
3/2024

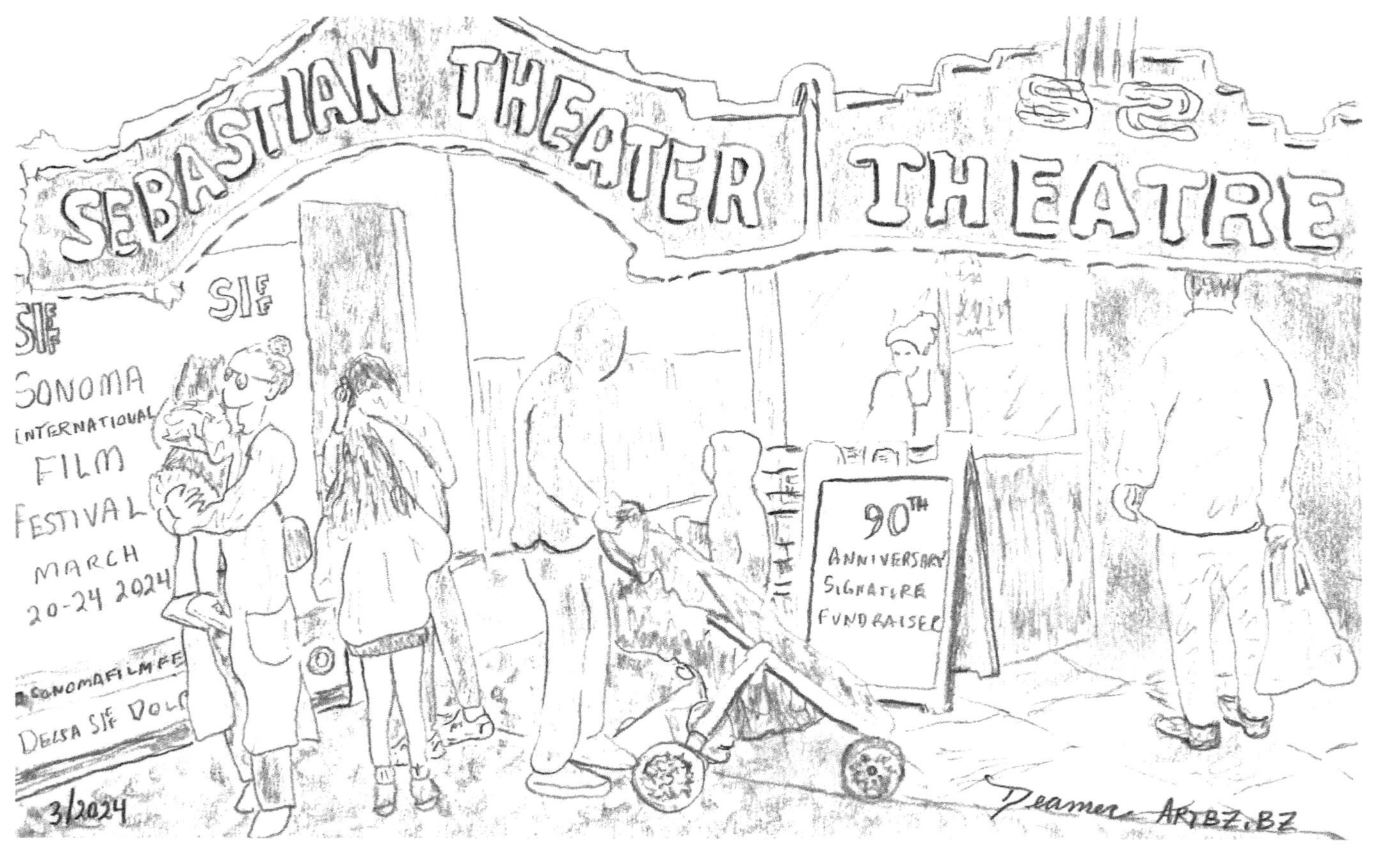
SEBASTIAN THEATER THEATRE
S2
SIF
SIF
SONOMA
INTERNATIONAL
FILM
FESTIVAL
MARCH
20-24 2024
SONOMAFILMFE
DELSA SIF DOL
90TH
ANNIVERSARY
SIGNATURE
FUNDRAISER
3/2024
Deamer ARTBZ.BZ

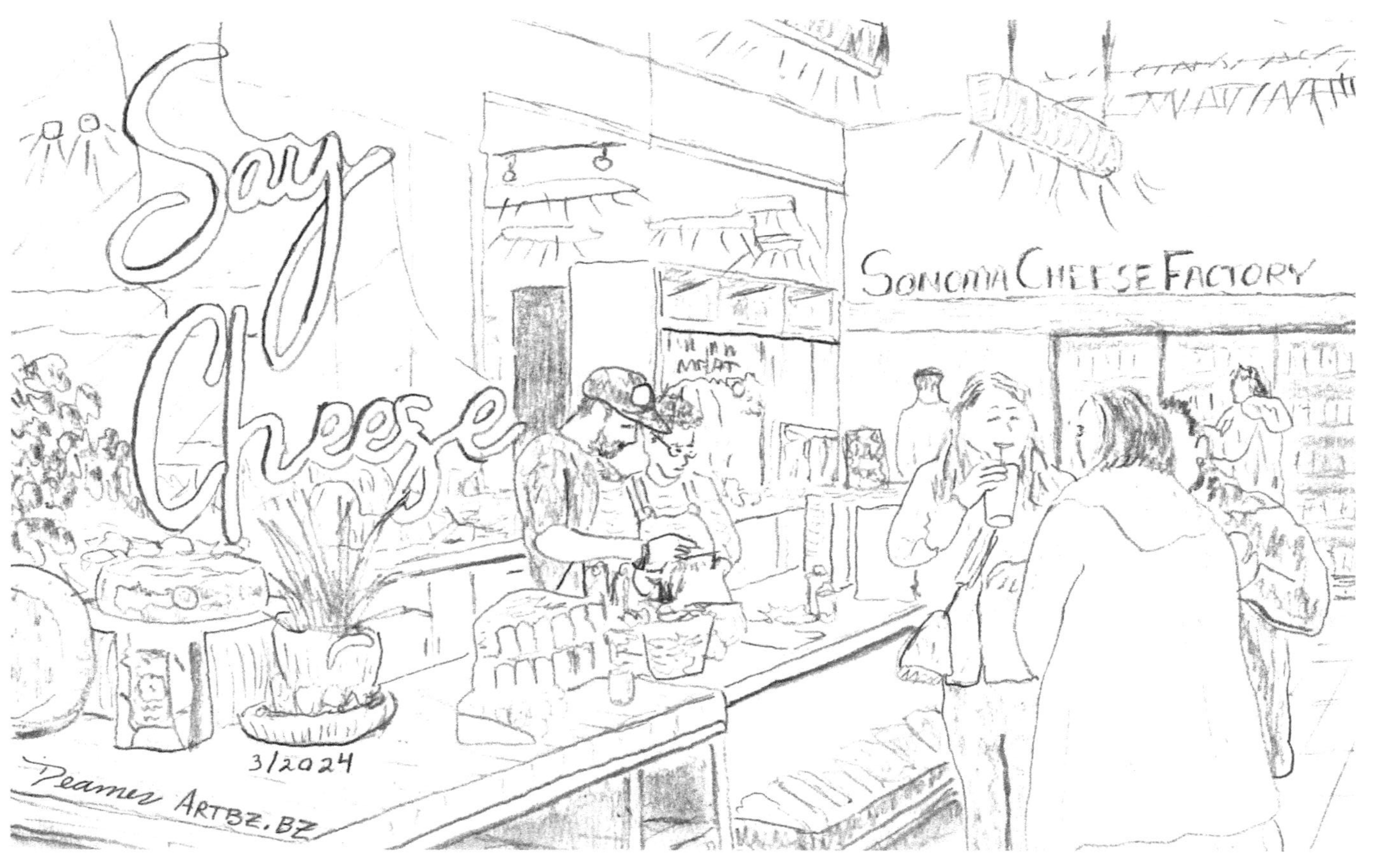
Say Cheese
Sonoma Cheese Factory
MEAT
3/2024
Deamer ArtBz.Bz

PAGE   INDEX OF IMAGES

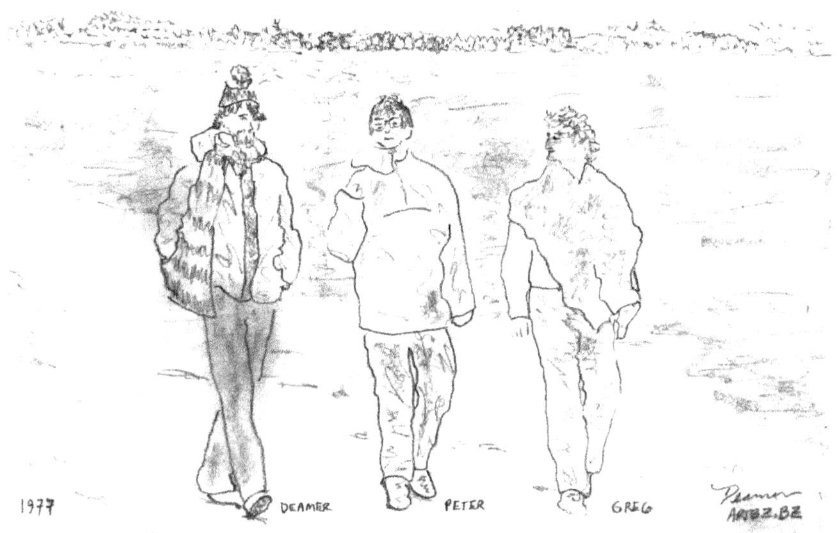

<u>Available Deamer Sketchbooks</u>:

SAN DIEGO, SAN DIEGO: LITTLE ITALY MERCATO, CENTRAL COAST CALIFORNIA, CHERRYBEAN COFFEE, SALINAS CA, TIJUANA MEXICO (DUAL LANGUAGE BOOK), UMBRIA, ITALY, SAN FRANCISCO, MUSEUM OF MODERN ART SAN FRANCISCO, SKETCH/COOKBOOK PS GRILL, NEW YORK CITY, MUSEUM OF MODERN ART NYC, HAVANA CUBA, HONG KONG, MAIN STREET SALINAS, MARKET DAY CARMEL, SEATTLE, LAS VEGAS, MUSEE D'ORSAY PARIS PARIS & LUGANO SWITZERLAND

<u>Coming Soon</u>:

SALT LAKE CITY, MIAMI, AUSTIN TX, NEW ORLEANS, SANTA FE NEW MEXICO

Deamer Sketchbooks: <u>http://artbz.bz/Books/sketchbooks.html</u>

Novels by Deamer:

Pickup a Deamer novel online or from your local bookstore:

https://www.amazon.com/author/deamerdunn

STRENGTH AND GRACE & FUERZA y GRACIA (Español)

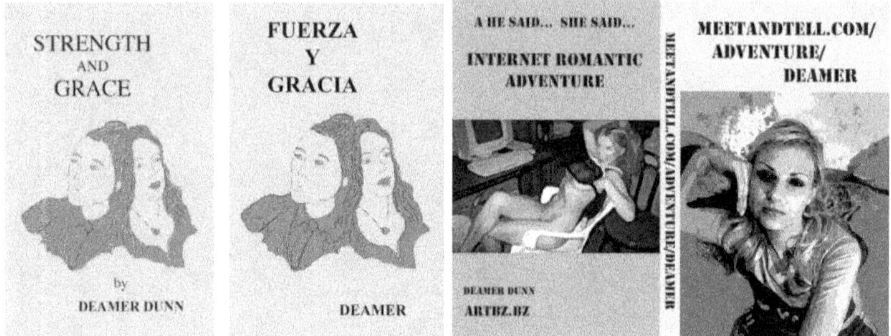

MEETANDTELL.COM/ADVENTURE

Chef Omar T Culinary Adventure Series
TRAVEL FICTION

Omar and his family travel to a different location for each of these culinary adventures. The travel fiction aspect is enhanced with descriptions of actual sites, restaurants, bookstores, galleries and shops—including sketches, favorite lists and recipes. Diversity in race, religion, culture, language and sexual orientation not only exists within Omar's family, it is celebrated in these tales. Each Omar T book is independent, you do not need to read them in the order of their publication, though there are some references for those who do.

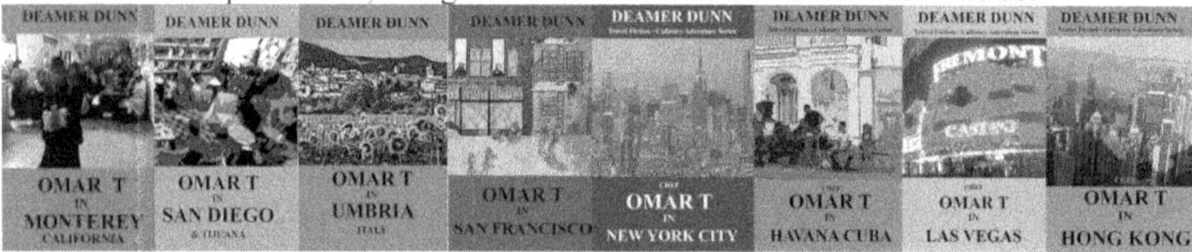

Published: Monterey California, San Diego/Tijuana, Umbria Italy, San Francisco, New York City, Havana Cuba, Hong Kong, Seattle, Las Vegas, Paris France & Lugano Switzerland

Coming Soon: Salt Lake City

In the Works: Miami, Austin Texas, New Orleans

Being researched: Santa Fe NM, Buenos Aries, Rio, Bogota, Madrid, Berlin, Prague, Vienna, Budapest, Bangkok, Singapore *and then????*

Also from Pajaro Street Publishing:

RM Blake EROTICA:
EROTIC REFLECTIONS
This book of erotica includes twenty-two stories, eleven told by a woman, eleven recalled by a man. With illustrations by Deamer.

Also Coming from RM Blake:
THE SEXUAL EDUCATION OF ZOE
AND
THE SEXUAL EDUCATION OF COLIN

These two companion novels mirror each other. Young Zoe approaches her favorite professor to help her further her education.
Colin, like Zoe is also from a difficult background. In this book, his much older professor of philosophy approaches her promising student with continuing his education in her bedroom.

RM Blake Love Song Journals Poignant stories of loss & love
Stephen and Lily
So many of us face addiction, obsession and a drive of compulsion. These drives can create beauty as well as destroy.

Joseph and Mickey
Love later in life can often be complicated. Relationships and history between each lover's families can put a strain on love.

Also Coming Soon:

UMBILICAL CORD A collection of African Stories
Deamer Dunn with co-author/humanitarian
Tererai Trent
*Named by Oprah Winfrey as her favorite all-time Guest!
a collection of African short stories

All Deamer and Pajaro Street books are available wholesale for bookstores and other retailers through both KDP and Ingram.

About the Author/Artist

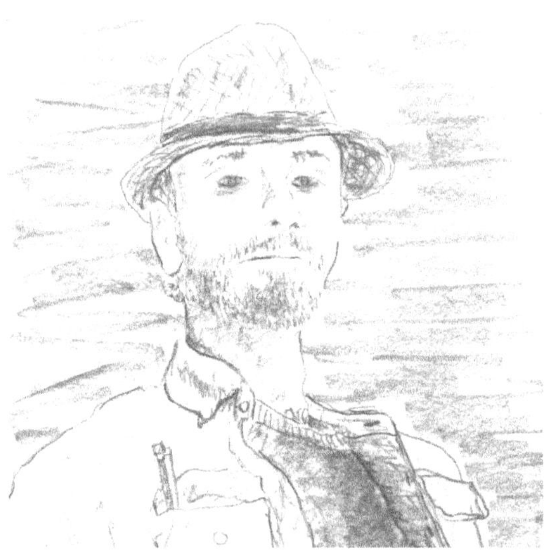

Deamer is a retired chef/restaurateur who travels the world with his sketchbook and laptop. For each city he visits he creates a Sketchbook (A book to make your own) and a novel with his recurring chef character, Omar T. These are culinary adventure stories he labels "Travel Fiction." Chef Deamer was born and raised in Salt Lake City, Utah. He lived in Switzerland and the Washington D.C. area before settling in Monterey County California in the early 1980's. "I had the incredible luxury of having a world class artist for a mother. Gradually some of her skills rubbed off on me." Deamer maintains a home in the birth city of John Steinbeck, Salinas California, the former location of his dinner only restaurant, Pajaro Street Grill. "I have a list of fifty locations where I hope to write Omar adventures…
Come join the journey!"

http://artbz.bz
"Everyday is a great day to read a book or color one!!!"

Keep in touch with Deamer, as Omar travels the world, deamer@artbz.bz Please pass on your impressions; write a review on Amazon and/or other sites such as Goodreads – your thoughts can really make a difference! Just about any bookstore, anywhere in the world, can get you a Deamer book through Ingram at the same price as Amazon ☺
https://www.amazon.com/author/deamerdunn You can also support your local bookstore via: https://bookshop.org/shop/deamerdunn

Romantic, Novelist, Obsessive Traveler, Sketchaholic

www.ingramcontent.com/pod-product-compliance
Lightning Source LLC
Chambersburg PA
CBHW071312140726
47996CB00005B/1736